M·Y·T·H·I·C BRITAIN

Logres

A Mythic Britain Expansion for the Saxon Lands

Published under license in the UK by Aeon Games Publishing

www.aeongamespublishing.co.uk

ISBN 978-1-91147-116-5

Printed in Great Britain

Mythras

THE DESIGN MECHANISM

Credits

Developed and written by
Paul Mitchener

Editing
Brian Pivik

Proof Reading
Inkwell Resources Limited

Design and layout
Alexandra James

Artists
Cover by David Benzal
Alan Gallo and Eric Lofgren (courtesy of Outland Entertainment)

Cartography
Colin Driver

Playtesters
Simon Beaver, John Bell, Chris Gilmore, Peter Griffith, Brad Milburn, Blain Neufeld, Andrew Sangar, Michael Schloss, Graham Spearing, Lawrence Whitaker, John Wolstenholme

Contents

Introduction

...Hengest and Esc fought with the Welsh, and took immense Booty. And the Welsh fled from the English like fire.

The Anglo Saxon Chronicle

The Saxons had harried the coasts of Britain since late Roman times. Vortigern, the High King, hired them as mercenaries to aid in his conquests of the Picts and then betrayed them, cheating of them of the lands they were promised. The Saxons defeated Vortigern in battle, and then at the peace meeting betrayed him in turn at the Night of the Long Knives, slaughtering him and all of his nobles in attendance at a feast.

To most Britons, the Saxons are the sea wolves who came from across the water, remorseless in battle, endlessly greedy for land and loot. In the lands they have taken - Logres, the lost lands - their rule over the Britons is total, and many who remain are reduced to the status of slaves or servants. They are relentless when wronged, and never forgive a slight. But who are they?

Mythic Britain: Logres is *their* story.

Why did they come?

The Saxon homelands are low-lying areas and for centuries they have raided Britannia's shores. Such raiding became easier when the Romans ceased defending the shoreline and retreated to the capital. The Saxons began to migrate en masse when rising sea levels caused frequent salt water flooding, making their lands all but impossible to farm. Instead of raiding further inland, where lived their kin, the Frisians, they set out to settle in another fertile land they were familiar with, namely Britain.

About this Book

This book is a supplement for the Mythic Britain setting for the Mythras rules. It includes an extensive background on the world of early Saxon Britain, including details of Saxon culture, descriptions of the Saxon lands and important people, and Saxon magic.

We round out this book with a short campaign of four linked scenarios for Saxon characters. These scenarios take place just after the scenarios in *Mythic Britain* and can be played independently.

Saxon Peoples & Kingdoms

Saxons is a blanket term for a group of Germanic coastal tribes who once raided, and are now settling, in Britain. They share a common culture, ideals, and similar languages. The various Saxon peoples are:

The Angles

The Angles have settled on the east coast of Britain, in the kingdom of Anglia. Under King Guercha, Anglia is the second most powerful of the Saxon kingdoms.

The Frisians

The Frisians did not come to Britain but remained in their homeland. They still sail and raid but, more than that, they trade-and maintain trade connections with their cousins in Britain.

The Jutes

The first of the Saxon groups to come to Britain, under the leaders Hengist and Horsa, were the Jutes. They are present across much of the south coast of Britain, although the old Jute kingdoms are now absorbed into Saxon lands.

The Saxons

The Saxons are the dominant group and give the peoples as a whole their name. The Saxon kingdom of Ceint is the most powerful of the Saxon kingdoms, although it faces challenges from both Anglia and the newcomer Cerdic. Cerdic is, for the present, expanding Ceint lands.

Besides the lands of Anglia and Ceint, Saxon expansion is also occurring in the regions of Mierce and the South Coast. The South Coast has a fringe of Saxon settlement, with further expansion being opposed by the Celtic kingdom of Dumnonia. Mierce is another border region claimed by both Ceint and Anglia, as well as the Celts. The dominant force in Mierce are the Angles.

Saxon Society: War & Blood Feud

The Saxons value lands, freedom and kin. The key way a Saxon advances in status and wealth is through military success. A warlord (called an ealdorman) holds his men to his banner through a supply of glory, loot and land. Saxon warriors (carls) are free men and not obliged to follow a lord who does not reward them or honour his promises. Unlanded free Saxon warriors are in a state of almost constant war.

A Saxon lord's decisions are made before an assembly of the carls who follow them, who must assent to his decisions. They do this by banging their weapons against their shields. A lord will also hold feasts, essentially celebrations involving as much drink as food. They mark victories, funerals, marriages and religious festivals.

Someone who is wronged by another brings the complaint before an assembly. The lord, if he agrees, gives them permission to right this wrong by pursuing a bloodfeud – a vendetta against the one accused of the crime.

Kin are the most important thing to a Saxon, as they are the only allies one can truly rely upon. In a bloodfeud, kin are allies, are expected to provide warriors to fight in a bloodfeud, or pursue it on behalf of a helpless victim. A bloodfeud is not just a right but an obligation. Not pursuing a bloodfeud indicates an acknowledgement that the wrong was merited.

Bloody death is not the only way a crime can be resolved; the one accused can also pay compensation to the victim in the form of wergeld, which usually takes the form of treasure. But one is not expected to pay wergeld unless forced to do so.

Structure of Saxon Society

Saxon society is hierarchical, although free men have considerable freedoms and can rise higher in society. At the top are the kings, and their relatives and potential heirs, the *athelings*. The kings hold that they are descended from the gods themselves, although in reality, in the new lands of Britain, one who takes enough power and land and has sufficient following can become a king.

Below the athelings are the Saxon war leaders, the *ealdormen*. Then come those with lands, the *thanes*. The highest status thanes are *King's Thanes*, who receive their lands directly from a king rather than an ealdorman. Then come the *carls*, the free folk of the Saxons. The ealdormen (and even kings), can only rule with the assent of carls in assemblies.

Then come those who are not free and have fewer rights. *Geburs* are peasants, bound to their lands and not permitted to attend assembly. Then there are *thralls*, who are slaves. Both fellow Saxons and conquered Celts can be thralls.

The *laece* (pronounced *leech*) are outside of this heirarchy. They are shamans, who both serve and master the spirits. Although they present themselves as healers, the laece mastery of magic and command of the spirits makes them powerful and dangerous indeed. Although they often serve Saxon kings and ealdorman, laeces are free to serve whichever lord they choose or, for that matter, none. They are feared and respected in equal measure.

Saxons & Britons

Recent archaeological evidence points heavily towards a high degree of assimilation between Saxons and Britons. It is likely the Saxons were resisted and, if sources like the Anglo Saxon Chronicle and Nennius are to be believed, battles were bloody. However, it makes sense for conquered Britons to have integrated with Saxon conquerors, whether willingly or otherwise, and to have adopted their ways, customs and language. Few invasions are successful without such assimilation, and while the Britons (known as welsh to the Saxons) were no doubt displaced to a large degree, many more became Saxons.

It is therefore highly likely that Britons who have chosen to live with their conquerors are found amongst the carls and, possibly, even the ealdormen. Saxons recognise loyalty and reward it, although such Britons would no doubt need to work doubly hard to gain trust and establish loyalty from born Saxons. An advantageous way of achieving that trust and loyalty is to marry into a Saxon family and produce children that will be raised as Saxons and worship the Saxon gods.

Names

Most Saxon names are made up of two elements with different meanings. These meanings are often associated with battle or weapons. You can create new Saxon names by combining elements in different ways.

Here are some examples from historic sources. These names are not those of major non-player characters in the setting or famous people from history, so you should feel free to pillage (or recombine) for your own use.

Many more Saxon names can be found on page 142 of the main *Mythic Britain* book.

Female Names

Aelfgifu	-	"aelf"=elf, "gifu"=gift
Aethelflaed	-	"aethel"=noble, "flaed"=beauty
Aethellind	-	"aethel"=noble, "lind"=serpent
Cyneburg	-	"cyne"=royal, "burg"=fortress
Dungifu	-	"dun"=dark, "gifu"=gift
Eadgyth	-	"ead"=wealth, "gyth"=battle
Ealdgyth	-	"eald"=old, "gyth"=battle
Eoforhild	-	"eofor"=boar, "hild"=fight
Frithuswith	-	"frith"=peace, "swith"=strong
Glaedburg	-	"glaed"=bright, "burg"=fortress
Hildraed	-	"hild"=battle, "raed"=counsel
Hildeleoma	-	"hilde"=battle, "leoma"=light. *Figuratively, this means 'sword'*
Leofflaed	-	"leof"=beloved, "flaed"=beauty
Mildburg	-	"mild"=gentle, "burg"=fortress
Mildgyth	-	"mild"=gentle, "gyth"=battle
Sunngifu	-	"sunn"=sun, "gifu"=gift

Male Names

Aelfnoth	-	"aelf"=elf, "noth"=bold
Aelfgar	-	"aelf"=elf, "gar"=spear
Aesc	-	"ash tree"
Aethelwine	-	"aedel"=noble, "wine"=friend
Aethelmaer	-	"aedel"=noble, "maer"=famed
Beorhtric	-	"beorht"=bright, "ric"=power
Cenric		"cene"=bold, "ric"=power
Ceolmund	-	"coel"=keel, "mund"=protection
Cola	-	"charcoal"
Cuthbeohrt	-	"cuth"=famed, "beohrt"=bright
Cynebeald	-	"cyne"=royal, "beald"=bold
Cynefrith	-	"cyne"=royal, "frith"=peace
Deorwine	-	"deor"=beloved, "wine"=friend
Dunstan	-	"dun"=dark, "stan"=stone
Eadgar		"ead"=wealth, "gar"=spear
Eadweard	-	"ead"=wealth, "weard"=guard
Eadwig	-	"ead"=wealth, "wig"=war
Ealhstan	-	"ealh"=temple, "stan"=stone
Eardwulf	-	"eard"=land, "wulf"=wulf
Ecgbeohrt	-	"ecg"=edge of a sword, "behrt"=bright
Eoforgar	-	"eofor"=boar, "gar"=spear
Garheard	-	"gar"=spear, "heard"=brave
Heard		"brave"
Hildraed	-	"hild"=fight, "read"=advice
Hrothgar	-	"hroth"=famous, "gar"=spear
Loefdaeg	-	"leof"=beloved, "daeg"=day
Naegling	-	"nail"
Osbeorn	-	"os"=god, "beorn"=bear
Paega	-	"peak"
Saewine	-	"sae"=sea, "wine"=friend
Sigeweard	-	"sige"=victory, "weard"=guard
Swithwulf	-	"swith"=strong, "wulf"=wolf
Wigstan	-	"wig"=war, "stan"=stone
Wilfrith	-	"wil"=will, "frith"=peace
Wulfric	-	"wulf"=wolf, "ric"=power

Saxons have no surnames but often carry titles and nicknames besides their main name. There is an element of family naming in that children often have the same or similar sounding first element in their names as their father and almost always the same first letter.

Pronouncing Saxon Names

Most consonants in the names in this book are pronounced in the same way as in modern English. The letter "h" is never silent and is sometimes placed before other consonants.

The letter "c" can be pronounced in two ways — either hard, as the letter "k", or softly, similarly to "ch" in modern English. So the word "laece" is pronounced "leech" or "leech-a'. The hard "k" is more common.

The letter "g"usually resembles the modern letter "g"but at the start of a word before an "e"vowel is pronounced similarly to the letter "y'.

Vowels and dipthongs (vowel combinations) are slightly more complex. Modern German is a fair approximation for most of them. The letter "y"is a vowel, and sounds either as the letter "i', or the sound "oo'.

A Note from the Author

I grew up on the south coast of England, in a village called Netley Abbey. It is named after the ruins of the abbey there and these ruins were familiar to me as a child. I also grew up with stories of the Saxons and with Cerdic, and was excited by them before I grew excited by Arthurian myth and other parts of history and fantasy.

According to the late medieval historian William Camden, Netley Abbey was the site of Cerdic's battle with the British king Natanleod, where the Saxons defeated the latter's armies and founded the kingdom of Wessex in 508. I always thought it odd that local people - even my school teachers - made little of this profound historical connection. It was only later on that I learned that another Hampshire village, Netley Marsh, was conventionally identified with the site of the battle. It was too late for me; my fascination with the Saxons and with "Dark Ages"history had already formed.

Recently I returned to one of my first historical loves, the Saxons, and pondered in public the possibility of writing a Saxons RPG. The Saxons in most stories are presented as the barbaric enemy in Arthurian literature, or the unfortunate victims of the Vikings or Normans in stories of later times, but there is much more to them than that. The roots of major portions of British culture, and the English language, go back to them. They wrote the epic hero poem *Beowulf*, as good as anything out there in classical literature.

Lawrence Whitaker saw my musings and got in touch to ask if I would consider writing a Saxons book for *Mythic Britain*. I admire *Mythic Britian*, both for its gritty historical feel to Arthurian myth, and its subtle but mystical view of the British magical landscape — in some ways barely supernatural but in other ways with the magic of it all being pervasive. I jumped at the chance.

I would also like to thank my partner Marjory who really got behind me writing this, encouraging me, listening to me talk about it and buying me lots of books on Saxon history to read - including things I would not have thought to seek out on my own.

I would also like to thank Richard Rohlin, a scholarly friend with great interests in Anglo-Saxon history and literature, who was kind enough to have a read through the culture chapter for me.

This book is the result. I hope you like it.

Paul Mitchener, September 2016

Saxon Characters

Character creation for Saxon heroes follows the *Mythras* rules, along with the guidelines in the *Mythic Britain* Characters chapter, except as noted here.

Culture and Community

For a Saxon character, their culture will be either Saxon, Angle,or Jute, depending on their tribe. These cultures are similar, as described in the first chapter of this book, but there are small differences in customs noted elsewhere.

Homeland/Tribe

This can be chosen by the players, chosen by the Game Master, or randomly rolled on the tables provided.

Religion

Saxons nearly all follow the Saxon Pagan religion. Christian Saxons are very rare, although Christianity is a small possibility for Celts who have come to otherwise embrace the Saxon culture.

Saxons following Celtic paganism are unlikely to still be a part of Saxon culture, as the religion opposes the Saxons on principle.

Cultural Skills

These are as described on pages 121 to 122 of *Mythic Britain*. A Fyrdman is a typical Carl warrior.

As well as the combat styles described in *Mythic Britain*, a Saxon character can also learn two other combat styles:

Saxon Noble (Seax, Sword and Shield, Trait: Mounted Combat)

Saxon Hunter (Seax, Spear, Bow, Trait: Skirmishing)

Regions of Logres

There are four regions of Logres, as the Celts name the Saxon lands of Britain. All are described in the *Saxon Lands* chapter of this book. The detail in that chapter may also provide some useful background ideas when considering Passions and a character's Background Event.

It is recommended that all characters start in the same place and are part of the same community. In the adventures later in this book, the characters are initially fighting for Cerdic on the South Coast, although later events take them further afield.

The random element of the Region table is there for those who prefer a more random approach to character creation.

Random Region

D100 Roll	Region	Land	Tribe
01-25	Ceint	Ceint	Jute
26-35	The South Coast	The South Shore	Saxon
36-50		The Island of Wiht	Jute
51-75	Anglia	Anglia	Angle
76-88	Mierce	South Mierce	Saxon or Jute
89-00		North Mierce	Angle

Social Class

D100 roll	Class	Wergeld	Money Modifier
01-10	Gebur	50	0.5
11-75	Carl	600	1
76-85	Thane	1,200	2
86-90	King's Thane	3,000	4
91-95	Ealdorman	5,000	6
96-00	Atheling	10,000 or more	8

Although percentages are provided in the above tables, these do not reflect class proportions in society but rather frequencies in an adventuring band. Certainly fewer than one in 20 Saxons in general are athelings, and geburs are at least as common as carls.

The social classes in Saxon society are detailed in the culture chapter. For convenience, here is a quick summary:

Thralls

Thralls are slaves. Their lack of freedom makes them unplayable as starting characters in a typical game. Thralldom need not be forever: one can become a thrall when captured in war, or to pay off wergeld, effectively paying for a crime through slavery.

Geburs

Geburs are the peasants of Saxon society, bound to an area of land, unless special dispensation deems otherwise. They are not warriors and obey slightly different character generation rules to Saxons of higher classes.

A gebur with a talent for magic might be taken in by a laece for training and thus transcend their birth. Otherwise, they are only likely to be a part of an adventuring party by the orders of a Thane or Ealdorman, when they have particular skills to add.

Carls

Carls are free Saxons; the free warriors, also called fyrdmen, have a say in decisions made by their ealdorman. They are the standard Saxon player characters in *Mythic Britian.*

Thanes

Thanes are Saxon landowners in charge of an area of land and an extended family including dependents and servants, as well as a few carls. The thane's lands usually host a single hall and eight to ten houses. The carls under a thane's rule are free to leave his service and seek employment elsewhere or can become thanes in their own right as a reward.

King's Thanes

A king's thane receives rights as a thane directly from a king, rather than a greater thane or an ealdorman. A king's thane has jurisdiction over several lesser thanes. An ordinary thane may also be raised to a king's thane for loyalty and distinguished services.

Ealdormen

An ealdorman is a leader of a warband, a Saxon noble, second only to kings and more powerful ealdormen. This is generally the highest rank a Saxon warrior can aspire to.

player character groups

The standard set-up for a Saxon adventuring group consists of free warriors, and perhaps a laece, serving an ealdorman or thane. As a default, the superior is a non-player character. A player character thane or ealdorman can work (and is allowed if you roll on the table) but typically this is a rank player characters aspire to rather than begin with.

A gebur who is part of the group is one with useful skills. You do not have to roll on the table; this is up to the group. If you do not roll, everyone is a carl.

athelings

Athelings are relatives of kings and can potentially become kings themselves if they gather enough support. However, a starting player character who is an atheling is but a minor member of royalty and, perhaps, even an illegitimate member. This rank grants some privileges, of course, as reflected in starting money and wergeld; and like other free warriors, athelings can aspire to greater things. By itself, the rank does not grant any powers of command over other Saxons.

careers

As with Celts, most Saxon player characters are warriors, with a secondary career as described on page 135 of *Mythic Britain*. Laeces are as described on page 136. Christian Saxon priests are not allowed. As well as the skills described there, a laece may also learn the trained skill Literacy for the Saxon languages (see *Mythras*, page 47).

skalds

Saxon skalds are not completely devoted to their careers in the same way as Celtic bards. They are warriors as well as poets. Generate skalds as follows:

- Skalds are exempt from the Superstition skill in the same way as druids and laeces.
- A skald character has 100 points to spend on Bard/Skald skills and 75 points to spend on Warrior skills.

geburs

A gebur player character is exceptional and more capable than the typical peasant.

- Pick a primary and a secondary career for a gebur player character.
- You have 100 points to spend on skills in your primary career and 75 points to spend on your secondary career.

events

When you generate a Saxon player character, you should roll once on the Background Events table on the following pages, which replaces the one from *Mythic Britain*.

background events

1d100	Event
01	Distinguished Older Sibling: An older brother or sister has made a name for themselves, becoming a famed warrior. How do you feel about this? Are you close? Will you follow in their footsteps?
02	Last Survivor: Enemies raided the village where you lived and slaughtered your kin. Being kinless, you are vulnerable- there is nobody to protect you in a bloodfeud, or to support your case should you need to pursue a feud or exact wergild. But never mind that. Who killed your folk? What are you doing to get revenge?
03	Enslaved: You were enslaved after being captured in battle but managed to escape. Who enslaved you? Were they Saxon or Celt? And how did you manage to get free?
04	Battle Glory: Your heroism was the key to victory in a significant battle. What was the battle? How were you rewarded? Who now knows of you?
05	Family Feud: One of your kin has been wronged and you are dragged into a blood feud against those who wronged them. Who was it? What happened – does your kinsman really have right on their side? Are you eager or reluctant?
06	Celt: You are not of Saxon blood, although the Saxons treat you as a free warrior. How did this happen? Do you consider yourself a Saxon or do your real loyalties lie elsewhere?
07	Newcomer: You are newly landed on the shores of Britain and have few friends here. Where did you come from? Why did you come to Britain? Who do you know?
08	Royal Blood: You are a descendant of the god Seaxneat and a distant relative of one of the tribal kings, although in all likelihood you are far from the throne. However, you could become an atheling should you amass the support. Do you want this? Could your wyrd have such things waiting for you whether you will it or not?
09	Heroic Drinker: No matter how much ale or mead you drink, you never become drunk. Is this an advantage or a disadvantage to you at feasts? Could it be a strange blessing of the gods? Do other people know of your "talent"?
10	Night Eyes: You can see in the dark as well as you can in full daylight. This is presumably a blessing of the gods but how do others really feel about this? Do they even know?
11	New Lord: You have left the service of your old ealdorman, maybe even your old king, to take employment elsewhere? Why? What attracted you to a new lord or what went wrong with your old one?
12	Heirloom: You have a weapon, shield or helm of fine workmanship with a name marked in runes. How did you come by it? What is its story and what could its powers be?
13	Accused: You have been accused of a crime severe enough that your accusers are pursuing a blood feud. What was the crime? Did you do it or were you framed? If the latter, by whom?
14	Heavy Doom: A laece once prophesied that you have a dark fate waiting for you, where you are destined to cause ruin. Do you know more details? Do you believe it? Have you told anyone?
15	Fated for Greatness: A laece once prophesied that your wyrd is to do a great and famous thing. Do you know or susppect what it is? Do you believe it? Have you boasted of it?
16	Saved your Lord in Battle: When you went into battle led by your lord, you saved his life. Did you win or lose the battle? How has your heroism benefited you?

Background Events

1d100	Event
17	Sporting Victor: You won an important sporting contest, which brought you temporary fame and glory. What was the nature of the contest? Who still remembers your victory?
18	Gift: Someone of importance – a king. ealdorman or laece – gave you a valuable gift: something impractical but too important to simply sell or give away. What was it? And why did they give you it?
19	Hopelessly Lost: You got hopelessly lost on a journey – perhaps blown off course on a sea voyage. You made your way back to familiar lands but you, and perhaps a few companions, know of a land few, if any, Saxon eyes have seen. Where is it? Do you know how to return?
20	Dream Visitation: A god or great spirit visited you in a dream to whisper secrets to you. Secrets you can only half remember. Who was it? What can you half remember?
21	The Power of God: You have witnessed the power of the Christian God in dreams and visions, or the word of His priests has awoken something in your heart. Are you a rare Christian convert amongst the Saxons or still resolutely pagan?
22	Work of Art: You once created a work of extraordinary artistic beauty, such as a piece of jewellery, a helm or a poem. The work is far beyond your normal capabilities. If you are not normally skilled in the craft you practiced, matters are even more mysterious. Did the gods work through you? What did you make? What happened to it?
23	Buried Treasure: A dying relative told you where they had buried a secret treasure. Where is it? Are you the only one they told?
24	The Body: When you were a child, you found the dead body of a warrior in a place you played. When you went back to the place after telling others about it, the body was gone. Who was it? What happened to the body? Did you ever find out more? Did one of your kin murder the warrior?
25	Bastard: You were born out of wedlock and you do not know your father, although your mother always said he was of high status. Do you have any other details? Are you even interested?
26	In Love: You are in love with someone of higher status. Before you can court them, you must prove your worth. What will you do to impress them and their kin?
27	Sibling betrothed to enemy: You have a beloved sibling and a bitter personal rival. Your sibling became recently betrothed to that rival. Is the match political or personal? How has this affected your feelings? What are you going to do about it?
28	One Eye: You lost an eye in battle. This does not affect your abilities, although some take your affliction to be a sign from Woden. But what could that sign mean? What nickname have others bestowed upon you?
29	The Plague: Your home suffered a terrible plague, wiping out most of your kin and neighbours. You were one of the few survivors and feel that you were visited by a god in your fever dreams. Now you are completely free of disease, not suffering a moment of illness since that time. What does this mean? Could there be a price for this blessing?
30	Past Love: You were truly, deeply, in love with someone and then the relationship went completely sour. Or perhaps it was always rotten, deep down. In either case, your past love is now your enemy – an enemy who knows many of your secrets. Of course, you also know theirs.

Background Events

1d100	Event
31	Quest: A dying grandparent gave you a task and made you swear an oath to fulfil it. What was the task? Why are you the one to complete it?
32	Bitter Friendship: As a young adult, you accidentally killed or severely injured a childhood friend in an accident. Perhaps it was a dare gone wrong. Their kin are now your enemy, although you paid wergild and there is no blood feud. What happened? Who are or were they?
33	Spirit Animal: Where you grew up, a great bear lurked near your home, eluding hunters and killing both livestock and the occasional thrall. Now, as an adult, you have seen the bear again and the killing has begun. What could this mean? Is it a sign from the gods? What are you going to do about it?
34	Killed a Druid: When fighting the Celts, you killed a druid and with his dying breath he cursed you. What was the curse? Do you even believe it? Is there any way to lift it?
35	Oldest Sibling: You have 1d8 younger siblings, whom you are expected to look after and set a good example. How do you feel about this? How do they feel about this? Do your parents still live or do you have sole responsibility?
36	Heavy Wergild: Thanks to an action of you or one of your kin, your family had to pay an immense wergild that left them impoverished. What happened? Was it your fault? What will you do to restore your kin's status and prosperity?
37	Family Curse: Your family is cursed and none have lived beyond the age of 30 for three generations; disease, accidents and deaths in battle have always carried them off. Does this knowledge weigh heavily upon you? Or can you put it to one side and enjoy life to the fullest for the short time you have on this Earth? After all, for a warrior, old age is already a rare fate.
38	Blood Feud: One of your kin has been accused of a horrible wrong and a blood feud is being prosecuted against them. What was their crime? Are they guilty? Will you stand by them?
39	Black Sheep: You have been disowned by your kin. It is as if you have nobody. Why did this happen? Is there a way to earn your way back into their good graces? Is this even what you want?
40	Military Disaster: You fought in a battle where your side lost catastrophically. There were few survivors. What happened? Was anyone in particular on your side to blame? Were you to blame?
41	Mismatched Eyes: You have eyes of different colours. This makes you an object of superstition and others believe you have magical power and, perhaps, fear it. The thing is that you do sometimes (at the GM's discretion) get visions of distant people and places. Have you told anyone? Do you act on these visions?
42	Freed Slave: You were sold into slavery, perhaps as a result of debts, but you managed to earn your way to freedom. What is your relationship with your former master? How do others who know of your past condition perceive you?
43	Never Lost: You never get lost. You always know where you are and how to retrace your steps if necessary, although your talent does not help when it comes to finding somewhere new. How do you use this special talent?
44	In Vino Veritas: When you drink heavily, you utter poetry that sometimes, according to those who have heard it, has the power of prophecy. You would not know – you can never remember such drunken poetic utterances. How do others perceive you? Do you make use of your strange talent?

Background Events

1d100	Event
45	Infamous Sibling: One of your brothers or sisters has made a name for themselves but not a good name; rather a notorious name, one of treachery and criminality. This reflects on their kin and you, although they have been officially disowned. What have they done? Are you still secretly in contact?
46	Exile: You are exiled from your old kingdom and cannot go back. Why? Have any of your kin left with you?
47	Riddler: You won a riddle contest cleverly and artistically in front of many witnesses. This has brought you much acclaim. What was the nature of the contest? And if riddling is not normally a talent of yours, did the gods speak through you?
48	Family Laece: One of your close kin joined the wise – they are a laece or medicine man. How does this help or hinder you?
49	Saved Someone's Life: In battle, you intervened to save the life of someone important: an ealdorman or even a king. What recognition has this brought you? How were you rewarded?
50	Near Fatal Accident: As a child or young adult you nearly died in an accident brought on by your own daring – or folly. What happened? How did you survive?
51	Forbidden Love: You love the partner of your lord and think your feelings are returned. Of course, not only are they beyond your reach socially but married to the one who commands your loyalty. What does this unfortunate situation drive you to do?
52	Second Sight: You can see into the spirit world; the spirits can communicate with you, although you cannot command them. The spirits sometimes lie, depending on the results of a Superstition roll. Do you use this power and have you told others?
53	Betrayed: One of your kin has betrayed you, selling you out to a personal enemy. Who was it? Who is your enemy? Do you have any idea why they betrayed you? And what are you going to do about it?
54	Spared Enemy: In battle, you spared the life of an enemy warrior when you could have killed them. They turn out to be very important. Perhaps your own side ridiculed you but do you have a potential influential friendly face in the camp of your enemies?
55	Love and War: You were betrothed to another from an enemy family or kingdom as part of an attempt to broker peace. You fell in love with them and they with you. Then you were separated when relations between your family or kingdom and theirs broke down and the fragile peace was shattered. But you are still in love. What will you do? What will they do? Will you choose your family or kingdom over the path of love?
56	Impoverished: Thanks to a disaster (the tides of war, plague, famine, fire), your kin are now impoverished. What happened? Can you help them?
57	Rescuer: You saved someone important or the child of someone important, from dying in an accident. Was this recognised? Were you rewarded?
58	Spared by an Enemy: In battle, an enemy warrior spared your life when they could have killed you in battle. Do you know why? Do you feel you owe them a debt?
59	Heroic Duel: You killed a personal enemy in a heroic one-on-one duel in front of witnesses. Now what do people think? What of the enemy's kin? Was the duel legally sanctioned?

Background Events

1d100	Event
60	Criminal Secret: You committed a crime such as theft, arson or even murder, and got away with it – so far. Why? What was your crime?
61	Blood of the Gods: Although not royal, descended from Seaxneat, one of your ancestor's a few generations ago was a god or so the stories say at least. Which god? Do you believe it? How does this affect your reputation?
62	Enemy of a Laece: You have done something to anger a magician – a laece – who lives near your kin. What was it? And what will the laece do now?
63	Murdered Sibling: Someone murdered your brother or sister. Do you know who? Surely you seek vengeance!
64	Ship: Your kin are skilled ship builders and indeed own sea worthy vessels. They were a vital part of a force landing on Britain's shores.
65	Drowning: As a child you nearly drowned, even ceasing to breathe before coming back to life with a laece's assistance. Since that time, you occasionally seen visions of people who have departed, even those not close to you. Are you one step closer than usual to the afterlife?
66	Berserker: In battle, a red mist descends and you can barely remember your actions afterwards. You may have folk magic you use instinctively when entering this state that boosts your prowess.
67	Wolf Pack: A pack of wolves has taken up residence near where you or your kin live. A laece has declared them a sign from the gods who cannot be harmed, but they are preying on livestock and have even attacked people. What will you do?
68	Failed Apprenticeship: You were apprenticed to a skilled and specialist craft, such as boatmaking or weaponsmithing but failed to complete your training. What happened? Are you still skilled?
69	Brush with Power: Your parents were important people, close to the king. Your father was an ealdorman or even an atheling and high in the king's council. Then your family lost their exalted status. What happened? How are you affected?
70	Walking through the Mystic Forest: A beautiful woman or man invited you into a forest glade. You do not really remember what happened there but when you emerged a year had passed. At the GM's discretion, you sometimes get odd glimpses of other realities. You can turn these glimpses into actual prophecies with a successful Art (Poetry) or Lore (Riddles) skill roll. Do others know of your power? What do friends and kin make of your long absence?
71	Failed Laece: You were apprenticed to a laece but for reason(s) you still do not know, your master turned against you, refusing to train you further and cast you out. What do you do now?
72	Court Summons: A king has recently summoned you to his mead hall for a festival. Do you have any idea why? Is it good or bad? Will you go?
73	Trade Connections: You have trade connections with continental Europe, perhaps through kinship with the Frisians or even the Franks. They can sometimes procure exotic goods which are generally unknown in Britain.
74	Mixed Blood: You are not a pure blooded Saxon; rather one of your parents was a Celt, although you are accepted by the Saxons as a free warrior and perhaps more. Who are or were your parents?
75	Tragic Romance: A past romance ended not just in disaster but with the death of your love, for whom you still mourn. What happened? With which friends or enemies from that time do you remain in contact?

Background Events

1d100	Event
76	Know a Secret: You know a secret about someone important – a king or an ealdorman. The secret is something they would rather stay hidden. What is it? How did you find out?
77	Forgiveness: Rather than seek vengeance or wergild from a past enemy, you forgave them. What did they do and why did you forgive them? Are you a rare Christian among the Saxons? Do those who know what you did think you weak?
78	Theft: Something precious of yours was stolen. What was it? You do not know the thief, or where it is, but you may suspect? What do you suspect? What are you going to do to get it back?
79	Commemorated in Verse: A famous skald mentioned you and used you as a theme for a poem. What about you attracted their attention? Was the poem flattering or insulting and what has it done for your repuation?
80	Widely Travelled: You have been to distant lands; not just the shores of Britain and Germany but further south and east, perhaps even to Byzantium. How have you come to travel so widely? What have you brought back from your journeys?
81	Long Distance Swim: You gained a measure of fame for an epic feat of swimming, perhaps as a challenge, perahps out of necessity when your boat capsized. Can you repeat it or was it a once in a lifetime achievement?
82	Religious Duty: A laece told you to perform a seemingly meaningless religious ritual, such as dropping a stone with a hole through it in a particular pool, or gathering a particular rare plant by the light of the new moon. The duty is at best inconvenient. Will you do it? Can you guess at the meaning?
83	Patron: You have a well-off and influential patron, perhaps an ealdorman, who supports your endeavours, supplying funding and support. He has asked nothing of you for this help – yet.
84	Grey Hair: After an encounter with the supernatural, you have prematurely grey hair. This hair will not take any dye; the colour always comes through. What did you encounter?
85	Cause of Strife: You made an inappropriate remark at a tense moment that caused not just strife but an outright feud between two families. How do you feel about that? How do those involved feel about you? Are you reviled or miraculously blameless?
86	Good Luck Charm: You carry a small good luck charm with you whenever you go and indeed have had a fair share of good fortune, avoiding some of the worst things that have beset those around you. But you know this will change should you lose your charm. What is it? What luck has it brought you?
87	Lost a Duel: You lost a personal duel with a rival. Worse, after beating you, they left you alive, although you do bear a scar from that encounter, as well as bitterness and humiliation. Now what are you going to do?
88	Cursed Someone: You lost your temper with one of your kin and loudly cursed them, calling upon the gods to bring them misfortune. A few days later they died. Was this a coincidence, or do you have powers? How do you feel? Do others know of this, and if so how do they feel?
89	Lost Companion: On a trip with companions through a forest, you took an afternoon nap. When you awoke, it was night time and one of your companions had vanished. There was no sign of them and you never saw or heard tell of them again. What do you think happened?
90	Lost Lore: Exploring Roman ruins, you retrieved an ancient cache of scrolls. Perhaps you do not know how to read them but what knowlededge could they contain?

Background Events

1d100	Event
91	Bitter Betrothal: To help your kin make peace with a rival family, you have agreed to marry one of your rivals. The problem is that there is too much history for you to easily forget and you and your betrothed simply do not get on at all. What on earth is marriage going to be like? What will you do?
92	Cursed Treasure: As spoils of war, you took a gold armband from a Celtic warrior and since then you have had an awful run of bad luck. What has happened? You have even tried throwing the cursed thing away but an honest thrall found the armband and returned it to you. What will you do now?
93	Bonds of Friendship: You have a firm friend (or perhaps more than a friend) in the camp of an enemy, perhaps an enemy who is not even Saxon. Could this lead the way to peace? Will you attempt to rise above the squabble? Or will you use your friendship as a weapon?
94	Sundered Family: Your relatives are arguing over an inheritance gained from the death of a well-off thane. The quarrel may escalate into outright violence. Have you chosen your side, or will you stay out of it? Or will you even try to intervene as peacemaker – after all, the argument weakens you all.
95	Lost Lands: Your family lost their lands through the tides of war, drought, or another disaster. Will you help them reclaim them? Or are matters beyond that, and will you go on to claim new land?
96-00	Reroll twice.

Saxon Culture

The Saxons are a loose alliance of Germanic coastal tribes who began raiding the coast of Britain in late Roman times and then settled in great numbers on High King Vortigern's invitation, following the promises of territory. They came in search of glory, land and riches; an additional push came when the harvests in their original homelands failed. The Saxons come from Denmark and Northern Germany, and although there are several tribes, they share a common culture and have closely related languages.

The Saxons therefore, are not a single homogenous group but have many customs in common. The word *Saxon* in this book is used to denote the peoples as a whole and when talking about the common cultures. Confusingly, one of these individual tribes are also called the Seaxa, or Saxons, the sons of the sword. They are arriving in great numbers on the south coast and King Aelle, who now rules Ceint and seeks to conquer all Britain, is part of the Saxon tribal group

Of the other tribes, the Frisians have largely remained in their ancestral lands. The Jutes, the tribe Hengest and Horsa belonged to, settled in Ceint and parts of the south coast, although many of the Jute rulers now belong to the Saxon tribe. The people of Yngvi, the god of the sword, also known as the Angles, have conquered most of eastern Britain. Further Saxons have settled in the borderlands they call Mierce, although they are far from united.

Social Hierarchy

The basis of Saxon society is kin and status. A man's or woman's kin are important allies who can be relied upon and they offer protection in matters of law. One who is kinless is vulnerable, having nobody to defend them, avenge them or who can be relied on to take their side in possibly violent arguments.

Within Saxon society, the important people, those with freedom and who make decisions, are the free warriors or carls. Carls are not strictly tied to a lord or king, have the right to bear arms and may participate in decisions made at an assembly. Carls who serve in a king's household are his housecarls and have superior status. Ahead of the carls in status are the thanes. A thane is in charge of a hide of land – a small estate of 120 acres or so, which is farmed by the thane's servants and dependents. Thanehood can be granted by either a king or ealdorman.

Those thanes with their status granted by a king are known as King's Thanes. A king's thane has more land than an ordinary thane and governs a number of lesser thanes. A thane is the head of his family and responsible for their kin, as well as dependents and servants.

These servants may be free men and women who serve the thane, sometimes including the thane's kin, and include a few carls. A thane's dependents and free servants work for him in return for a livelihood, representation and protection. The carls are free to leave to find service elsewhere; they stay through reward and personal loyalty. Some servants, however, are not free; these are thralls and are treated by the law as property rather than people. A thane's thralls work for him because they must.

Most thanes earn their lands and status as a reward for an active life as a free warrior. Saxon expansions within Britain mean that land is there for the taking by one who can both seize it and defend it. A thane's status therefore requires success in defending his land, and protecting and providing for kin and servants. One whose servants are murdered by a rival, and who fails to exact due vengeance or obtain an appropriate wergeld (see below), is unlikely to keep his position.

The most powerful of the Saxon free warriors are the ealdormen. An ealdorman leads a warband of carls, called a fyrd, and can be lord of several thanes. He is also a ring giver, distributing rewards and plunder to followers and this is considered the duty of every ealdorman. An ealdorman can often only maintain status through waging almost continual war for new lands and plunder. This explains the raids into British territory even from settled Saxons who should be content.

Carls in a warband are not bound to their leader or any code of law; rather they follow out of personal loyalty and the expectation of material rewards. A carl who feels he does not receive his due from an ealdorman is free to seek service elsewhere or strike out on his own, maybe putting his own warband together. When the Britons say that the Saxons are little more than mercenary raiders, there is an element of truth – but most do not understand the nature of Saxon society and the freedoms that they enjoy which leads to this behaviour.

Languages

The languages of the Saxon tribes – the Angles, the Frisians, the Jutes and the Saxons – are dialects of a common Germanic tongue and the relevant language skills default to each other at a Hard grade of difficulty.

Kings & Succession

At the top of Saxon society, commanding several ealdormen and their warbands, are the kings and their noble families – the athelings. Most kings claim to be descended from Seaxneat, the mortal son of the god Wotan, but in reality an ealdorman who masses enough power and territory can claim to be king in his own right, with his own ealdormen, thanes and carls. New lands present an ideal opportunity for an ealdorman to become a king. A carl, apart from a housecarl, owes no unending allegiance to a king and some noted Saxon warriors and even ealdormen sell their services to several kings.

There are no clear rules for succession when a king dies and no clear principle that a king's oldest son inherits, although in the more established Saxon kingdoms, especially among the Jutes, some form of succession of this nature is emerging. Ideally, a related atheling is proclaimed king by the carls who served the old king. More typically, however, the old king's holdings and thanes are divided amongst several other disputing successors – an act that provides the opportunity for more wars and plunder.

One Saxon king stands out from the others: Aelle, King of Ceint. He has named himself *Bretwalda*, king of all Britain, consciously positioning himself as a Saxon replacement for the old British high kings. He seeks to unite all of the Saxons, indeed, all of Britain if he can, under his rule and a number of lesser kings pay him tribute.

The recent arrival of the Saxon lord Cerdic on the southern shores of the land boosts the Saxon forces but also promises Aelle a rival to his claims to leadership of all Saxons. King Guercha of Anglia also does not recognise Aelle's claim and he is powerful in the north.

Geburs & Thralls

The carls, let alone thanes, ealdormen, and kings, occupy a privileged position in society. They are free to bear arms, to move about the country and serve any lord they wish. Below them are the unfree Saxons, the gebur. A gebur's duty varies and can be arduous. They are bound to a particular thane and must give up to half their time in labouring for their lord, earning their own living in the time remaining to them. In some places, geburs can be called to arms by their thanes. Geburs are the largest class in Saxon society and most conquered Britons in Saxon lands serve as geburs.

Beneath the gebur, both in status and rights, are those who are truly unfree: the Saxon thralls. Thralls are slaves and by law considered property rather than men. Most are the property of the thanes and labour on their land, while a few thralls serve an ealdorman or king directly. Legally, an injury or death to a thrall counts as property damage, with any wergild paid directly to their owner. Men, women and children can all be thralls and the child of a thrall is also a thrall. Ownership of thralls, especially new and wilful thralls, is not something a Saxon goes into lightly, and they are legally responsible for any of their thralls' actions. An owner is legally entitled to punish or even kill their own thralls as they see fit.

Even amongst the thralls, there are status levels. An unskilled agricultural worker (the most common thrall) has no status and is treated like any tool or implement. By contrast, a skilled craftsman may even earn a small amount of wages, although they are still of course unfree and required to obey their master's commands. Thralls are allowed their own possessions but are not allowed to carry weapons, including the traditional seax.

The typical outcome for a people who are newly conquered by the Saxons is thralldom. It is also the fate of other Saxons taken prisoner in battle. A man may sell himself into thralldom to pay off debts or provide for his family and criminals sometimes do this to raise money to pay wergild.

However, thraldom need not be forever; selling oneself as a thrall is for a set period of time, although usually at least a decade. An owner can will their thralls to be free when they die or can pass them on as property to their kin. An owner can also free a thrall in a religious ceremony to the god Tyr, held at a crossroads, which symbolises the former thrall is now free to choose their own path.

In many Saxon lands, almost all Britons still present serve as thralls and geburs. The biggest exception is the land of Ceint, where the Saxons have been present long enough that the British are no longer a newly conquered people and Aelle has a relaxed attitude towards the British who do not resist him. Blood is still important, however, and British free folk have half the wergild of their Saxon counterparts. Trusted Britons can, and do, become carls, thanes and, in a few cases, ealdormen — as long as they swear they allegiance to Aelle.

Laeces

Saxon laeces, or shamans, know how to travel the spirit world and how to contact and bind spirits. Part of the role of the laece is protecting the world from spirits. They also bind them to their own service, for their own sake and for the sake of the Saxon people.

Laeces are also healers. They are skilled in herbalism and mundane medicine, as well as in casting out spirits who cause madness and disease. Laece are also expected to be knowledgeable about mystical matters, such as matters of cosmology that are obscure to the common man.

Becoming a laece requires both a period of training lasting several years and an inborn talent. The talent is no respecter of class and can appear in a thrall or gebur just as often as in an atheling. By custom, a laece who notices the talent in someone adopts them for training, regardless of their prior station in life.

Laeces exist to an extent outside of society. They are not warriors and do not make decisions in an assembly. They need not be loyal to ealdorman or even a king and travel throughout the Saxon lands, advising and dealing with the spiritual and medical matters they find. Not all laeces are nomadic but even those who settle down usually do so in isolation, just outside of ordinary settlements. Ealdormen, athelings and kings go out of their way to attract the patronage of a skilled and powerful laece; there is always advantage in having the spirits on your side.

Most laeces see themselves as above mundane politics, not favouring one Saxon faction over another, although they still try to stay on good diplomatic terms with the powerful people in ordinary Saxon society. A king usually has a laece as an advisor and would be wise to heed their words.

Women, Marriage & Children

Men and women have equal legal and social standing in Saxon society; the Saxon word *mann* means an adult person of either gender. Women may own property and land and free women have as much liberty as men to pursue a profession. Women are as well educated as men; or even better educated, considering the emphasis on martial prowess in manly training.

Some women are warriors – shield maidens – and free female warriors are as respected as their male counterparts, with the same right to make decisions in assembly. Female thanes are rare, however, and a female ealdorman is almost unheard of. Even women who are not warriors wield influence and often take the lead in matters of diplomacy and ceremony.

An arrangement for marriage is a contract between the groom and the bride's father. The bride's consent is required; she cannot be forced to marry against her will and a woman is not subordinate to her husband. A married woman keeps her own property and her father's status, rather than taking on the status of her new husband. Marriage usually takes the nature of a practical contract to form an allegiance between two families.

Before the wedding, the bride's kin gives her a dowry. The dowry goods are the bride's alone and legally untouchable by her husband. At the wedding, the groom gives the bride's kin a valuable gift – handgeld – to symbolise his financial well-being and ability to look after his new bride. The bride, for her part, gives her new husband a gift of a sword or seax, depending on status. The morning after the wedding, the groom gives his new bride a further morning gift, to further ensure the bride's independence should anything happen to him.

For richer families all of these gifts are valuable but for the poor they can be tokens. The gifts are expected to be appropriate to one's status and of similar value, meaning weddings between those of very different status levels are rare.

Before the wedding ceremony, it is normal for both bride and groom to bathe and wear their best clothes. The bride wears a wedding wreath of flowers. A skald or man of high standing, perhaps a local thane or ealdorman, officiates at the ceremony. He witnesses oaths of loyalty the bride and groom make to each other and blesses the union in the names of the goddess Freja and Frigga.

A wedding is an excuse for a feast for the kin of the bride and groom and, for important families, many other guests. The month after the ceremony is hunigmonath (honey month) for the bride and groom, so called because they are entitled to drink mead if they can afford it, regardless of their usual stations

Marriage is more than just a way of binding families. Only married thanes can be given land, whether grants of existing land, or newly conquered land to administer. Both men and woman can be thanes, although most are men, who gain the status after a successful life as a free warrior. If a thane dies, their spouse gains thane status and inherits their land. However, their other goods return to their kin.

When it comes to children, both boys and girls are important and they gain their father's status. They are typically brought up in roles according to their gender. Girls learn housekeeping, household management if of high status, brewing and cooking. The fashion in some newly rich households is to teach the girls – although not necessarily the boys – to read and write. Boys have a more martial upbringing, practicing weapons from an early age. Depending on their family, they also learn how to farm.

Funerals

At a Saxon's funeral, their friends and kin gather, and a skald recites a poem to honour the deceased and commend them to the gods. They then typically cremate the body, although there are exceptions to this, and bury the ashes in a pottery urn or bronze bowl. Grave goods, which are buried along with the body or ashes, are a part of the custom and include things that will be useful to the deceased in the afterlife. Warriors are buried with combs, razors, weapons, helms and shields. Women are often buried with jewellery and combs, although some also have the accoutrements of warriors. Poorer individuals are buried with more basic items, such as beads, knives, belts and pots containing food. The Saxons inter infants with pots of food to ensure they will not go hungry on their journey to the afterlife. Married couples and children are often buried together. Along with the grave goods, the Saxons bury animal skulls with their dead to indicate the protection of spirits.

A feast of the fallen person's kin follows the funeral. When an ealdorman or king dies, or after a battle where there are many fallen warriors, feasts can be grand affairs.

When they have time, Saxons will also burn or bury those they defeat in war, or executed criminals. They do not wish to displease the spirits and gods by not respecting the dead. However, Saxons do not bury their enemies with grave goods, unless they wish to honour a defeated enemy in some way.

The grandest of all Saxon funerals, reserved for the greatest of kings and richest of ealdormen, is a ship burial. In this case, the kin of the deceased place their body and grave goods on a ship, which they set ablaze – either on land or drifting out to sea. The ship is of course valuable, so using one in this way is a great indication of wealth and prosperity; the symbolic value in Saxon beliefs is that Saxon nobles are carried to the afterlife in boats.

Rulership & Law

Assemblies

An assembly is a gathering of carls before an ealdorman or king. The assembly as a whole, not just the lord, makes decisions involving policy and legal cases, and are held in an ealdorman's or king's feasting hall. Public religious ceremonies also take place at an assembly, and the proceedings are rounded off by a feast, with its accompanying entertainment.

If an ealdorman or king dies, or has been deposed, the carls and thanes gather at an assembly to attempt to choose a successor, although such successions are seldom clean and often lead to splintering factions and even war.

The role of a king or ealdorman at an assembly is to listen to complaints, speak in judgement and suggest actions. The free warriors signal assent to a decision or judgement by banging their weapons against their shields.

There is some hierarchy to assemblies: those held in the mead halls of kings are more important than those held by ealdormen. All carls serving an ealdorman can attend a local assembly. Only the ealdormen, thanes and other men of importance in the king's service will attend a king's assembly, although the most important ealdormen are more powerful than the least important kings.

Blood Feud & Wergild

Saxon law is basic. When a free man or woman is wronged – robbed, assaulted or murdered – they and their kin have the right to appeal for a blood feud before an assembly. A blood feud allows them to pursue a legal vendetta against both the criminals and any kin who defend them. Blood feuds can escalate on both sides but by legally containing them, a lord usually manages to prevent such things escalating into a full-blown war.

Not only is a blood feud legally allowed but it is expected; one who does not pursue a blood feud when wronged is at best a coward and at worst admitting they deserve whatever happens. This is one of many ways that kin is important. Without kin, a Saxon has nobody to take their side in a blood feud, avenging or protecting them.

Fortunately for the stability of society, there is a recent innovation that provides an alternative to the blood feud, namely wergild or 'man payment'. Wergild is treasure that one accused of a crime, or their kin, pays in compensation. Since Saxon society lacks a formal concept of money, there is no fixed amount for wergild but the higher someone's station, and the more severe the crime, the greater the wergild.

A freeman seeking to pursue a blood feud in assembly can honourably accept wergild as recompense instead of the death of a criminal, although they are not obliged to take it. Wergild is a nuanced system, as it does not just apply in cases of death but also for injury and other crimes. There are different quantities of wergild for different injuries; the amount depends on a person's class (so a thane is worth more than a carl), age and usefulness to society.

Blood feuds and wergild are the rights of carls and their kin. Servants and dependents have no such rights, although harming a free man's dependents is the same as damage to his property or theft and he may take legal action to seek amends, in the usual forms of pursuing a blood feud or demanding wergild before an assembly. A thane or ealdorman, after all, is expected to protect and provide for his dependents and servants.

Saxons at Work and Play

Food and Drink

Feasting is the pleasure of the rich and the solace of the poor. They mark victory celebrations, marriages, religious festivals and funeral wakes.

The central feature of a king's or ealdorman's feast is meat, typically chicken or pork, with beef and mutton on special days. They eat barley bread and some vegetables along with the meat, all washed down with copious quantities of ale or mead and in some halls, wine they import from the continent. A skald – a poet who recites his own work to a harp accompaniment – is part of the entertainment, as are after dinner speeches and toasts.

The drink is just as important as the food and after dinner speeches and toasts are part of any good feast. As more drink is consumed, entertainments become less refined. Carls wrestle, swap ribald jokes and riddles, and fall into drunken brawls, which sometimes turn into serious fights.

Poorer Saxons do not eat meat on any regular basis except at feasts, where chicken, bacon and pork sausages feature. As with the British, the great staple of the Saxon diet is barley. They make round flat loaves of barley bread, which is baked on the hearth stones of a fire. Another typical peasant meal is a boiled broth called briw, consisting of barley with peas, beans and other vegetables. Poor Saxons also eat fish (including fish dried for long-term storage), cheese and chicken, duck or goose eggs. One difference between the Saxons and the Britons is that the Saxons lack a tradition of hunting for game.

The main vegetable the Saxons cook is the leek, although they also make use of beetroot, carrots, curly kale, onions, parsnips and turnips. Vegetables, along with garlic, are used as much for flavouring as anything else, as Saxons use herbs in medicine rather than in cooking. For sweetening, the Saxons use honey and fruit, with apples, pears, plumbs, blackberries, strawberries and raspberries being the most popular.

The main drink for rich and poor, and young and old alike, is a weak barley beer and those with access to cows and sheep also drink milk. On feast days or when they simply desire stronger drink, Saxons drink ale. Mead, a distilled honey drink is reserved for kings and guests at a king's feast. Some ealdormen and kings are beginning to acquire a taste for imported wine from continental Europe.

Saxons eat from wooden or bronze bowls, using a wooden spoon for briw, or bread and knives for more solid dishes. Poorer Saxons drink from wooden cups, although thanes and richer carls use drinking horns.

Clothing

Saxon men and women have distinct styles of clothing, although female free warriors — shieldmaidens — dress similarly to men for practical reasons.

Everyday clothing for a man consists of a long-sleeved undershirt reaching to the hip, a loincloth and wool trousers held up with a leather belt threaded through loops, similar to a modern belt and usually have decorative buckles. On top of this, a man wears a knee length long-sleeved tunic. Richer tunics are decorated at the neck, wrists and hem. Trousers have no pockets but a man will hang pouches and a long knife, called a seax, from their belt.

Women wear a long-sleeved wool or linen underdress with a drawstring neck. The sleeves are also fastened; poorer dresses with string and richer dresses with metal clasps. An outer dress called a peplos goes over the underdress. The peplos is a tube of colourful material, featuring shoulder clasps and a belt to hold it to the underdress. Just as men do, women hang pouches and accessories from their belts. Richer women use decorative shoulder brooches rather than clasps and also wear shawls, fastened to the shoulder with the brooch. These wealthier women also wear rings, bracelets and necklaces of beads, although brooches are the most common form of jewellery.

In colder weather, both men and women wear cloaks, which are fastened with brooches or clasps. High status people wear clothing in bright, light colours, especially light blue and purple, as well as having more ornamentation. The clothing colour of those of low status, and especially those who are not free, is usually dull brown.

Typical Saxon footwear consists of wool socks and leather shoes, which are fashioned from a single piece of material and fastened with laces or toggles.

Both men and women have long hair and take great care of it. Almost everyone carries a comb and in the case of the richer members of society, these are rich and ornamented, while ordinary combs are simply carved from bone. The importance of combs is such that they are buried with the dead as treasures to be taken into the afterlife.

Houses, Villages & Halls

The Saxon building material is wood and built over a rectangular pit. It is two stories high, with the lower storey below ground, with a thatched roof. The earthen floor is covered with sand or flints. A group of eight to 10 such houses, along with a hall forms the holdings of a thane and around 30 people, including the thane's extended family and servants, live in such a holding.

A thane's hall is a larger and grander building with a hearth in the centre. It is a communal gathering and eating area.

A group of such holdings forms a village, which is ruled by a more powerful thane (often a king's thane or in the case of the largest, towns in their own right, sometimes an ealdorman). A town or village has a stone wall or wooden stockade fence.

Some towns cluster around older Roman fortifications, which the Saxons now use for their own purposes. The Saxons do not usually repurpose old Roman towns, although when they do they build new houses within the old Roman walls. More typically, they simply plunder them for building materials.

The feasting halls or mead halls of ealdormen and especially kings stand out from common dwellings. Such halls, like the lesser halls of thanes, are built around a long room with a stone floor. Benches line the walls and a king's housecarls (or unmarried free carls in an ealdorman's service), both dine in the hall and sleep there on mattresses, with their weapons close to hand so the hall can immediately be defended.

The roof of a hall is tall and gabled, and the timber is clamped with iron. A king's hall has further decoration on the roof. The walls are covered with tapestries and the benches have embroidered covers.

Away from the hall are private chambers for the king and queen, or ealdorman and his wife, and their most important retainers. A hall also functions as a fortress: the doors are securely barred and it is surrounded by a wooden palisade with a barred and guarded gate.

As well as the hall, within a palisade are some other buildings called burs. These outbuildings serve as lodgings for guests and families, storage places and workshops.

Metalworking

The most esteemed craft among the Saxons is metalworking and it is more than just a skill, it is an art form to make helms, swords and jewellery. The helms of famous warriors are richly decorated with abstract patterns in bronze or silver, and animals with bodies divided into sections to match the pattern at the fringes of the design. Heavier jewellery bears similar patterns.

Sometimes these patterns, especially on brooches, carry visual tricks, so that the shape resembles an animal from one angle and a human face from another. These tricks are the visual equivalent

Sword Names
Hildeleoma — 'battle light'
Hrunting — 'thrusting'
Naegling — 'nail'
Scirmael — 'brightly patterned'
Graegmael — 'grey mark'
Wyrmmael — 'serpent's mark'

of a riddle and are both for amusement and occasional magical significance.

Swords are a prestige item, not carried by the common warrior but rather by the famous, the powerful and the rich. They are also personal items and carry names. A sword requires both time and great expertise to make. A swordsmith will fold four different types of iron to give a blade a sharp edge, and make it strong yet not brittle; the process gives the sword a distinctive patterning down its blade. Swords are expensive both because of the time and skill needed and the cost of the materials.

Weland, the smith of the gods, has high status in Woden's feasting hall and some legendary helms and weapons are said to have been made by him — including, in some Saxon eyes, Arthur's sword Excalibur. Mortal smiths have a high rank in society; they are free men, with the same status as warriors, even if they do not fight.

Games & Sports

As well as the riddle game described on page 30, Saxons are fond of dice and board games, and gamble at both. They play a form of knucklebones and tacfl, a board game which most closely resembles modern draughts or checkers.

More physical games include sword dancing, swimming, running and archery. Riding and horse racing are starting to catch on as pastimes for nobles.

Money & Possessions

Saxon trade is based on barter. They do not make use of money, although they do keep gold coins from the Frankish lands or old Roman coins from Britain, as ornaments. Jewellery also serves to an extent in place of currency; Saxons exchange treasure for practical goods, although not at a fixed value. The term 'ring giver' used for a king or ealdorman indicates their habit of doling out such treasure to their followers. Incidentally, the word ring used here means more than just a finger ring — it includes bracelets, arm rings and collars such as the Celtic torcs.

The Saxons do not wear the same style of jewellery as the Celts as a general rule but brooches are almost universal for women. As noted previously, both men and women carrry combs and the combs belonging to people of high status are valuable and highly decorated, sometimes with precious materials.

The Saxons are a superstitious peopleand wear charms on a cord round the neck to protect from the ill workings of fate and hostile magic or spirits. The most common charm is a small ornamental hammer, symbolising the protection of the thunder god Donnar. Kings and athelings with ambition wear an eagle's talon around the neck to gain the blessing of Wotan, king and war leader of the gods. The common folk will sometimes drill holes through coins, especially old Roman coins, and wear them round the neck on a

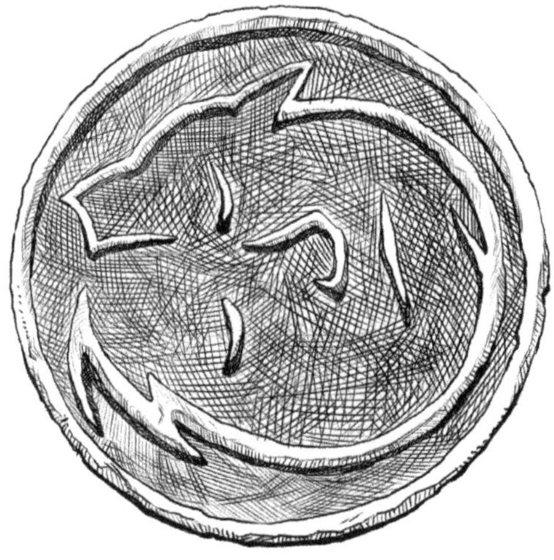

piece of string as a symbol of prosperity. One folk belief among many Saxons is that the Roman coins were magical charms created by the old rulers of the land.

All free Saxons, both men and women, carry the long-bladed seax knife. Thus, free Saxons are always armed and never defenceless. The seax, however, is primarily a tool rather than a weapon and a Saxon will use his or her own seax to cut their meat at a feast.

Saxon Armies

Saxon armies are small, usually numbering at most a few hundred men. Saxon warriors are most commonly armed with shortspears and axes of various sorts, including battle axes, great axes, and hatchets as throwing axes. They also carry round shields and some Saxons also make use of the longbow in ranged combat. Rich and esteemed warriors wield longswords, which have a symbolic as well as a martial value and are a sign of nobility, as swords are both precious and expensive weapons.

Saxons warriors fight on foot; they have no cavalry as such. Rich warriors will ride into battle, although they may dismount before fighting. Saxon forces also include a few scouts as well, who are the best riders and know how to fight from horseback. An ealdorman leads a warband, numbering between a dozen and hundreds of warriors. The men in the warband follow a successful lord because of personal loyalty, respect and pay in the form of loot. Successful ealdormen gather more and more followers; a free warrior is under no obligation to stay with the same lord, especially if they fail in battle or do not treat their warriors well or richly.

The seax carried by all Saxon carls provides an emergency close quarters weapon.

Boats and Ships

The Saxons are still a seagoing people and take pride in their skills as sailors. The rivers of Britain and the seas around it are their trade and communications channels of choice, not the decaying Roman roads. Saxon boats and ships are the most advanced of the era and carry both oars and sails. Saxon boats and ships have figureheads at each end and can be rowed forwards and backwards equally well; they do not as such have a front or back.

The Saxons beach their ships when they land by sending everyone to stand at the aft of a vessel to tilt it before riding up the beach. They do not need to wade ashore, even when landing larger craft.

Smaller boats have four oars and two sails, and are manned by four sailors. These small boats stay close to the shore or sail on rivers. Larger sea-crossing ships carry a crew of around 45, including 30 oarsmen. There is room for additional passengers; enough for a fleet of ships to transport Saxons en masse to Britain's shores.

Language & Culture

The languages of the Saxon tribes are the ancestors to the tongue known in the modern day as Old English. They are grammatically complex and closer to modern German than to modern English; for example, nouns have three genders: masculine, feminine and neuter, with endings depending on five cases, as well as whether they are singular, plural or dual. This can be important in Saxon poetry (see below), just as it is worth noting that the sun is grammatically feminine but the moon masculine.

The Saxon alphabet is the 24 letters of the elder Futhark runes. These runes are not used in literature but are carved into jewellery, weapons, including both swords and spear tips, and even tools such as spinning wheels and combs. They are most often used to record names and for magical purposes, such as invoking the spirits or divination. The act of naming someone or something with runes is a part of Saxon magic.

Few in Saxon society are literate, although many know and use a few runes, such as those which spell their own names. The literate people are often laeces.

Poetry & Riddles

Saxon society has a rich tradition in oral poetry. Life is uncertain, bloody and often short, with glory impermanent. Poetry reflects these themes and is expressed in alliterative verse, where

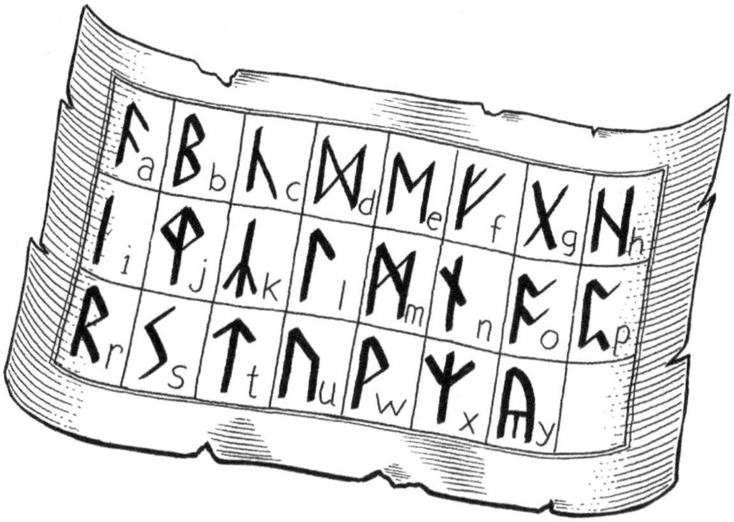

the rhythm is important and the sounds starting sentences and phrases match.

extract from beowulf

Time passed away. On the tide floated
under bank their boat. In her bows mounted
brave man blithely. Breakers turning
spurned the shingle. Splendid armour
they bore aboard, in her bosom piling
well-forged weapons, then away thrust her
to voyage gladly valiant-timbered.
She went then over wave-tops, wind pursued her,
fleet, foam-throated like a flying bird;
and her curving prow on its course waded,
till in due season on the day after
those seafarers saw before them
shore-cliffs shimmering and sheer mountains,
wide capes by the waves: to water's end
the ship had journeyed. Then ashore swiftly
they leaped to land, lord of Gothland,
bound fast their boat. Their byrnies rattled,
grim gear of war.

The Wanderer, which reflects on the misery of an exiled atheling cut off from previous delights, is typical both in its melancholy tone and verse structure. The contrast between the thriving and the decaying is a feature of Saxon verse and nautical themes are also common. The alliterative structure, melancholy and contrast between prosperity and ruin features in the best-known example of Saxon poetry, namely Beowulf. Beowulf comes from a later time in Saxon history, although it looks back nostalgically to earlier, more heroic times – such as the times of *Mythic Britain*.

A skald is a poet who composes and recites poetry. Recitations are accompanied by a harp. The skald will recite standard much-loved pieces and compose poems concerning recent events and elegies for the dead. Skalds are usually attached to a king's or ealdorman's mead hall, where as well as being an entertainer, they serve as a historian and preserver of oral traditions. A few wandering skalds also visit lesser mead halls, playing for food and lodging as well as appropriate gifts.. A skald will be present at a king's great feast, a celebration or to commemorate the homecoming of a warband.

It is a great thing for a warrior to be commemorated by a skald in life and to have their elegy composed and recited at death. An ealdorman or even a king gains status by having a talented skald in their service.

Poetry also has a magical function and was passed down to man by Woden, who drank magical mead to gain poetic insight. Skalds are closer to the spirit world than most men and have access to secret, or at least obscure, knowledge. A skald can destroy reputations through mockery, as well as make or celebrate them, and thus are as much feared as well as honoured.

Kennings

Within poems, kennings, a type of figurative expressions, are often used in place of ordinary words. Some examples are:

Battle Light: A sword

Bone House: The human body

Ring Giver: King or ealdorman

Wave Floater: A ship

There are several kennings describing the sea, including *Whale Road, Fish Home* and *Seal Bath.*

Extract from the Wanderer

Where is the horse? Where the hero?
Where the treasure-giving prince?
Where the seats at the feast, where the delights of the hall?
Alas, bright goblet! Alas, mailed fighter!
Alas, princely power. How that time has passed away,
Grown dark beneath night's helmet, as though it had not been.

In a more playful mode, the Saxons are fond of riddles, swapping them for entertainment at feasts, trying to guess answers. Riddles sometimes make use of poetic kennings and a skilled riddler makes them up on the spot.

Two people can play the riddle game, a contest of wit and poetic talent. The two players take turns posing riddles for the other to guess and ends when one party fails to guess a riddle. The game is best played in front of a vocal audience, where a nonsensical riddle is disallowed, or an answer allowed if it fits the riddle, even if it is not what the riddler intended. Usually, the game is more of a performance than a cut-throat contest – it is done as much to entertain the audience as anything else.

However, the Saxons also play the riddle game for more serious stakes, as a form of gambling, or as a usually non-violent way to settle a dispute.

Mythras Rules for the Riddle Game

In a formal riddle game, one player challenges the other, with the challenger posing the first riddle.

To pose a riddle, make a Standard roll using Customs (Saxon), Lore (Saxon) or an Easy roll with Art (Poetry), Lore (Riddles) or a similar skill.

If, as a player, you actually present a riddle, you get an Easy bonus to your skill.

A Games Master may wish to present a riddle to a player for them to solve; in this case, the GM rolls normally with no bonus for the NPC riddler and then presents the riddle if the roll is successful.

Critical Success

Hard riddle; opponent needs a critical success in their roll to answer.

Success

Successful riddle; opponent needs a successful roll to answer.

Failure

Riddle easy; no roll needed to answer it.

Fumble

Riddle disallowed; disqualified from contest.

To answer a successfully posed riddle, the player makes a Standard roll with Insight or an Easy roll with Art (Poetry) or Lore (Riddles). These skills are all capped by the PC's skill in the Language of the riddle contest.

The degree of success needed is in the above table. If a player gets a critical success where an ordinary success would do, the character gives a logical answer to the riddle that is different to the one intended but perfectly correct and elegant; this meets with the acclaim of the crowd.

If your GM has explicitly prepared an actual riddle and rather than just rolling you answer it successfully as a player, you do not need to roll for your character.

Most Saxon riddles are short, sometimes making use of poetic kennings and usually improvised. The following is typical:

A wonder on the wave,
water became bone

(Answer: Ice on the seashore or shores of a lake)
Some riddles are more sophisticated in form.

Examples of Riddles

A wonderful warrior exists on earth.
Two dumb creatures make him grow bright between them.
Enemies use him against one another.
His strength is fierce but a woman can tame him.
He will meekly serve both men and women
If they know the trick of looking after him
And feeding him properly.
He makes people happy.
He makes their lives better.
But if they let him grow proud
This ungrateful friend soon turns against them.
(Answer: Fire)
When I am alive I do not speak.
Anyone who wants to takes me captive and cuts off my head.
They bite my bare body
I do no harm to anyone unless they cut me first.
Then I soon make them cry.
(Answer: An onion)
I saw a beast breasting the waves,
it was strangely stuffed with wonders,
It had four feet beneath its belly
and eight upon its back;
had two wings, twelve eyes
and six heads. Say what it was.
It flew over oceans but was no bird,
yet showed some likeness to
horse and man, hound and bird,
and women's beauty too. You will, if you know
how to, tell the truth about
the way in which this creature moves.

(The answer to this last riddle is a boat but some of the references perhaps need some explanation. It refers to a fairly small vessel. The four feet are four oars and the eight feet belong to the four rowers. The two wings are sails and the six heads and 12 eyes belong to the four sailors and two figureheads, on fore and one aft)

Many riddles are more ribald, as one would expect for a game played after many drinks.

Swings by his thigh,
a thing most magical!
Below the belt,
beneath the folds
of his clothes it hangs,
a hole in its front end,
stiff-set and stout,
it swivels about.
Levelling the head
of this hanging tool,
its wielder hoists his hem
above his knee;
it is his will to fill
a well-known hole
that it fits fully
when at full length
He's oft filled it before.
Now he fills it again.

(Answer: A Key)

The Saxon Calendar

The months in the Saxon calendar correspond to 28 day lunar cycles. There are 12 months in the year and the Saxons insert an extra month outside of the normal ones when the calendar drifts out of sync with the seasons.

The Saxon months are, as they roughly correspond to the modern ones:

- Aeftella Geola – Second Yule: January
- Sol-monath – The Month of Cakes: February.
- Hreth-monath – The Month of the Goddess Hretha: March
- Eostre-monath – The Month of the Goddess Eostre: April
- Thrimith-monath – The Month of Three Milkings: May
- Sere-monthath – Midsummer Month: June
- Aeftella Lipa – Second Midsummer: July
- Weod-Monath – Plant Month: August
- Haerfest-Monath – Harvest Month: September
- Winterfelleth – Winder Full Moon: October
- Blot-Monath – Month of Sacrifice: November
- Aerra Geola – First Yule: December

When the Saxons add an extra month to the calendar, they fit the month of Thrilitha, or Third Midsummer, between Sere-monthath (June) and Aeftella Lipa (July).

In the Saxon calendar, days begin at sunset (rather than sunrise, as in the Roman tradition). Thus the night is part of the day following it and, poetically, night comes before day. Some festivals and feasts begin at sunset, marking the start of the new day.

Religious festivals are a part of the Saxon calendar and influence the names of several of the months. These include:

The Festival of Cakes

The Festival of Cakes is held when the snow first melts and winter shows signs of lifting. Families and especially children celebrate by eating the cakes and offering thanks to the gods.

The Festival of Hretha

Hretha is the goddess of death and winter, and must be placated with animal sacrifices before she lifts her hold on the land and spring begins. Warriors eat these animal sacrifices at a feast.

The Spring Festival

The Spring Festival is sacred to the goddess Eostre, goddess of the spring and the dawn. It begins at dusk, when celebrants light bonfires that burn through the night. Water drawn from wells and springs the following morning is said to have healing properties.

Midsummer Festival

On the night of the Midsummer Festival, children gather bones, which the Saxons burn on fires. Young warriors also run around the fields with brands lit from these fires, before putting them into a wheel which they roll around. The fire and brands are to drive away spirits of disease and poison, and the wheel symbolises the turning of the year, at which time the spirits can more easily cross over from the spirit world.

The Harvest Festival

The time of harvest is backbreaking work and when it is over, it is natural for those who work the land to hold a feast to celebrate. A folk belief is that a spirit resides in the last grain harvested. The farmers beat the grain to the ground to chase the spirit out and plant that final grain back into the ground when the seeds are sewn the next year to bless the new crop.

Winter's Beginning

At winter's beginning, farm animals not expected to survive the winter – or who appear likely to be too expensive to feed – are sacrificed to the gods and the Saxons hold a feast at dusk.

Yule

Yule is the midwinter festival, celebrated for three nights starting with midwinter night. It is the major festival of the Saxon year. A special Yule Log is brought into the house and burned over the three days of the festival. Baneful spirits are invited into a household should the Yule Log be extinguished. At Yule, a special feast is held and ealdormen and distinguished warriors travel to the king's feasting hall to toast their king, staying for the winter season if travel is difficult. Even ordinary families save an animal to sacrifice, so they can eat meat at the Yule feast.

Days of the Week

In the era of *Mythic Britain*, the Saxons do not name the days of the week. The modern English names for the days come from later Anglo-Saxon times.

Gods, Spirits & Magic

Saxons know the gods, spirits and magic are real and living. This chapter explores the Saxon view of the supernatural world.

The Aesir

The Saxon gods, the Aesir, govern the higher affairs of the universe and preserve it against the hostile forces of the Ettins or devouring giants. They are neither all-knowing nor infallible but are far above mankind in terms of power. They seldom intervene in mortal affairs but must be propitiated with rituals and sacrifice.

The Aesir are also responsible for the fate of men after their death: the *Waecyrien* are spirits in the form of winged battle maidens who take warriors who fall in battle to the paradise of Neorxnawang to feast in the halls of Woden, king of the gods. They are destined to fight by Woden's side against the Ettins and the forces they raise at the end of the world. Those who die peacefully go instead to the realm of Niflhel, to be judged by the goddess Hel.

Saxon kings are (at least theoretically), linked to the gods. The royal houses of the Jutes, Angles, Frisians and Saxons all trace their descent from Seaxneat, earthly son of the god Woden born of a mortal woman. The number of generations the houses claim for their divine descent varies; the Angle king Guercha claims this is relatively immediate for him and trumpets the claims of divine blood the loudest of any of the Saxon kings.

The gods require respect and ritual acts to honour them but not formal worship as such. The largest and most important rituals take place on certain holy days of the calendar, as described on page 32, and involve an entire community. Minor rites are a more frequent occurrence, especially when a Saxon invokes the gods for a favour, such as fair weather or a good battle.

Invoking the Aesir

The Aesir seldom intervene in mortal affairs but seldom is not the same as never. A Saxon character can seek to invoke the gods for aid before beginning an endeavour. To do this, you choose a god relevant to the undertaking and make a sacrifice to them, usually in the form of a ritual slaughter of an ox. The sacrifice must take place outdoors and during the sacrifice, the one petitioning the god must shout appropriate ritual phrases to seek their favour.

The player then makes a Superstition skill roll. On a critical success, the god looks favourably upon your endeavour and you gain a blessing. A blessing allows you to increase the success level of a single skill roll during the undertaking. Thus, you can use a blessing to turn a critical failure into an ordinary failure, a failure into a success or a success into a critical success.

You can only have one such blessing at a time. If you do not use a blessing during the endeavour where you sought divine aid, it is wasted.

Of all the gods, warriors most frequently call upon Woden's son Thunor, the thunder god. Thunor is a hero of the myths, mighty in battle, who wields a hammer. Many warriors wear a stylised hammer amulet on a chain to symbolise Thunor's blessing. The superstitious also invoke Thunor to protect them from hostile supernatural forces, by touching an amulet or making the sign of the hammer. But even this is a ritual form of protection rather than anything like a Christian prayer.

Wyrd

The concept of wyrd means fate or personal destiny. A mortal's wyrd is ordained at their birth by the Norns. There is nothing anyone can do to change their wyrd. One who is born to be a warrior will be a warrior. One who is born to be a leader will be a leader. One who is born to be a thrall will be a thrall.

Wyrd encompasses even the Aesir as well as ordinary men. The gods can no more fight their own fates than mortals. Wise gods and laeces can divine the role of wyrd in lives and the cosmos, and the goddess Frigg is said to know all wyrds but a mortal can never attain such knowledge. A mortal might have serious hints about their fate but will never know the exact workings, or everything in detail

Although this seemingly leads to a fatalistic view, wyrd does not mean there are no choices in life. No mortal can fully know their destiny and prophecies can be misleading as guides, or have the potential for varying interpretations. A man can choose how he faces his destiny and how he reacts to the pull of fate. A man may be destined to be a warrior and die in battle but a warrior may choose to fight well and earn a glorious reputation, or to be cowardly and despised.

A king may choose to rule well and kindly or be a bloodthirsty tyrant, even if his personal wyrd does not depend on this choice. There is a tension between wyrd and free will but any man or woman can face their destiny either laughing or cursing, making the best they can out of events or despairing. These things are not foreordained and are all the same to wyrd.

The weary spirit cannot
withstand wyrd,
nor does a rough or sorrowful mind
do any good.
Those eager for glory
often keep secure
dreary thoughts,
in their breast.
- The Wanderer

Each of us must await the end of his path in this world,
and he who can, should achieve renown before death!
That is the best memorial when life is past
and a warrior's days are recounted!
- Beowulf

The Seven Realms

In Anglo-Saxon cosmology, there are seven different realms. Under ordinary circumstances, it is impossible for an ordinary mortal to cross between them and even a laece can only explore aelfham, the spirit world. However, some beings and influences do come from other realms and not all circumstances are ordinary ones.

The Realms Above

The Realms Above are sometimes simply called Heofen or Heaven. They are not the same place as the Christian Heaven but rather the realms of the gods and the blessed dead.

Esageard

Esageard is the home of the Saxon gods, the Aesir. They dwell similarly to the mortal kings, in wooden feasting halls, and host feasts and entertainments every day for both lesser gods and spirits, and the blessed mortal dead. However, everything is grander than in the mortal realm; the feasting halls are truly vast and rooved with gold, and the mead of the Aesir is a potent and magical drink.

Neorxnawang

Neorxanwang, the fields of contentment, is a paradise, a heavenly meadow without toil, worries, hunger or sorrow. The dead who are rewarded by the gods and warriors who die in glorious battle dwell here. Noble deaths besides those in battle may be rewarded here, for all that, in Saxon lore, death in battle is the surest route to Heofen.

The Realms Between

Middengeard

Middengeard, or Middle Earth is the everyday mortal world. It can be a magical place at times but the magic comes from other realms rather than being native here.

Aelfham

Between Middle Earth and the worlds above and below is the spirit world, Aelfham. Some spirits here are conduits between Middengeard and more distant realms. Others, especially the Aelfar, which give this realm its name, are native here.

When a laece travela to the spirit world, or communes (communea) with the spirits on their own ground, he projects his souls here, while his bodies remains in Middengeard.

The Realms Below

If the worlds above are more exalted than the mortal world, the worlds below are dark and dreary places, often though not necessarily full of woe.

Nastrond

Nastrond, or corpse shore, is hell, a place of punishment. The foul dragon Nidhogg dwells here, far from the sun, chewing on stinking corpses. The constant drizzle of rain here is the acidic venom from Nidhogg's breath. Those guilty of the worst possible crimes (murder, oath breaking and adultery) and those who fail to redeem themselves by dying in battle are sentenced here for by the goddess Hel for their afterlives.

Niflhel

Niflhel is an indistinct world, full of mists and fogs. It is a realm of ice and cold with seven great frozen rivers defining its bounds. It is the abode of the goddess Hel, one of the Aesir, who judges those of the dead who do not die in battle. Those who have not lived notable lives, and are refused the rewards of Asageard or Neorxnawang, or evil ones, who Hel sentences to the realm of Nastrond, spend their afterlives here.

The realm of Niflhel is not a place of suffering or punishment, but neither is it a reward. It is a limbo.

Ettinham

Ettinham, although one of the worlds below, is separated from the Aesir's realm of Esageard by the river Ifing. It is a cold dark icy place of snow and storms, and home to the Ettins, the devouring giants, the enemies of the Aesir and ultimately the whole of creation. Many mythological stories of the Aesir tell of their adventures into Ettinham and some of the Aesir have Ettin ancestry.

Spirits

Saxon wise men believe in a variety of spirits, existing between the gods and man, crossing the spirit world between heaven and earth. Some spirits are conduits between the mortal realm and the gods and others act of their own volition. They dwell in the spirit world, between Heaven and Earth; that is, between Neorxnawang and Middengeard.

Saxon laeces, or shamans, know how to travel the spirit world and make contact with the spirits. Spirits are not cooperative without coercion and many are hostile. Part of the role of the laece is protecting the world from spirits. They also bind them to their own service, for their own sake and for the sake of the Saxon people.

Binding spirits is a tricky business because they are not cooperative. Even those who are not inherently hostile, such as the cofgodas and landvaettir, resent any form of service and must normally be coerced to help. The aelfar are an even more dangerous matter. They play evil games, possess people and can bear lifelong grudges when bound or defeated.

The Celtic and Saxon spirit worlds do not intersect. A Saxon laece on a spirit journey will not interact with, or even encounter, Celtic spirits. However, Celtic and Saxon spirits can fight or otherwise interact with each other. The only way a laece can defeat a Celtic spirit is by use of a Saxon spirit. Similarly, a druid can only battle or drive off a Saxon spirit by means of one of their spirits.

To the Saxons who know such things, there are several types of spirits.

Holy Ground

Saxons do not have sacred buildings or churches but worship the gods outdoors. The laeces hold certain spots to be sacred, places where the spirits can cross more easily or suitable for burials. Some of these sites are on top of older Celtic pagan sites, although the Saxons avoid using Christian holy ground in this way. Saxon burial grounds in particular can be on top of ancient sites indeed, with Saxon mounds mingling with barrows that predate not just the Romans but the Celts.

One reason the laeces order such sites to be reused is to replace the spirits lingering from old worship with new Saxon spirits, thus adapting the land and adjacent spirit worlds to the new Saxon landholders. The placement of symbolic objects, such as stones marked with runes, is a part of the ritual of replacement.

Aelfar

The Aelfar (singular: *aelf*), or elves, are the most common spirits native to Aelfhem and thus the ones the laece most frequently deal with. Pale of skin and fair of face, some would call them beautiful but it is an evil beauty, for they are capricious, malevolent and vengeful. Many ailments and diseases in the mortal world are due to the malice of the Aelfar, so a laece must know how to cast them out. If bound, one can be useful for cursing an enemy. Essentially, to survive long as a laece, one must know how to deal with Aelfar.

Most Aelfar are Sickness Spirits in *Mythras* terms (*Mythras* page 152). They have powers to attack within Aelfham and discorporate those in the physical world, as well as to inflict ailments. One affected by an Aelf's sickness is said to be "Aelf shot".

Animal Spirit

Saxons venerate the wolf, the boar and the eagle as ferocious spirits of wild nature. These animals are often represented in Saxon art. Spirits of all three types of animal can be found in the spirit world in places corresponding to concentrations in the mortal world.

These spirits are Animal Nature Spirits (*Mythras* page 151), with the power to Dominate Species and a Stealth skill of 50%+INT+CHA.

Animal Spirits are somewhat mutable: a leace, when they bind an Animal Spirit, can change it to a Predator Spirit (*Mythras*, page 151) or a Shape-Shifting Spirit (*Mythras*, page 152). Mutating the spirit as such deprives it of free will.

Animal Spirits will ignore people in general, even a laece travelling the spirit world. However, an Animal Spirit will fiercely resist any attempt at control, coercion or binding with all the desperate force it can muster. Further, an animal spirit will never forget an attempt to bind it; a laece can take one by surprise once.

Cofgod

In *Mythras* terms, a Cofgod (plural: *cofgodas*) is a guardian spirit (see *Mythras*, page 149). In some households, people lay out offerings to the Cofgodas, hoping to attract their attention and favour. A Cofgod blesses a place it favours by acting as a guardian, preventing supernatural harm from coming at the spectral hands of other spirits, such as the malicious Aelfar. The Cofgodas more often help common folk rather than laeces, thanes and ealdormen.

However, one of the Cofgodas will soon leave somewhere to its own devices should the offering cease — and the offerings are never a reliable way of attracting one and thus a laece will sometimes bind a Cofgod to a place to protect it. Like other Saxon Spirits, Cofgodas resent servitude and distrust those with the power to potentially bind them.

Landvaettir

The landvaetir are spirits of the land, with one foot in the spirit world and one foot in the mortal landscape. A landvaettir is tied to a particular place, such as a grove of trees or a hill; some mighty landvaettir might be spirits of larger areas, such as an entire forest but more usually landvaettir in such a place are part of an allied group of spirits.

There are also Celtic spirits of the land in Britain but the Landvaettir are already there, not just in conquered areas and are different to their Celtic analogues. However, in the Celtic lands they sleep; it is only in Saxon lands (when a laece contacts them over a period of time), that they awaken.

Landvaettir have the powers of both Nature Spirits (*Mythras*, page 151) and Curse Spirits with the Dominate Region special ability; their powers are equally beneficial and baneful.

Niflung

The Niflungar are spirits that haunt treasure hoards, especially buried treasure. A good Saxon king or ealdorman will distribute wealth to followers rather than hoard it and the attention of a Niflung is a curse affecting misers. That said the Niflungar are more prone to seek out the buried treasure of the dead and thus dead kings and their buried treasures are best left undisturbed, not only out of respect but out of respect for and fear of the evil spirits who protect their treasure. Sometimes a laece will deliberately call down a Niflung to protect treasure.

In *Mythras* terms, Niflungar are elemental spirits of darkness (see page 148). They appear as indistinct dragons.

Nikor

Nikor are monstrous river spirits. Like the landvaettir, they vary in scope. Most Nikor are tied to ponds, streams or stretches of river but the mightiest are linked to entire rivers and lakes. Active Nikor can be hazardous to travellers who do not pay obeisance by making a sacrifice when crossing a river, typically in the form of a minor valuable thrown into the water.

In Mythras terms, Nikor are Water Spirits (see *Mythras*, page 148).

Scaedugengan

The Scaedugenda are forest spirits, cloaked in shadow, somewhat human in shape, though larger and distinctly monstrous. The most famous of these spirits in Saxon stories is Grendel, the first monster in Beowulf. Scaedugengan are particularly fearsome as they are half dead yet bound to the mortal world, meaning they can hurt those in the material world without being vulnerable themselves.

Scaedugenga have the same power as Wraiths (see *Mythras*, page 153). Unlike Wraiths, they are not confined to one place,

Grendel

Grendel's hatred began,
...the monster relished his savage war
On the Jutes, keeping the bloody feud
Alive, seeking no peace, offering
No truce, accepting no settlement, no price
In gold or land, and paying the living
For one crime only with another. No one
Waited for reparation from his plundering claws:
That shadow of death hunted in the darkness,
Stalked Hrothgar's warriors.
ked with runes, is a part of the ritual of replacement.

although they usually focus their predations on a particular area. A laece who really wants to curse an area and does not care about having control of the curse, will call down a scaedugungan.

Waecyrien

The Waecyrien (the equivalent of the Norse Valkyries) are spirits who serve Woden, king of the Aesir. They take the form of winged warrior maidens and their function is to bear off the spirits of the dead who fall in battle to the higher realms. Those found in the spirit world are either bearing one of the dead away or waiting, just across from a battlefield, for fallen warriors. It is rare and inadvisable for a laece to interfere with a Waecyrie, for they are both powerful and directly serve the king of the gods. For a laece to hinder a Waecyrie fulfilling their function threatens the workings of wyrd and will bring doom.

In *Mythras* terms, a Waecyrie is a Death Spirit (see *Mythras*, page 148). As well as the usual powers of a Death Spirit, a Waecyrie is a messenger of Hoefen and recipient of prophetic wisdom, as it pertains to their function. To this end, a Waecyrie has the skill Lore (Battle Foretelling) at a level of 60+INT+POW.

A laece who succeeds in binding a Waecyrie can ask her a single question about upcoming battles in return for her release. Occasionally, a laece will wait at a battlefield to ensnare a Waecyrie to perform such a divination. However, this is dangerous. A Waecyrie is a powerful spirit with an Intensity of 4 or higher. A laece known to the Waecyrien could face multiple opponents in the spirit world and binding a Waecyrie for any purpose other than divination invites disaster as she calls for help from her fellows.

Lore (Battle Foretelling)

With this skill, a Waecyrie knows about present and near future battles in the mortal world, including positions of outcomes and warriors whose wyrd is to fall. Future predictions are never entirely reliable; even Woden, king of the gods and lord of the Waecyrien, is never certain of wyrd and unanticipated factors can change its perception. Once a mortal knows the role of wyrd, the sight of it becomes more warped.

Nevertheless, with this skill, a Waecyrie can tell probable outcomes and who will probably die.

The Wild Hunt

The Saxons as well as the Celts believe in the wild hunt. In Saxon stories, it sweeps through the forests on winter nights, carrying off those who are caught out of doors, either to join the hunt or to be chased by it. The hunt travels at the direction of Woden.

The key role of the Wild Hunt is not to ensnare people in the mortal world but to hunt down those in Aelfham. Spirits of the Wild Hunt, whether they take the role of hunter or hound, are Bane Spirits (see *Mythras*, page 147). On the nights when the hunt

> Let no one be surprised at what we are about to relate, for it was common gossip up and down the countryside that after February 6th many people both saw and heard a whole pack of huntsmen in full cry. They straddled black horses and black bucks while their hounds were pitch black with staring hideous eyes...
>
> ...Reliable witnesses who kept watch in the night declared that there might well have been twenty or even thirty of them in this wild tantivy as near as they could tell.
>
> The Anglo-Saxon Chronicle

rules, the spirits can the skill Discorporate at 50+INT+POW %, as well as their other powers.

The White Dragon

To the Britons, the Red Dragon deep in the spirit world symbolises the magic and prosperity of their people, whereas the White Dragon symbolises its ruin and invasion. When both dragons stir, as at the moment, the land is in conflict.

A few more mystical Saxon Laeces have learned of the British Dragons and are seeking to find a way to access and fully waken the White Dragon from Aelfham or elsewhere in the Seven Worlds. They see the potential of the White Dragon not being a force for the ruin of Britain but a spiritual force favouring the new Saxon rulers. Some even say that it is wyrd that the white dragon is to be the banner of Saxon kings over all the land.

Laeces & Magical Practices

The word "laece" is pronounced "leech", not as in the parasite, but as in a doctor. A laece is an animist, healer, mystic and binder of spirits — a "medicine man". Laeces are proficient in esoteric lore and herbalism as well as more magical arts. They are also amongst the few in Saxon society who can write — although the act of naming someone or something with the Futhark Runes that form the Saxon alphabet is itself a magical one and part of a binding ritual.

All laeces are trained to the level of Shaman (*Mythras*, page 197), meaning they can travel in a trance state to Aelfham and bind or negotiate with the spirits there.

There is no hierarchy amongst the laeces and no leadership, instead having traditions passed down from master to apprentice. In particular, there is no equivalent to a High Shaman or Spirit Lord in *Mythras* terms.

Healing & Herbalism

One of the main roles of the laece is healing. As far as the common folk are concerned, this is a laece's primary function in society, although the laeces themselves, and some kings and ealdormen, often believe otherwise.

A laece's healing is mundane as often as magical. Laeces know how to dress wounds, perform simple battlefield surgery and apply herbal poultices and medicines, but when it comes to herbalism a laece's healing skills are closer to the magical.

As part of a laece's training, they know that herbs are at their most effective when gathered in a ritual fashion. Part of the ritual is gathering herbs by moonlight and digging them out of the ground without damaging any part of the plant rather than cutting them.

In rules terms, if a laece has time to gather fresh herbs in a ritual way, they can reduce the difficulty of a Healing roll by one level, for example from Formidable to Hard, from Hard to Standard or from Standard to Easy.

Further, a laece may gather suitable herbs to assist in the magic of spiritual journeys or binding spirits. With fresh ritually gathered herbs, a laece can use his Healing skill to Augment his Trance and Binding skills (see *Mythras* page 130-131).

Runes & Names

The Futhark Runes were invented centuries ago. They were derived from the Latin alphabet, when Germanic tribes first came into contact with the Romans. The purpose of the Runes is not

Literacy

A character who has the Literacy skill, at any level, in any of the Saxon languages, knows the Futhark runes and can both read and carve them. Such knowledge is a necessary skill for most laeces but of little use to the common man.

The Futhark runes are used to record names and epithets. They are not used to keep records or write literature. There is little or no need for a character to raise their Literacy skill in the Futhark Runes above the base level.

records or literature but naming things: people, but more especially spirits.

Names written in runes are magical. Part of the act of binding a spirit is naming it, for spirits in their original form usually have no names. In order to bind a spirit into a fetish, a laece must carve the spirit's name into the object to contain the spirit.

The most common objects carved with runes (and so used as fetches to bind spirits), are jewellery, belt buckles, combs, spinning wheels and weapons, especially spearheads or seaxes.

Riddles

Riddles also have a role in magical practice, as well as being a game or excuse for ribaldry. Some riddles, to those spiritually attuned, symbolise magical truths. Spirits are bound with a riddle as well with the power of a laece's will.

Not all riddles take the form of words; images and concepts can also be riddles and signify ambiguity, transformation and hidden truths. Any results of divination take the form of riddles.

The god Woden is a contradiction and a riddle. Is he benevolent, as chief of the Saxon gods, or baneful, as god of the hanged man, and death in battle, or is he neither and a representative of hidden wisdom? Such questions are mortal ones and do not properly apply to the king of the aesir, however similar to mortals the gods seem in some tales.

Woden's horse, Sleipner, is a symbolic riddle. He is a stallion with eight legs that can transport the rider between worlds, and from Middle Earth to the worlds above or the worlds below. He symbolises four men (who of course have eight legs between them), carrying a bier on which to cremate the deceased, thus transporting them between worlds.

Binding Spirits

Much of a laece's power comes from binding spirits. A laece will bind spirits to gain their power or to neutralise the power of a possessing spirit. They do this cautiously, for a laece's expenditure of personal magical power only returns slowly and the spirits are dangerous. Even spirits a laece wants on their side will only help to any extent if bound and fight against being bound.

Some spirits, such as the Aelfar or the Wild Hunt, are hostile and dangerous even before a laece seeks to control them.

If a laece is to bind a spirit, their first act is to prepare a fetish, as described on page 135 of *Mythras*. Part of this process is naming the object and the spirit that is to be bound there, with runes the laece carves upon it.

The next step is for the laece to find an appropriate spirit. They must travel to a suitable place in the mortal world, where the spirit resides, just "across", in Aelfham. The table below indicates where a laece must visit.

Spirits

Spirit Sought	Where to Find It
Aelf	Anywhere
Animal Spirit	Near a concentration of the animal
Landvaettir	By a notable natural feature (hill, forest, etc)
Niflung	Amidst an old treasure hoard
Waecyrie	Battlefield
Wild Hunt	Midwinter Nights

Having travelled to a relevant location, the final step for a laece set upon binding a spirit is to go into a trance to reach the spirit world, and defeat it in spirit combat, as described from page 137 in *Mythras*. If they win, they have successfully bound it.

The maximum number of spirits a laece can bind at once is equal to half their CHA. This number includes a fetch, if any, and spirits in fetishes which they have given to others. A player character laece begins with one bound spirit of their choice.

Fetches

A Fetch is a laece's spiritual double, a spirit taking the form of an animal (not necessarily just the usual wolf, boar and eagle animal spirits, although those are the most common) who reflects the laece's inner nature. The form of a player character laece's fetish is up to the player, although the GM and other players can make suggestions.

A laece player character does not begin with a fetish. Gaining one means going on a spiritual quest, with three traditional stages, although there are variations. The steps below are typical of this spiritual quest.

- The first stage is following a spirit in the Wild Hunt back through the spirit world in a trance state, once the hunt ends. The laece must do this undetected or else the hunter will turn and attack them. Whether or not they prevail, this attempt at the quest is over for the laece and they must wait for another night.
- If the laece follows the hunter spirit successfully, it leads them to a hill at the edge of Ettinham. The final stage of the quest is inside the hill, which has a single hidden door. Getting in requires gaining admittance by trickery.
- Within the hill are many hunter and animal spirits. Among them is the animal spirit who will be the laece's fetch. This spirit is an Awakened Fetch, as described in *Mythras* on page 149. The laece must defeat the Fetch in spiritual combat, binding it. Failure means the laece is discorporated and trapped for good in Aelfham, while the body left behind never awakens.

All of the Fetch abilities (*Mythras*, page 149) are appropriate except for Elemental and Spellcasting.

Prophecy

A laece can use their Lore (Saxon Pagan) skill in divination, casting runes carved into bone and reading hints of names in the results. This grants a laece insight into the ebb and flow of wyrd around people and events. The act of divination is asking for information, although usually the GM will only supply fragments and hints.

The laece can seek information about a person, place, event or object. The standard difficulty applies to a task if the information is in the observable present and neither hidden nor obscure, meaning many people know it.

Bump up the difficulty by one level (to Hard, Formidable, Herculean, then Impossible) for each of the following that apply:

- The information involves events of the future.
- The information involves a person, place or object distant to the laece, either physically or metaphorically.
- The information is hidden or obscure.

Events are such that information can easily change, especially for events in the future. Further, if the laece has attempted a recent divination, this muddles the flow of wyrd. For each such divination the laece has tried in the previous week, bump up the difficulty again by one level.

For example, Brogan the Wise, a laece, wants to find a lost golden torc, looted from the Celts, that Thane Tormund had given to his wife. Brogan is doing this to impress the Thane but little does he know that Tormund's wife was having an affair with one of Tormund's carls, a man called Durgar, and she gave the torc to Durgar as a secret gift.

The laece tries divination. This information involves the observable present, and people nearby, but it is hidden. This is a Hard task. However, Brogan has used his divination skill last four days ago, making the task not just Hard, but Formidable.

If he succeeds, Brogan will learn that Durgar has the torc, and a riddle that hints at the affair.

Roleplaying the Quest for the Fetch

A laece player character's quest for their fetch will not involve everyone in the group. It does not have to take a full game session but it is more than just a short digression. More than one allied laece can quest together for their fetches, helping each other along the way but an all-laece group will be unusual.

One way to keep everyone involved is to have other forces assail the laece's body while they are in a trance state in Aelfham. Perhaps spiritual turbulence leads to a gathering of predators, led by a hostile animal spirit. Or perhaps an enemy laece or druid chooses to attack while the player character is vulnerable. The GM can cut between scenes involving the spirit world and scenes involving the physical world.

Alternatively, the other players could portray spiritual allies of the laece, turning this into a quest for the whole party in Aelfham. In this case the quest could be more involved and dangerous, with further encounters than the three part outline here.

The final option, and perhaps the easiest, is to play through the quest as a short one on one game outside of the usual game time, perhaps immediately before or after the main game session.

Logres: The Saxon Lands

Logres is the term Britons use for those lands in the east of the country the Saxons now control. The Saxons do not use the term themselves, instead referring to the various kingdoms that have been estabished: Ceint, Wiht, Anglia and Mierce.

Ceint & the South Saxons

Ceint is the most powerful and prosperous of the Saxon kingdoms and includes all Saxon lands south of the river the Saxons call the Thames and the Romans called the Thamesis. It includes three formerly independent Saxon kingdoms, unified under the rule of the Bretwalda, King Aelle, who claims high kingship over all the Saxon lands and seeks to expand his rule still further.

The easternmost and oldest of these kingdoms was the land granted by Vortigern to Hengist and Horsa and their Jute followers, who initially ruled as joint kings and then seized it when Vortigern attempted to withdraw his offer. The east of Ceint shows fewer signs of violent initial conquest than the other Saxon kingdoms. Some of the old Roman-British settlements are still occupied and the divisions of the domains of the Ealdormen reflects centuries old Roman divisions. Even the Jutish name, Ceint, derives from the old Brythonic name, Cantus, and its Romanisation, Cantium.

The Jutes of this region maintain trading relations with the Franks and Frisians across the sea in continental Europe. Some of the younger carls are even beginning to see a way to worldly success and glory that lies not in loot from conquest but in the still greater riches that come from trade and occasional raids. The more traditional Saxons say that the Jutes were always strange and here they are going soft.

To the south and west of Hengest and Horsa's old kingdom lie coastal lands of the South Saxons. These lands were not united until the coming of King Aelle, who unified these lands under his rule, assimilated the Jute lands in Ceint to the east, and conquered the Britons to the north, past the chalk hills called the South Downs.

The northern part of Aelle's kingdom stretches from the South Downs as far as the River Thames and the old Roman capital of Londinium. This portion of the kingdom consists of newly conquered British lands. Aelle's policy here was to drive out only those Celts who mounted effective opposition, enslaving those he defeated as thralls. Those who did not resist and were willing to swear fealty to him by paying tributes, Aelle allowed to keep their lands.

Now, in Ceint, both the north and eastern regions, live those of Celtic blood who are carls, and even Thanes, as well as geburs and thralls. Celtic villages, maintaining some or all of their old customs, exist alongside Saxon homes. Even some Roman towns and fortresses were never wholly abandoned and the Jutes and Saxons have occupied them, although the more dramatic of the Roman remains are either pillaged or avoided as objects of fright and superstition. King Aelle, ever practical, has had many such demolished, pillaging the worked stone for building work elsewhere.

Ceint is the most prosperous of any of the Saxon lands. The climate is one of the warmest in Britain and the soil is fertile. The kingdom does not want for food and the thralls and geburs easily grow fruit that would be a great struggle in the colder parts of Britain. As well as orchards, Ceint has plenty of good pasture and grazing land on the chalk hills.

It was also the part of the country first in contact with the Romans, trading with them before they came to British shores, and the first to be conquered, although many of the Celtic kings here became 'clients' of the Romans rather than resisting and paying the price for that. When the Hengist and Horse came, hundreds of years later, they were less merciful; they were in part pursuing vengeance against the British and seizing land they were refused. As noted above, King Aelle in his expansions of territory, is more practical and ultimately more successful than they were.

King Aelle's decision to name himself Bretwalda, the high king of all Britain, has cast his prosperous kingdom in an even more prominent light. Unsurprisingly, no British lords have responded to this claim. The response from the Saxons has been mixed. The people of Ceint have, by and large, responded to the claim with great enthusiasm.

Further afield, the warlords in the Mierce borderlands have ignored Aelle's claims and Guercha, King of the Angles, has not sworn fealty. The newly arrived Ealdorman Cerdic, to the south, has sworn fealty to King Aelle, but his thoughts are similar to Guercha's; namely that if one Saxon can become Bretwalda, so can another. The office is now out there and that could be Aelle's real legacy rather than the empire he is building.

Notable Settlements of Ceint

Anderida

Anderida is King Aelle's capital. Somewhat ironically, it was once a Roman fortress, built as part of their defences to keep the southern shores of Britain safe from Saxon raiders. After Roman times, it passed into the hands of a Celtic warlord, Glaes. Aelle conquered Anderida after a three month seige. When Aelle's eldest son, Cymen, went to negotiate a surrender, Gleas had him murdered. Aelle then summoned all his forces to overwhelm Anderida and slaughter everyone within.

The fortress was badly damaged in the siege but Aelle has had it repaired, the old Roman stone shored up with wooden palisades and earthworks. It occupies a strategic position, surrounded by marshes and the open sea near an excellent harbour, with a single well-protected road leading north.

Surprisingly, given its history, Anderida thrives and the surrounding town grows year by year. It has a mixed population of Jutes, Saxons and even Britons, although here the Celts are severely mistrusted. Its position as Aelle's chief city means Saxon nobles come here to pay homage and many new Saxons who land on Britain's shores come here first of all.

Anderida also hosts a thriving and surprisingly cosmopolitan market, dealing not just with food and goods from Ceint but looted valuables from Dumnonia to the west and goods from the Frankish lands on the continent. There is a thriving market for imported wine, which Aelle's housecarls have acquired a taste for and which the king serves at his feasts as a sign of prosperity.

Naturally, Saxons drink their wine unwatered and it is stronger than ale or mead; Aelle's feasts can be even more drunken affairs than usual. Being able to hold one's drink is especially important for Aelle's senior housecarls and attendant Thanes and Ealdormen.

Caer Ceint

Cantiacorum, known as Caer Ceint to the Britons, was the leading Roman capital of the area, known for its theatre and large temple to the war god Mars. When Roman rule ended in Britain, the people abandoned the city and it remains remarkably intact but now crumbling.

The city, especially the temple, is an object of superstition to the Saxons, who fear the old war god. It is still a coming of age ceremony for local youths to spend a night in the city or the temple — and occasionally youths come out of the place with visions of armies and eagles, or go missing entirely. The superstition accounts for the intact nature of the place; the local geburs never dared quarry the stone of the buildings.

Sometimes those fleeing from a blood feud, or otherwise fugitives from justice, shelter in the city, trusting in the superstition of those pursuing them from following. Perhaps such fugitives account for those who go missing... perhaps.

Cissacaestre

Cissacaestre was once the Roman town of Noviomagus Regnorum. The town was repurposed as a fortress when the Saxons first began raiding the south coast, when the Romans still ruled Britain. The stone walls of the fortress are over six feet thick; it was too strong for the Saxons to ignore it and indeed was occupied by a sequence of Celtic then Saxon warlords. It never fell by force of arms, only by treachery or, when Aelle came, by surrender.

Today the fortress is called Cissacaestra — Cissa's fortress — and is now the seat of rule of Aelle's son Cissa, who is a king in his own right, though subservient to his father, and rules over the domain formerly belonging to the South Saxons. A new Saxon town has grown up around the old Roman fort, built with stone taken from the Roman ruins. Over a thousand people now live there, and the new town has a bustling market with goods both from all over Ceint and across the water from Frankish lands.

Hrofaecaestre

Hrofaecaestra occupies a strategic location near a Roman bridge over the river Medway. It is an ancient British town with Roman walls, reinforced first by the Britons and then by the Saxons when they took the town a few years ago. They did this under the lead of one of Aelle's Earldormen, Hrof, and the Saxon name for the town translates as "Hrof's castle". From his castle, Hrof rules over the northern portion of Aelle's kingdom.

Hengist and Horsa fought Vortigern near here, establishing the Kingdom of Ceint when Hengist was victorious, although his brother Horsa fell in battle. Hrofaecaestre is a major centre of agriculture and has been since Roman times. The climate and fertility of the region attracted numbers of wealthy Romans and the ruins of their villas are common in the nearby land. Now it, and Hrof's successes, attracts wealthy Saxons. Becoming Thane in this area is a rich reward, although the land attracts raids from the Angles to the north; a free warrior with land here does not retire from action entirely.

Londinium

Londinium was the Roman capital of the province of Britannia and was once the largest city in the country. It began to empty even before Roman rule in Britain ended, although some people remained, holding onto a Roman style of life in villas, each fortified in their own right, by the river in the south west of the city. Meanwhile the rest of the city suffered from looting and fire, and both Britons and Saxons quarried the stone of the once mighty public buildings for their own fortresses.

Still, a community of 1,000 or so remained until King Aelle expanded his conquests to the north, when most fled. A few dozen people remain and have sworn fealty to Aelle, who allows them to keep their outmoded styles and customs as long as they pay him tribute. These few dozen people, living in a ruined city, are truly the last Romans in Britain.

Thanet

A thin stretch of water, the Wantsum Channel, separates the Isle of Thanet from the mainland and it is possible to cross the channel on foot at low tide. The island is an important part of Saxon history, for King Vortigern awarded it to the Saxon leaders Hengist and Horsa, and their men, in return for their military service. It holds the first Saxon settlements in Britain.

"Then came three keels, driven into exile from Germany. In them were the brothers Horsa and Hengist... Vortigern welcomed them, and handed over to them the island that in their language is called Thanet, in British Ruoihm."
Nennius, Historia Brittonum

There are no large towns on Thanet, just a scattering of arable villages and a harbour. In the earliest Saxon times, Thanet was a place where ships usually landed before seeking the mainland, and a centre of trade, but as the Saxon territories have expanded, Thanet has become more isolated. It is now ruled by Esc, who is Thane of the island, answering to King Aelle. Esc son of Hengist was once king of Ceint but now he lives in virtual exile, although some of his housecarls remain loyal to the old dynasty.

Saxons and Jutes who would replace King Aelle sometimes come to the island to plot and talk with Esc but the former king pays them little heed. Ships that would sooner not deal with Aelle still land here rather than Anderida. Esc's councils are watched by men loyal to King Aelle.

Rutupiae

On an island in Wantsum channel are the remains of a Roman fortress, known by the learned to be called Rutupiae. One side of the walls, along with the bridge linking it to the mainland, have collapsed but three walls and a lookout post, which the later Romans converted from a massive commemorative statue to the Roman invasion of Britain, are still intact.

Rutipiae is important in the Roman history of Britain as the first place the Romans landed in the invasion under Emperor Claudius and the place the legions gathered and the ships set sail with them when Roman rule ended. The ruined fortress bookmarks the era that has ended, to be replaced with the time of Britons and Saxons.

Specific Customs and Dress

The people of Ceint are more accepting of other peoples than other Saxons; something of King Aelle's pragmatic attitude has rubbed off on them. Other Saxon cultures, Britons and even Christians can live there as long as they are loyal to the kingdom and its social structures.

The Jutes have a different tradition of kingship to most others. In a Jutish kingdom there are two kings, not one, although one of the two is senior. Further, rather than all of the royal family being athelings, potentially competing for the throne and dividing the kingdom, only the son of a king (either king) can become king.

The first kings of Ceint were the brothers Hengist and Horsa. When Horsa died in battle with Vortigern, Hengist and his son Esc ruled as joint kings and Hengist was succeeded by Hengist's other son, Octa. Two years later, Aelle launched his invasion. Esc surrendered to Aelle and Octa fled with a number of his people to the Isle of Vectis (see page 49). Now Aelle and his son Cissa rule as joint kings.

The Jutes are long-standing trading partners with the Franks, and the Ceintish elites have adopted brightly coloured clothing and the custom of Frankish nobles of sewing small gold or even jewelled bees into their cloaks. The Jutes also have a unique style of brooch known as the quoit brooch, taking the form of a bronze or silver ring embossed with decorations in the geometric shapes, face masks and pairs of symbolic animals, most notably horses.

Another way that Jute customs differ from the Saxons is in the matter of burials. Due to the soil and lack of wood in their homeland, the Jutes commonly bury their dead directly in the ground, with no use of coffins, rather than cremate them. Cremation is an honour reserved for famous kings and Ealdormen. Along with the bodies, they of course bury suitable grave goods (see page 23).

Allies and Enemies

Aelle, through positioning himself as Bretwalda, has followers but no real allies. His chief enemy is Dumnonia to the west, which is the chief victim of his raids and attempts at expansion and in particular Natanleod, who commands the western marches.

The exiled former king of Ceint, Octa, is on the isle of Wiht, and sometimes attacks ships trading with Ceint, his arrangement with Dumnonia allowing him to do this. Aelle hopes to solve this issue with diplomacy rather than force of arms.

Ceint has a rival to the north in the form King Guercha of Anglia, who has not sworn fealty to Aelle as Bretwalda and covets the title for himself, although the time is not yet ripe for him to claim it. However, perhaps Aelle's most dangerous rival is the newly landed Saxon Ealdorman Cerdic, who has recently landed on the south coast of Britain with many ships and men, and is winning great victories over the Britons. For now, Cerdic answers to Aelle but his men are already urging him to take his place as a king.

Notables of Ceint

King Aelle

Hailing from the land of the Angles, Aelle is an ambitious, ruthless warlord who has successfully carved out a kingdom in southern Britain that includes the old Roman cities of Anderida and Londinium. With his sons, Aelle is intent on conquering the whole of Britain, in time. It is his belief that the Celts have had their day, that their gods have deserted them and that this Britain is now the rightful inheritance of the Saxon tribes and he shall be the first Saxon king, the Bretwalda, of these new dominions.

Aelle is known for his ferocity and ruthlessness as a warlord. When Anderidda defied him, after he had offered reasonable terms, he massacred every Celt in its walls to make an example of what happens to those who defy him. He has continually pressed the borders of Dumnonia, battling Uther, Arthur, and the other warlords who protect it; and he has sent his sons to press the northern Britons by strengthening the wild midlands known as Mierce.

Guercha is another Angle who claims kinship with Hengest and Horsa and challenges Aelle for rulership of Mierce. Now that Cerdic has arrived, there is now another warlord intent on making Britain his. These three Saxon chieftains are destined to clash. If they are not stopped they will found new kingdoms, in time, which will come to truly shape Britain's destiny: Ceint, Wessex, Mercia and Anglia and others. Aelle is not the first, but he is one of the most dangerous.

King Cissa, Son of Aelle

Cissa is King Aelle's eldest remaining child, after the death of his brother, Cymen. He is now the King's junior co-ruler. People still speak of Cymen fondly as a proud, bold and skilled warrior. By contrast, many do not know what to make of King Cissa. He is soft spoken, polite with his enemies and coddles his thralls.

Even more strangely, he has an obsession with learning. He can read Latin and will reward warriors who bring him old Roman texts of interest. Slight and scholarly, some call Cissa soft and lacking the strength and ruthlessness of his father and deceased brother. Against this, those who serve Cissa directly love him.

At present, King Aelle has sent Cissa north to Mierce with a warband of Ceintish men to carve out now territories for the kingdom. The king presumably sent him north to prove himself. Cissa is accompanied by a veteran Ealdorman, Osdaeg, in these conquests.

Esc, Son of Hengest

Esc and his brother Octa were kings of Ceint before Aelle came. Unlike his brother Octa who fled into exile to the island of Wiht,

Esc remained and swore allegiance to King Aelle, acknowledging him as both king and Bretwalda. He worried about his wife and four children too much to oppose Aelle.

The former king is now a mere Thane, ruling over the Isle of Thanet. He knows there are plots there against Aelle but is careful to maintain enough distance to claim plausible ignorance. He will not get involved in them or expose them to Aelle's men. He claims he has once ruled as a king and is now content on his island.

In truth, Esc is almost as much of an exile as his brother. He is now fond of eating and drinking to excess and the riddle game. Enormously overweight, he can no longer ride a horse, let alone go effectively into battle. He cultivates a jolly, well-meaning facade and his former glory ensures he has a modicum of respect, although his brother Octa now professes to despise him.

Behind the facade, although, Esc is a bitter man. He stepped down from power to preserve his family and regrets that his family are no longer royal. His sons will never rule as kings but he is a realist and knows how effective Aelle is as overlord. In some ways, the worst thing for Esc is that Aelle treats him and his family kindly and with respect.

Hrof

Hrof is the most powerful of Aelle's Ealdormen, ruling directly over the northern portion of his kingdom. He is a fierce grizzled man with a black beard and hair – unusually dark for a Saxon. Once he was an absolute terror on the battlefield, seeming more bear than man. Now past his prime, Hrof is still frightening when he loses his temper. However, he is loyal to Aelle, for the Bretwalda has rewarded him for his prowess as richly as any of his own sons.

Hrof's daughter, Ealhwyn, is betrothed to Aelle's youngest son, Wlencing; this political marriage ties the powerful Ealdorman to the King. Ealhwyn is Hrof's only heir and he brought her up to fight better than any man. Ealhwyn is as fierce and frightening as her father and has won several victories leading warbands against the Angles and Britons.

Neither Ealhwyn nor Wlencing are altogether happy with the coming marriage. Wlencing is displeased at being married off to a convenient noble like a useless daughter. Ealhywn sees her future husband as an arrogant princeling and a marriage as interfering with her career as a warrior. She does not see being married to Aelle's son as an honour for her; she would much sooner win renown in her own right. However, for now, both Ealhwyn and Wlencing are obedient to their fathers.

Those from outside the families do not realise how little it would take to upset matters and potentially even Hrof's subservience to Aelle. Hrof is a proud and honest man but he has been rash before in the face of disrespect or perceived insults.

Wiht & the South Coast

The island of Wiht (known to the Celts as Ynys Wyt), and south coast between Ceint and the River Itchen, is newly conquered Saxon and Jute land, although the mainland areas under Saxon control do not at present stretch far from the coast. The mainland coastal area is relatively flat and a rich source of clay; in more settled times, pottery was a major industry in the area.

The Saxon area of influence extends as far as the chalk hills to the north. In the hills themselves, and further north, things are wild and no large kingdom claims dominion. People there often have a very local attitude, being suspicious of all outsiders, perhaps for good reason. After all, those who visit from outside the area come as conquerors or raiders.

In this hilly area is Old Wintan-Caestre Hill, a hill fort abandoned when the Romans came and never reoccupied. In this hill are ancient burial mounds from a time before the Celts, when men used tools and weapons of bronze rather than iron. Treasure perhaps awaits in these ancient mounds but so too perhaps does something fearsome and in all the long years of the hill, none have dared to excavate it but the Saxons are not all prone to the old superstitions.

There is no unifying king of the region but rather several competing earldormen, with the newcomer Cerdic gaining dominance. Some of the earldormen acknowledge Aelle of Ceint to the east. They are reluctant to pay tribute but are happy to join his warbands raiding Dumnonia to the west. Others are fiercely independent and the exiled former king of Ceint, Octa, hates Aelle and actively works against him.

The biggest unified domain is Wiht, a diamond-shaped island 20 miles across, once known to the Romans as Vectis. Until recently, the island was under British control, until a small group of Cerdic's Saxons conquered it. After the initial battles between Cerdic and the British on the mainland, Octa son of Hengist, exiled from Ceint, landed a fairly large force here and now rules as King of Wiht. The island provides an excellent base for his raids on both Saxon and Celtic shipping and coastal villages.

Much of the coast of Wiht consists of sandstone cliffs, with a few harbours. Overall, the landscape is surprisingly varied considering its size and features flat arable land, forest and chalky hills, although no one feature dominates.

There are smaller islands of importance in this area of coastline; one of these is Heglingeg, separated from the mainland by a narrow stretch of water, Swaere Deep, that is nonetheless still impassable

The situation on Wiht and the South Coast, as described here, is late in the year 495. It takes place after the *Mythic Britain* scenario *Suppose Your Time Were Come to Die*. It assumes the player characters were fairly successful, so Cerdic's Saxons did not defeat Dumnonia and the Britons in battle but the Britons were unable to completely repel the Saxon invaders, leaving them territory on the south coast and room for Octa to settle the island of Wiht. Also, neither Cerdic nor Cynric were captured or killed.

in stormy weather. The island has no permanent settlement but it was holy ground to the Celts and the pagan Romans and although abandoned by the Christians, it is holy again to the Saxons. It is said that the god Yngvi, king of the elves, now lives here and those who visit the shrine and sacrifice a pig receives visions — although more fearsome visions await those who would go into the half-ruined Roman temple.

When King Octa arrived on Wiht, he came with many of his Jutish followers. Octa's policy was not Aelle's policy of letting Britons who acknowledged him as ruler continue in their old ways but rather that inherited from Hengist and Horsa of complete conquest. Most Britons who remain on Wiht are thralls and when Octa and his Jutes came, many fled to Dumnonia or to the hills to the north of the Saxon domains on the mainland.

However, Octa has recently begun treating the Britons more kindly and opened up diplomatic relations with Dumnonia. He has an arrangement with Dumnonia where he attacks ships associated with Aelle's kingdom, for he hates that king far more than he does the Britons. Some refer to Octa as the "pirate king", although in truth he is no more than a nuisance for Aelle.

However, Octa's convenient relationship has been upset by the Saxon Cerdic, who is now using the island as a base of operations. Cerdic has many carls with him and although they acknowledge Octa as ruler, Cerdic and his men act as they will and Octa feels himself being slowly forced out. Soon he will have to make other plans.

Anglia & Mierce
Key
Forest
Marsh
Car Dyke
Scale
0 10 20 30 40 50 miles
0 10 20 30 40 50 km
Mierce
Anglia
Lunden
Tomworthig
Ratae
Medeshamstede
Northwic
Westwic
Boede
Elig
Lokenhyte
Cytringan
Aeglesburgh
Londinium
N

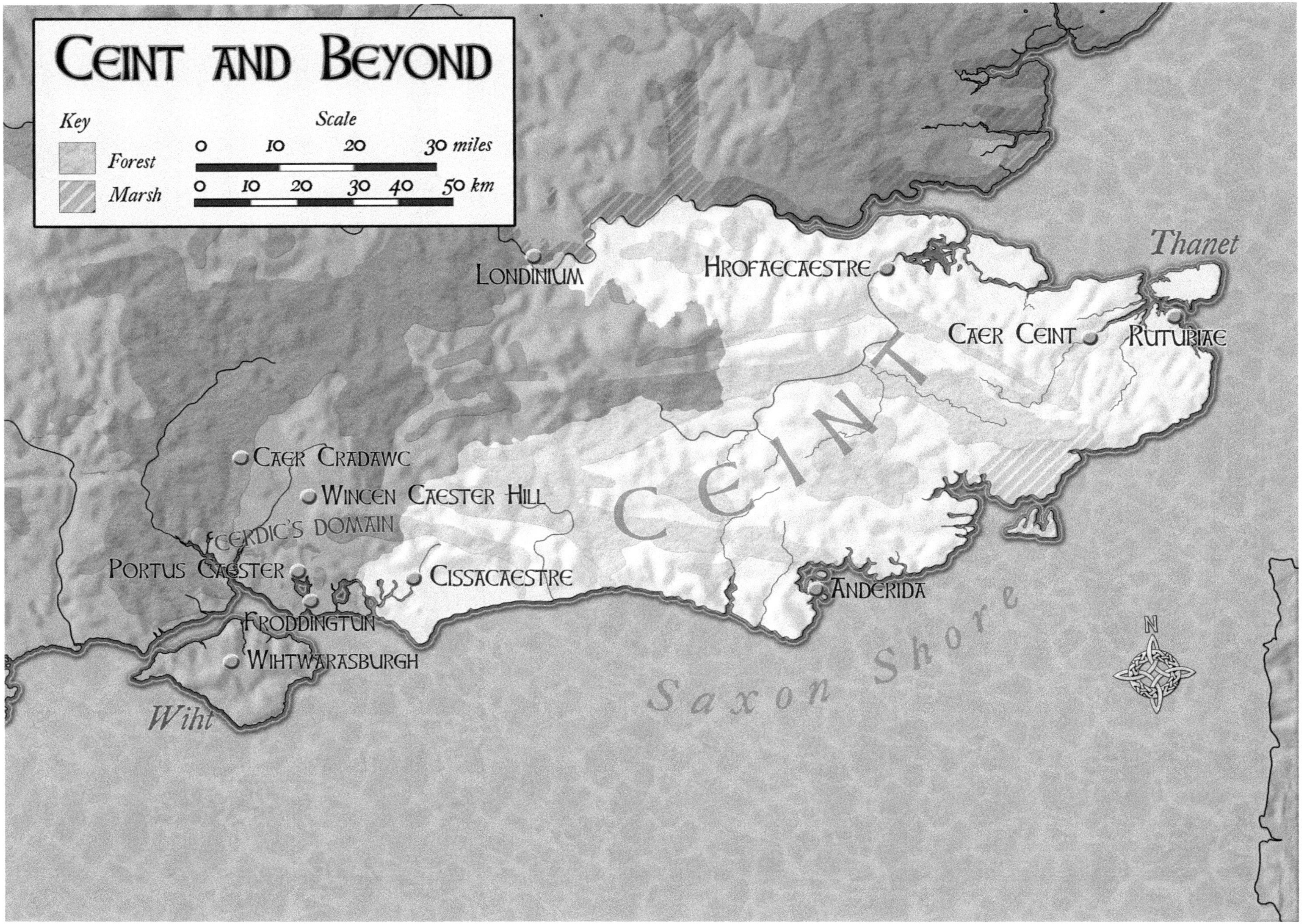
CEINT AND BEYOND
Key
Forest
Marsh
Scale
0 10 20 30 miles
0 10 20 30 40 50 km
LONDINIUM
HROFAECAESTRE
Thanet
CAER CEINT
RUTUPIAE
CEINT
CAER CRADAWC
WINCEN CAESTER HILL
CERDIC'S DOMAIN
PORTUS CAESTER
CISSACAESTRE
ANDERIDA
FRODDINGTUN
WIHTWARASBURGH
Wiht
Saxon Shore
N

Notable Settlements of Wiht and the South Coast

Froddingtun

Froddingtun is a newly founded Saxon village in the centre of Portus island, to the south of the fortress of Portus Caester. Despite the good farming land, there were no earlier settlements and in Roman times, the sea levels were more uncertain, making settlement hazardous. Perhaps they are still but the place is a good harbour.

The Thane, Frodda is a huge bearlike man, with both a ready temper and a ready laugh. Although loyal to Cerdic, Frodda sees the relationship more as that between allies rather than him being Cerdic's man. Frodda and the people of the village are fiercely independent of all other rulers, although as long as Cerdic recognises this, he is welcome to land on the island.

One thing that helps maintain this presence is that Froddingtun is something of a religious centre. Several laeces dwell here, and tell the people that they are safe from the sea for as long as the gods are pleased. These laeces often travel to the old temple sites on the nearby island of Heglingeg. Further, Saxons of all allegiances in the South of Britain sometimes travel here to consult them.

Portus Caester

Portus Caester has long been the dominant fortress on this stretch of the south coast and was the most important of the Roman fortifications built to resist the Saxons on this part of the coast. After the Romans left, a line of Celtic chieftains continued to occupy the fort for the same purpose, with support from Dumnonia. The last of these was Dyrnloc, who fell in single combat to Cerdic's nephew Stuf when his forces sallied out to face besieging Saxons.

Cerdic executed all of the warriors in the fortress and made the others thralls. Stuf now commands Portus Caester and its conquest opens the area up fully to the Saxons.

The fort has a commanding presence on a hill overlooking a harbour and there is a surrounding town of both Britons and Saxons doing business with the harbour and the residence. It is still an impressive series of buildings, with a surrounding wall, great hall and lookout tower. Some say that Cerdic plans to use the place as his future capital, as King Aelle does with Anderida. Cerdic often visits Portus Ceaster to receive important guests.

Wihtwarasburgh

Wihtwarasburgh is the most important town on Wiht and King Octa's capital. It is inland, near the centre of the island, and at the top of the navigable reaches of the River Medina. It is newly built on top of a Celtic village and despite its inland location it is a major port, although it is secondary to Portus Caester commanded by Cerdic's son Cynric.

Many of the ships here are raiders, as guilty of riding other Saxons as Britons. Many of the crews of such ships are exiled from other Saxon lands. Wihtwarasburgh has already become a rough place for those fleeing blood feuds in other Saxon kingdoms. King Octa is willing to give warriors seeking new lords another chance, although many are immoral cut-throats, even compared to other looting and raiding Saxons. The town, with its population of a few hundred, has a lawless feel.

The central point in Wihtwarasburgh, and a bastion from the general chaos of the place, is a fortress of wood and stone that Octa had built on the ruins of a Roman villa. The fort is plain in appearance, but secure, and houses the king and his housecarls.

Specific Customs and Dress

The free people of Wiht and the south coast are independent, determined to make decisions themselves. Any who would rule them can only do so as first among equals. The Saxons have already deposed local rulers they did not like. The Celts before them had similar habits and even the Romans could only rule there in partnership. This sadly means there is unlikely to be any slackening in tensions between the Celts and the Saxons; both people are equally warlike, the Saxons will not give up their conquests and the Celts are likely to resist to the death.

The Saxons and Jutes here take great pride in the glory of battle. They are not just expanding because they seek land and loot; they are expanding because they seek foes to fight. They are also bitter and unforgiving when seeking to right wrongs against them, or seeking vengeance — wergild is seldom enough here to avert a blood feud.

Although effective in battle and personal combat, the Saxons here are challenged magically and the spirits on the mainland still oppose their laeces. On Heglingeg, the laeces are in the process of binding the local spirits, although the ancient pre-Roman spirits work against them. In particular, the mighty river spirits, Thamesis of the Thames to the north and Ancester of the Itchen to the east oppose them and make any attempts to claim the land around and beyond them difficult indeed. For this reason, perhaps, with the exception of Frodda-ing Tun, the Saxon people see little use for religion and believe the spirits and gods only work for those who work for themselves.

Allies and Enemies

The politics in the area are complex, as Cerdic and Octa are both allies and rivals; Cerdic and Aelle of Ceint are both allies and rivals; and Octa and Aelle of Ceint are enemies. Octa and the Celtic Kingdom of Dumnonia are almost allies but Dumnonia is an enemy of both Aelle of Ceint and Cerdic.

The enemy of your enemy need not be your friend here.

Notables of Wiht

Cerdic

Cerdic is a cold and unswerving man. Those who look into his eyes can see no mercy or compassion but equally he has no lust to kill or punish. Although fairly new to the land, in exile from Germany and not even a king, Cerdic shows signs of being the most dangerous foe the Britons have yet faced. He has yet to lose a battle, although the last grand assault on Dumnonia was indecisive. He made the mistake then of relying on magic; he wt make the same mistake again.

It is Cerdic's success that wins him followers. He has the biggest following of any of the Ealdormen in the area and even more who consider themselves allies. The fruits of success are rich ones and Cerdic awards his followers and allies generously, both with lands and the spoils of battle. He has effortlessly conquered the island of Wiht, ousted the British warlord Dyrnloc from Portus Caester, installing his son Cynric there as ruler.

Cerdic's wife Elisedd was not Saxon but British, an exile from Dumnonia who dwelled with the Saxons in continental Europe. She died in childbirth and Cerdic has not since remarried. Cerdic's deceased wife could be the reason behind his ambitions for conquest of Britain, Dumnonia in particular. Cerdic's son by Elisedd, Cynric, and his nephews Stuf and Whitgar, are the Ealdorman's most loyal followers.

In particular, Cerdic trusts his son as a roving ambassador and problem solver. Whitgar is stationed on the island of Wiht, where he serves with King Octa but also keeps an eye on the king for Cerdic.

Stuf

Cynric is Cerdic's nephew and is the most able of Cerdic's warriors. Whereas his uncle commands in matters of strategy, Stuf is deadly in personal combat and on the battlefield he seeks out enemy champions and commanders. Stuf's enemies say that he is a dirty fighter, without a sense of personal fairness or honour.

Cerdic has recently given Stuf command of the newly conquered fortress of Portus Caester and the surrounding town and harbour. Despite the brutalities visited upon the Britons when the Saxons took the fortress, Stuf has been experimenting with promoting those of British blood to senior positions and has even made Britons into Thanes.

Stuf's rivals say that this is because he has some British blood, although they are not foolish enough to think Stuf weak. Like most other Saxon rulers of note, Stuf is ruthless towards those who oppose him and his punishments for those who betray him are imaginative and gory.

Dunflaed

Dunflaed, although still a fairly young woman, is the most respected of the laeces who regularly attend the sacred isle of Heglingeg. She has no fixed home since her family's farm on the east coast of Wiht burned to the ground but can most often be found on Wiht, or in the village of Froddingtun.

The laece claims to be related to royalty, although she is vague concerning precisely which royal house. She insists she is a descendant of the gods, as royals are, and whatever the truth of this, she does have connections with the most powerful Saxons in the area. Both Cynric and Octa have consulted her for advice and are said to owe her favours.

Dunflaed's power is that of prophecy, blessings and curses. She leads the other worshippers at Heglingeg when she is in attendance but it is not the only base of her power. She both fears and respects the Briton Merlin and claims once to have been his lover. Dunflaed spreads exaggerated stories of her power and events she has foretold or brought into being.

As far as she is concerned, it is hard to tell truth from lies, what her real power is and which stories are true. Much of this is of the laece's own doing; Dunflaed likes being mysterious; despite this aura of distrust, in person she is compelling and hard to dislike.

Octa

The son of Hengist (the first king of the Saxon peoples on Britain's shores) and formerly one of the two kings of Ceint, Octa is a bitter old exile, clinging onto power from his base in Wihtwarasburgh on the island of Wiht. Those under his banner are the few housecarls from Ceint who have remained loyal and various pirates, murderers and traitors who the king has attracted through his policies of attacking Aelle's ships and those trading with him, and being willing to take on any man, no questions asked, often in a position of power.

The king of Wiht does not care that those serving him abuse their power, as long as they are willing to strike at his enemies; and he has many enemies. He hates the Britons for what they did to his father and even more than that, he hates the people of Ceint for supporting King Aelle who ousted him and his brother. He is beginning to hate Cerdic, who is gaining popular support at his expense, despite the Ealdorman being so cold.

Although he is not nearly as powerful as he once was, Octa's hate makes him dangerous and there is no telling what he – or the desperate ruthless people who serve him – will do in an attempt to stay in control and important.

Anglia

The kingdom of Anglia comprises two regions. The east is a network of fens and marshes; the Romans had attempted to reclaim some of the area as dry land but their walls have long since collapsed or flooded over. The Celtic population of the region was low – there is little dry land after all – and when the Angles landed, they found it easy to take over. Many of the Celts there were staunch Christians, dedicated to non-violence and they surrendered rather than fought.

The low population and natural environment (mainly unsuitable for larger settlements), makes the fens an ideal hiding place for criminals, exiles and those fleeing bloodfeuds. There are dangers in the fens and not all of these dangers are human. Anglia is a deeply magical land, where the spirits of Britain are old and strong.

Anglia was the centre of Queen Boudicca's power when she rebelled against the Romans and she had the help of the bloody victory goddess Andraste. A temple to Andraste, only ever receiving a surface conversion to a Christian church, still stands in the reputedly haunted ruins of the capital of the Iceni, Venta Icenorum. The Angles have not dared settle there but have founded the villages of Nothwic and Westwic nearby.

When the Angles came, they brought with them many laeces to subdue the spirits of this new land and bring their own to new homes here. In some ways the spiritual battle was tougher than the physical one.

The western edge of the fens is marked by Car Dyke, a ditch over 80 miles long dug by the Romans. Car Dyke is both a physical and spiritual boundary, although the Romans built it for the purpose of draining the fens, reclaiming more dry land. They never completed the project and it is now a narrow but deep waterway, which the Angles use to transport goods and people inland by boat.

Within much of their territory, especially the fens, the Angles get around in small boats rather than by road, making use of Car Dyke, rivers such as the Mede and Wensum, and numerous small streams. Even inland towns have some of the character of ports.

Beyond Car Dyke, the kingdom is dryer and has a higher population. Although the climate is dry, the land is good and fertile, and most of the area is still farmed, either by Angle geburs or the British now labouring for new masters. This part of the Angle kingdom stretches from the Thames to the south to borders with the ill-defined border region of Mierce to the north and west. The Anglians also claim Mierce. In this they are partially thwarted, not so much by the Britons but the Jutes and Saxons from Ceint.

The ruler of Anglia, King Guercha One-Eye, is still making a bid for power in Britain and has more and more Angles arriving from his allies and relatives in Germany with promises of lands and loot, so he can build up his power. This is a strategy that will pay off in the short term if it succeeds but is storing up longer lasting problems for Guercha.

Notable Settlements of Anglia

Boede

In Roman times, Boede was the coastal fortress of Gariannonum, guarding what the Romans called the Saxon shore. It is King Guercha's capital and the oldest large Angle settlement in the area. After Roman rule ended, the fortress had been abandoned and the Angles occupied it in order to have a secure place for expansion. Boede is located between the rivers Laek and Lyn, making it an ideal location for river traffic with the rest of Anglia.

The Roman walls and bastion are intact and mark an area just over 200 yards across. Within the walls, the Angles have demolished any remaining Roman buildings to build their town, reusing many of the materials. Guercha and his housecarls dwell in the bastion.

Boede sees frequent traffic with newcomers from the continent. The new arrivals often want to let off some tension, meaning there are numerous feasts, and sellers of beer prosper here. Some visitors comment that the whole town smells of beer and drunken fights are a frequent occurrence. Guercha's housecarls only get involved when fights look like they may lead to bloodfeuds or are otherwise getting out of hand.

Elig

Elig is a village on an island of higher rocky ground, surrounded by the fens. It was founded by the Angles and is placed in a commanding position over the surrounding low lying land. The village is little more than a cluster of wooden huts within a wide surrounding stone wall, where the founders built Angle houses within older pre-existing stone fortifications.

The ruler of Elig is Paega, the leading earldormen of Anglia. Preparing to fight for his belief that he, not Uffa, should be the successor of old king Guercha, Paega has fortified Elig, in imitation of Guercha's capital of Boede. Cities that Paega has seen in his adventures in Mierce have also been an inspiration. Naturally, King Guercha does not know that Paega plans to revolt against his son.

At present, the few skilled masons available have been coming to Elig from far afield to work on the fortifications and free warriors have been steadily arriving, drawn by promises of loot and glory, as well as backing a future winner, in Paega's planned play for power.

Lokenhyte

Lokenhyte was the first landing place of Angle colonists on Britain's shores and a Carl called Laka distinguished himself greatly in the battle against the Britons here, earning for himself the rank of Ealdorman. The village here, Lokenhyte, is named after him, and his rule by the founder's daughter, Lakswith, a King's Thane and the highest ranking woman in Anglia.

The village feels even more communal than most Angle villages, with the individual buildings often having a single function rather than being family homes. Not just unmarried Carls dwell in the Thane's hall; unmarried Carls and their families sleep in the adjoining rooms.

Lokenhyte, whatever its pedigree, is isolated on the fens, although it does see some coastal traffic. Recently its numbers have been swelling, as Lakswith has taken in Carls who have nowhere else to go, including many criminals who have been hiding out in the fens. Lakswith does not need to know about earlier crimes, as long as these Carls are prepared to swear service to her.

Those close to Lakswith whisper that war and glory awaits, as the Thane is planning on doing something spectacular with her new men. She at the very least has her sights set on rising to become an Ealdorman.

Medeshamstede

Medeshamstede was once a British market town, conveniently located on the dry side of Car Dyke, where the River Mede drains into the fens. It has a mixture of British and Angle styles in its wooden houses. In the centre is a large market square and a dock by Car Dyke allows small boats to access the town directly.

The town and market still sees considerable trade, not just with the Angles but with Ceint, the Britons and even people from overseas, especially Frisians. The town bustles with visitors and is the most cosmopolitan place in the Angle territories. Compared to most Angle and Saxon towns, the British population here is free and fairly well-to-do. They did not fight the Angle invaders and now pay regular taxes, keeping up their trade connections and giving the Angles a small but steady source of revenue other than loot.

The Thane of the town, Ardan, is a Celt who has fully embraced Angle ways, has taken an Angle wife and has both Angle and British followers. Most Britons have not gone as far as Ardan's embrace of Saxon ways. Before the Angles conquered the area, the people of Medeshamstede were Christian and now, most have renounced the religion but a few still practice it in secret. Ardan is aware of this practice and allows it but now worships the Saxon gods.

Northwic and Westwic

The villages of Northwic and Westwic are settlements near the old Iceni capital and its haunted Christian chapel, which was once a temple to Andraste. Northwic is north of the river Wensum, Westwic is to the south and west, and both villages are by convenient streams. Like other Angle settlements, the villages feature streets in regular grid patterns and wooden palisades.

The people of the villages include both the Angles who founded them and Britons from the surrounding countryside. Both Angles and most Britons fear to approach the ruins of Venta Icenorum, which are often surrounded by a low-hanging mist coming from the river.

There is a fierce rivalry, bordering on blood feud, between the Thanes of the two villages, Cengar and Aelfdaeg. Both sides have at times paid weregeld to the other, and legally that should be an end of it, but the two Thanes both claim pieces of farmland nearby and thefts of livestock are common. There have yet to be new deaths after the last settlement but it is only a matter of time before hostilities erupt again.

Specific Customs and Dress

Much Angle art and designs on jewellery is geometric and even their towns and villages have roads in regular grids. The flat terrain here permits this; under the instructions of the laeces, the grids usually line up precisely in north-south and east-west compass directions, to better guide the spirits.

The Angles place great store in land, feeling that possession of land is a measure of a man's worth. On that land, it is important to them how things are positioned and placed, to the extent of it being a superstition. They also believe in following omens – flights of birds, strange weather and features of the landscape are all treated as omens. The Angles have a greater proportion of laeces than the other Saxon folk of Britain and one of their jobs is to read omens. All Ealdormen, and many Thanes, have laece advisors. The most effective laece advisors mix honesty with a skill at telling their masters what they want to hear.

Like the Jutes, the Angles bury rather than cremate their dead, although important people are buried in coffins rather than directly into the ground. The feet of the body point east, and the head points west, to symbolise the Angles looking to Britain rather than homeward. The grandest of all Angle burials, reserved for their kings, is the ship burial, where a whole ship is a coffin. The honoured dead body and most magnificent of treasures and arms is loaded onto a small ship, which is buried whole in a vast mound.

The clothing of the Angles is dark and dull compared to the people of Ceint, and they see bright colours as impractical. However, both men and women of status wear jewellery and eat and drink well. The Angles place nearly as much importance on ostentatious displays of wealth as they do on land and it is unsurprising that they seek loot and conquest.

As well as jewellery, the Angles take even more pride than most of the Saxon people in their hair. Those of high rank, both men and women, do not wear it loose but rather comb it to one side and tie it in a knot.

Allies and Enemies

Although Anglia has its eyes set on the British land of Elmet, at present its expansion is bogged down in Mierce, partially because of its rivals there from Ceint. King Aelle's claim as Bretwalda is an annoyance to King Guercha, who craves the title himself. At the very least, Guercha would like to keep Aelle's men south of the Thames.

The Anglian kingdom does not border on any British kingdoms, being surrounded by Mierce and Ceint. The logical allies for Guercha may well be Aelle's rival Cerdic, his enemy Octa and the British kingdom of Dumnonia to the south, but at present Cerdic is loyal to Aelle, Octa is too weak and distant, and Dumnonia also too far away. Thus Guercha is relying on greater numbers of steadily arriving Angles to beat his rival Aelle; his real allies are in the Germanic homeland and, unlike some of the Saxon kings here, Guercha came to seek opportunity rather than as a result of exile.

Notables of Anglia

Guercha One-Eye

Guercha is King of Anglia and now an old man. He has always proudly proclaimed his descent from the god Woden and, like his ancestor, is said to have given up an eye for wisdom. He is both a temporal and spiritual leader of his people, although he now delegates leadership in battle to his Ealdormen. He still has his people's admiration and loyalty – he led them out of floods and famine in Germany to the new land they now call Anglia, which was ripe for colonisation and conquest.

Those who support Guercha know he stands alone, without peer or true successor, for all that his son Uffa is his heir. Neither Uffa nor Guercha's Ealdormen can match the king's combination of wisdom, firm rule and skill at war.

But Guercha, being a proud man, will always have more. When King Aelle of Ceint proclaimed himself Bretwalda, Guercha not only refused to bend the knee to his neighbour but vowed to supplant him, as is only right for one of his wisdom and divine ancestry. Anglia's conquests in Mierce are as much about getting ahead of King Aelle as they are anything else.

Uffa

Uffa is the only son of King Guercha and should be in line to inherit the throne. However, he is a mediocre warrior and uninspiring leader. Uffa's interests do not lie in rule or fighting. He has no ambitions for power, his own glory or the glory of Anglia. Uffa is keen still to do his duty, and will do it for the sake of his father, a rather overbearing personality.

Although the atheling does not want the throne, he will take and defend it out of this sense of duty; he is not soft, only distant. His housecarls, and most of those of King Guercha, will defend him also out of habit and the symbol of Anglia he represents. However, if he does not provide them with the opportunities for expansion that they crave, this support will evaporate and Uffa's reign will be short. The Kingdom of Anglia could then disintegrate, whatever the laeces advising King Guercha have prophesied.

Uffa's real talent and interest is for poetry and riddling, his mind often drifting down imaginative, impractical pathways. Were he not the king's only son, Uffa sometimes muses, he would have made a very fine skald. He could still make a good king if he can divert his intelligence, memory and sense of empathy into more practical applications.

Paega

Paega is a battle-hardened warrior, a veteran of the wars in Mierce and responsible for retaking Ratae for King Guercha. He is a relatively new Ealdorman but much respected. Paega is loyal to Guercha but does not see his oath of loyalty as including the king's son, Uffa; instead, seeing himself as next in line. He has been encouraged in this ambition by Aelfstan, the chief of Anglia's laeces.

Although both hard and ambitious, Paega is not uncompassionate and treats his thralls well, whether British or Saxon. He will often free the British he has taken prisoner after a short service of one or two months and even has a few British carls in his service.

Paega has a certain notoriety for his romantic affairs and he has been married six times. His latest wife, Briette, is a freed British captive. The marriage has caused ripples in Anglia and Paega's enemies say he is either foolishly besotten, or deliberately seeking to offend. For his part, Paega is secure enough in his position to not care what other people think of his marriage. He cares more about the whispers that Briette is a witch who has enchanted him.

Aelfstan

Aelfstan is the chief of the laeces in Anglia and advisor to the king. He looks the part, being balding with a long grey beard, although tall and unbent. He wears a necklace of spiritual symbols hanging from a chain and is also cryptic, often speaking in riddles. Aelfstan will sometimes give direct advice but of his own volition rather than when others ask or demand it of him. He is also a skilled healer and travels around Anglia, and even into Mierce, to practice this art.

The laece has a vision of the future that he is keen to share, where Anglia dominates the island of Britain. Thus, Aelfstan has advised Guercha to declare himself as Bretwalda and encouraged those close to Guercha to back this claim. Guercha has so far not done this but neither does he accept Aelle's claims as Bretwalda. Uffa, the king's son, has observed that the king does not fully trust Aelfstan's motives, although he believes he has Aelfstan under control.

Aelfstan now seeks the king's permission to travel into Mierce and use his talents in the coming conflict to ensure that Anglia dominates in the new frontier.

Mierce

The name Mierce means "border" in the Saxon language. The region stretches from the Thames to the Celtic kingdom of Elmet and is still one of the main fighting grounds between the Saxons and the Celts. Areas have already changed hands several times, with nobody gaining the upper hand everywhere. The land is centred upon the River Trent, which the Angles in Mierce use for transportation.

The River Trent is also the border between the spheres of influence of Anglia and Ceint. The Angles dominate the Trent, most of its tributaries and the lands to the north, while the Jutes and Saxons loyal to Ceint, by contrast, control much of the land south of the River Trent. The boundary between these zones is far from smooth. In particular, King Guercha of Anglia does not recognise it and asserts that Ceint has no claim to any lands north of the Thames.

Despite this, although there is tension between the Angles and folk from Ceint, there has yet to be outright war. The main fighting is still between Britons and Saxons in general in Mierce, in the form of numerous local conflicts. The Saxons, whether from Anglia or from Ceint, are a long way from controlling everything and resistance can be fierce, sometimes springing up again as soon as would-be conquerors have left.

The conflict between the British and the Saxons is not purely physical. The Celtic spirits, encouraged by local druids and those in the neighbouring British kingdom, strive to make Mierce unwelcoming for the invaders. The Saxon laeces, on the other hand, are bringing their own spirits and awakening the Saxon spirits of the land, so that Mierce can be theirs mystically as well as physically.

The Britons are helped in their resistance by the fact that Mierce is a wild land, heavily forested; much of it is difficult to travel and individual towns and cities are often isolated. The key routes are the old Roman roads from north to south and the rivers from east to west. There was never any unified ruler of Mierce since the Roman times ended, and this is Mierce's strength but it is also the Britons' weakness; they are not in a position to mount any organised resistance to the Saxons or even to exploit the divisions between Ceint and Anglia.

Mierce has a more extreme climate than the other Saxon lands in Britain, having very cold and wet winters, often with large quantities of snow. Even the Roman roads are impassable when snow falls. Summers by contrast are dry, comfortably warm and sunny. One place the snow never falls, which is mild even in winter, is the Arawn's Gorge, a place named Cheswell by the Saxons.

Arawn's Gorge was a major site of the old people, who were here before even the Celts. They lived in the caves here and their art, portraying hunted animals and fertility symbols, still adorns their walls and ceilings, and the caves are still haunted by death spirits who were friends of the old people. Others fear to go there but occasionally a desperate fugitive or overly curious explorer will find their way here. Rumours abound that there may be ancient secrets hidden deep in the caves.

The isolation between settlements in Mierce means some have adopted an unusual way of life. In the cities of Ratae and Lunden, the people continued a broadly Roman way of life until they were conquered by Angles. The villages of Cytringan are Saxon villages whose histories go back prior to any Saxon conquests in Britain.

Be that as it may, the Angles have a communications network in much of Mierce and dominate the rivers of Mierce, including the River Trent and the valley of the Anker, a southern tributary. However, recently the Anglian forces faced a major defeat and the leading Ealdormen in Anglia, Wiglaf and Hengwulf ,have not been seen since the Britons retook the city of Ratae.

The Anglians have since reconquered Ratae, and are here in great force, but are spread out. The Ceintish forces, by contrast, are relatively fresh and unified. King Cissa, son of King Aelle, and the Ealdorman Osdaeg lead the men of Ceint.

Notable Settlements of Mierce

Aeglesburgh

What of Hengwulf & Wiglaf?

Hengwulf and Wiglaf are described in the main *Mythic Britain* book. The political situation in Mierce dates from late 495, after the events in the scenario *Logres Burning*, when the British forces reconquered Ratae. Since that time, an increased Anglian presence has again forced the Britons out, although it opened up an opportunity for King Aelle to send forces in to grab loot and territory.

Aeglesburgh is the main Ceintish base of operations in Mierce, lying two dozen miles north of the river Thames. It is a secure fortress, built on top of a conquered Celtic hill fort, surrounded by a ditch, earth wall and wooden rampart. A few hundred people, mainly Jutes, live in Aeglesburgh.

The town was named by King Cissa to honour Aegle, a Jute hero who fell to the Britons in the town's conquest. Scouts have noted that the Britons in the area who have apparently submitted to their rule have become restive when Fyrdmen are withdrawn from Aeglesburgh. Cissa is currently in town trying to solve this problem, finding another way to rule the Britons nearby rather than being forced to eradicate them. Perhaps there is a firebrand to seek out?

Such unrest is a problem that Cissa would gladly pass on to others and with it the rule of the town. He would like to be free to pursue other operations in Mierce but Cissa knows where he is needed.

Cytringan

Cytringan, a collection of farmsteads and villages, is one of the oldest Saxon areas of settlement in Britain, having settled here since late Roman times, before the coming of Hengest and Horsa, when they served as mercenaries with the Roman armies. The Saxons never left, even intermarrying with the surrounding Britons, but maintained their own culture.

The people of Cytringan are as fierce in keeping their independence against the invading kingdoms of Ceint and Anglia as any Celts. That said, Osdaeg has recently negotiated a cessation of hostilities, where the people of the area can keep their independence as long as they do not oppose Ceint. However, Cytringan is not at present a part of the Ceintish lands of Mierce.

Cytringan's closest connection with the rest of Mierce is an alliance with the town of Tomworthig. This alliance goes beyond mere trade and non-aggression, consisting of pacts of service in the event of invasion, but for all that Cytringan is nominally on the Ceintish side and Tomworthig on the Anglian. A war between Ceint and Anglia in Mierce, if it is fated to come, will be messy indeed.

Lunden

Lunden is a Roman city on the slopes of a hill by a deep lake, leading up to a fortress. The rivers Trent and Witham place it on the Angle communications network. Until recently, the Roman features of the town – the forum surrounded by statues of horsemen, the public baths, even the aqueduct and fountains – were still intact, and the people carried on a way of life they saw as Roman, but that all changed when the Angles came.

The city tried to resist conquest and the Angles lost half of their invading force in the attack, thus the resulting looting was angry and destructive. Every Briton still in the city was killed, regardless of whether they took part in the fighting, and the Angles put the town to the flame. All that remains is the fortress, firmly under Angle control, and is a major assembly point for Angle forces heading into Mierce.

Ratae

Ratae consists of two settlements – the town of Ratae and the hillfort of Caer Leonis – on the bank of the river Soar. About a year ago, the Angles conquered both Ratae and Caer Leonis; the Britons then reconquered both, inflicting significant damage to Angle efforts to expand further in Mierce. However, the Angles have recently invaded Ratae again, under the veteran Ealdorman Paega, although the fortress is still occupied by resisting Britons.

Until fairly recently, Ratae was a well-preserved Roman town but repeated conquests have left it little more than an armed camp inside damaged Roman walls, hastily repaired with stone obtained from the surviving Roman buildings. The leader of the camp is the Ealdorman Stangar, who is becoming increasingly frustrated as the hillfort resists his siege and repeated assaults.

Ratae and Caer Leonis, at least as they were before the latest invasions, are described in more detail in the scenario Bran Galed's Horn, on page 245 of *Mythic Britain*.

Tomworthig

The town of Tomworthig straddles the River Anker. The lands around Tomworthig are the southernmost Angle holding in Mierce, however Tomworthig stands aloof from the Angle factionalism, even as far as possible from the conflict between Anglia

and Ceint. Although nominally Angle, it has an independent alliance with the Ceintish lands of Cytringan.

Icel, the lord of Tomworthig, sees the town as a place of brokering alliances and unions. Tomworthig is a classic Angle town, with streets in a grid each side of the river Anker, and the two halves of the town are linked by a wooden bridge. Both the east and west halves are surrounded by a tall wooden fence, far enough from the buildings of the town to allow room for expansion.

Lord Icel claimed the area around Tomworthig and founded the town in the name of King Guercha, although any permission to do this came after the deed was done. With permission came Angle settlers; the area is, after all, an important bulwark against Ceint's ambitions. However, something of the localism of Miercan politics has already affected the settlers and they are loyal to their new town and lord Icel first, with Anglia coming a distant second.

One of Icel's main aims for Tomworthig was for it to be a centre of trade rather than a military bulwark and he has succeeded in this aim. The town has the biggest marketplace in Mierce and merchants of all nations are welcome if they come in peace – even the enemies of the Angles.

Specific Customs and Dress

The people of Mierce, both the Saxon settlers and the Celts who were there before, have a certain immediacy to their attitudes. They do not feel any sense of the distant past now that the final "Roman" cities, Ratae and Lunden, fell to the Angles. What they care about is the present and near future, although they sometimes admire dreamers who look further ahead. With the exceptions of the conquering Ealdormen and their bands from Anglia and Ceint, they do not care about distant kings and rulers; what they care about is their own immediate rulers.

This attitude can lead to a certain defiance, even in the face of threats and atrocities. Conquerers who do not stay and rule seldom manage to keep hold of the land they have conquered and most people here, Saxon and Briton alike, believe they will never fall to Ceint or Anglia, even as those two kingdoms squabble over influence here.

Clothing here is usually plain and practical, with little decoration, even for the rulers. They favour colours in deep green and red. The exception is the cloaks worn by the Britons, and adopted by some Saxons, which have checks in many different colours; the finer the cloak, the more colours that are used.

Allies and Enemies

The neighbouring British lands, Elmet and the lands of the Parisii, have friendly trade relations with the British in Mierce and even the Saxon town of Tomworthig. They have little connection, either as allies or enemies, in matters of war. This could prove their undoing should a unified Saxon force take Mierce, as they will be next, but this seems unlikely in the immediate future.

The main conflict in Mierce is between Ceint and Anglia, as both of these kingdoms desire to conquer the land. They have fought each other in many skirmishes, although things have yet to come to all-out war.

Notables of Mierce

Stangar

The Angle Ealdorman Stangar is stationed in Ratae and has the responsibility of taking the hillfort of Caer Leonis. He is young for a warrior who bears the responsibility of an Ealdorman and, like many young warriors, Stangar is impatient for both more recognition and more glory.

However, any glory will have to wait until he has conquered Caer Leonis. In his impatience, and wish to terrify the Britons into surrendering there, Stangar has indulged in a series of calculated brutalities against British thralls and prisoners. Men, women and children are all slaughtered or die an agonisingly slow death.

This brutality has backfired and the Britons in Caer Leonis know that they must resist Stangar at all costs. What will happen to them and those they hold dear should they fail is unthinkable to contemplate. Worse, the Britons in north Mierce hate Stangar more than they do any of the other conquerors. To Stangar, this is most unfair; he claims to take no joy in his brutality, although some he commands doubt this. It is just as a means to an end, like any other weapon of war, and if the Britons had simply surrendered when asked, none of this would be necessary. As things are, they have left him no choice.

Icel

Icel is an atheling, being the nephew of King Guercha. However, he has formally renounced any claim to the throne and is content to rule Tomworthig rather than Anglia. He is not a great warrior or war leader but knows how to work with those who do have such talents. Rather, Icel's talents lie in organisation. He is expanding his territories, not by conquest, but by securing his borders, having his lands prosper and steadily attracting more settlers.

On the surface, Icel is a modest man. Although he has warriors in his employ, he calls himself Thane rather than Ealdorman and lets others lead in battle. Some of Icel's most prominent warriors are mercenaries, including Saxons and even Britons.

Icel's apparent modesty is misleading. His ambitions are greater than his enemies or even his fellow Angles have guessed. He does not want to be King of Anglia but he does want to rule over all of Mierce as king, independently of Anglia, Ceint or anywhere else. To this end, he is making Tomworthig both prosperous and mighty and hiding this ultimate aim. He knows he cannot succeed at present through force of arms and hopes the other kings will be pragmatic when he finally comes into his power.

It is early days in Icel's grand plan but he is still a young man and has accomplished much already. He has also yet to marry and a suitable marital allegiance could bring further influence.

Osdaeg

Osdaeg is an old experienced Ealdorman, who was leading warbands as a young man in the time of Hengest and he now serves King Aelle of Ceint. Osdaeg has lost as many battles as he has won but has never lost catastrophically. He is a cautious war leader, striking when he has a definite edge, retreating when outnumbered or matters are too uncertain, and preferring slow steady progress to glory. Most of the men in his warband are older than the average Saxon warrior and have a similar attitude.

King Aelle ranks Osdeag's skills very highly, at the same time noting that his lack of glory-grabbing makes him unlikely to be a threat to his own rule, even in distant Mierce. Indeed, Osdaeg has a "get the job done" attitude in Mierce. He is publically deferential to his co-commander, King Cissa son of Aelle, while advising him in private. His conquests are both without brutality and without any particular mercy; he allows his men time to loot but not to ruin new conquests.

As well as a general, Osdaeg has talent as a negotiator, a rare skill for a Saxon. At present, Osdaeg is in the north of the Ceintish controlled parts of Mierce, where he has arranged a non-aggression treaty between the Ceintish forces and Tomworthig, allowing him to hold the rest of the river Trent against further incursions from the Angles. Osdaeg is currently trying to talk to British leaders, again making use of the near neutral ground in Tomworthig, trying to recruit them to fight the Angles, who ravaged the cities of Ratae and Lunden, in exchange for independence and protection.

Mythic Saxons

Mythic Saxons contains game statitstics for the various people described earlier in the book, plus statistics for generic Saxons that can be used as the need arises.

Aelfgifu

Aelfgifu is a Saxon mercenary warleader from Cytringan. She is tall, grey-eyed, quick and graceful in her movements, although she gives the impression she can never remain completely at rest. Aelfgifu initially worked with the Ceintish forces in Mierce but now goes her own way, along with the men who follow her. She has no official title or status above that of a free Carl but those she works with treat her as an Ealdorman, although she swears fealty to no king. Aelfgifu initially worked with the Ceintish forces in Mierce but now goes where the pay is greatest. She has even fought for the Celts in the past.

Among Aelfgifu's kin, there is nothing unusual about the women learning to fight and Aelfgifu's mother was a warrior before she settled down with her family. Aelfgifu has an almost instinctive grasp of personal combat and tactics but her real talent is in understanding fortifications – both how to breech them and how to hold them. Aelfgifu is the best engineer in Mierce and those who follow her know and respect her talent for battle.

In her heart of hearts, Aelfgifu wants for something more – not just battle but a cause to fight for. For the past year, she has been in the service of Thane Icel of Tomworthig and thinks he could be the one. Icel is a worthy leader and what she hopes for the future of Mierce; he has even confided in her some of his longer term plans. If he were to take on honours for himself and offer Aelfgifu a prominent role, she could finally settle down and fight for something as well as just a good share of loot.

Aelfgifu

Characteristics	Attributes
STR: 11	Action Points: 3
CON: 12	Damage Modifier: 0
SIZ: 12	Magic Points: 14
DEX: 14	Movement: 6 metres
INT: 16	Initiative Bonus: 15/10
POW: 14	Armour: Leather, Plate Helm
CHA: 12	

Skills: Athletics 60%, Craft (Fortifications) 45%, Culture (Saxon) 72%, Endurance 54%, Engineering 77%, Evade 73%, First Aid 60%, Gambling 75%, Influence 54%, Language (Angle) 73%, Language (Saxon) 68%, Lore (Strategy and Tactics) 77%, Perception 75%, Ride 63%, Streetwise 75%, Superstition 38%, Willpower 53%

Passions: Love (Thane Icel) 58%, Loyalty (Tomworthig) 54%, Norse Gods 59%

1d20	Location	AP/HP
1–3	Right Leg	0/5
4–6	Left Leg	0/5
7–9	Abdomen	2/6
10–12	Chest	2/7
13–15	Right Arm	0/4
16–18	Left Arm	0/4
19–20	Head	5/5

Combat Style: Fyrdman (Battleaxe, Seax and Shield, Trait: Formation Fighting) 85%

Weapon	Size/Force	Reach	Damage	AP/HP
Seax	*M*	*S*	*1d4+2*	*6/8*
Battleaxe	*M*	*M*	*1d6+1*	*4/8*
Saxon Shield	*L*	*S*	*1d4*	*4/12*

Aelfstan

Aelfstan is the leading laece of Anglia, a land already rich in such folk, and advisor to King Guercha. He is cryptic, speaking in riddles, and manipulative. He looks the part of the chief laece of the kingdom, being tall, bearded and with a necklace of spiritual symbols and skulls of small animals. These skulls are in fact fetishes which hold spirits.

The laece travels as a healer but this travel is, however, a cover for more political activities. Although he has publically advised that Guercha should declare himself Bretwalda, and declared he sees Anglia leading the isle in the future, he has also come to believe that Guercha's line is not the one that will ultimately rule.

Certainly the king does not know that Aelfstan has also gone out of his way to advise the leading Ealdorman, Paega that Guercha's son, Uffa, is not fit to reign after him. In this he is backed by Uffa's wife, Briette. However, Aelfstan's motives are not to bestow power upon Paega as a worthy successor. The laece believes that

Aelfstan

Characteristics	Attributes
STR: 10	Action Points: 3
CON: 10	Damage Modifier: 0
SIZ: 13	Magic Points: 17
DEX: 12	Movement: 6 metres
INT: 15	Initiative Bonus: 14/13
POW: 17	Armour: Furs
CHA: 12	

Skills: Binding (Saxon Tradition) 96%, Culture (Saxon) 70%, Deceit 97%, First Aid 54%, Healing 97%, Influence 89%. Insight 94%, Language (Angle, Jute, or Saxon) 67%, Literacy 40% Lore (Norse Gods) 80%, Lore (Saxon) 70%, Perception 97%, Sleight 91%, Stealth 97%, Trance 98%, Willpower 104%
Passions: Loyalty (Anglia's Future) 57%, Norse Gods 64%, Love (Conflict) 64%

1d20	Location	AP/HP
1–3	Right Leg	0/5
4–6	Left Leg	0/5
7–9	Abdomen	1/6
10–12	Chest	1/7
13–15	Right Arm	0/4
16–18	Left Arm	0/4
19–20	Head	0/5

Combat Style: Hunter (Seax, Spear, Bow, Trait: Skirmishing) 62%

Weapon	Size/Force	Reach	Damage	AP/HP
Seax	*M*	*S*	*1d4+2*	*6/8*
Bow	*L*	*-*	*1d6*	*4/4*
Spear	*M*	*L*	*1d8+1*	*4/5*

in the coming conflict, a stronger man will emerge as victor and a worthy contender to put forward Anglia's strength.

Whatever his intentions, Aelfstan is an agent of conflict and chaos and has yet to be caught in his tricky ways. Aelfstan is not above murder to forward his aims but has not yet sunk that low, at least in Anglia. He now seeks an excuse to travel into Mierce; Cissa and the Ceintish alderman Osdaeg could profitably be set against each other, after all, and Aelfstan is sure he could find the right lever to pull there. All for the greater good of Anglia and the Saxon peoples of Britain, of course.

Aelfstan has a fetch and two spirits bound into fetishes which form a part of his necklace. These bound spirits are a Niflung- an elemental spirit of darkness, and a Cofgod - a guardian spirit.

The Fetch

Aelfstan's fetch has the abilities Covert, Discorporate, Persistent, Imperishable and Sagacity.

Characteristics

INT: 15

POW: 17

CHA: 12

Skills: Discorporate 82%, Lore (Strategy and Tactics) 130%, Lore (Norse Gods) 130%, Lore (Strategy and Tactics) 130%, Stealth 80%, Spectral Combat 79%, Willpower 79%

The Niflung

The Niflung (a dragon-shaped spirit of darkness) when called forth will seek to envelop an opponent in darkness. This attack does 1d6 damage to every hit location and can only be evaded, not parried. Further, escaping the freezing darkness requires an opposed Athletics, Brawn or Evade roll.

Characteristics	Attributes
STR: 36	Action Points: 3
DEX: 15	Spirit Damage: 2d6
INT: 13	Magic Points: 21
POW: 21	Movement: 10 metres
	Initiative Bonus: 10
	Protection: 2
	Hit Points: 39

Skills: Brawn 92%, Evade 66%, Perception 56%, Willpower 92%
Combat Style: Elemental Combat 78%P

The Corgod

Aelfstan's guardian spirit will interpose itself between the laece and magical attacks.

Characteristics

INT 9

POW 20

CHA 9

Skills: Spirit Combat 76%, Willpower 90%

Briette

Briette was a Celtic captive from Mierce. The most powerful of the Angle Ealdormen, Paege, fell in love with her and not only lifted her from thralldom but married her, in defiance of all convention. Some say that Briette is a witch because of this lucky turn of events and also due to the fact that her eyes do not quite match in colour, being different shades of blue, in contrast with her raven black hair.

A second rumour says that Briette is a Celtic princess. She presents herself as cultured and graceful, and takes delight in singing and dancing. There is a practical side to Briette's talents too; she first came to the attention of the Angle nobles through her skill at healing and her willingness to heal "the enemy".

The latter rumour is not true; Briette is of lowly birth and grew up in a village in Mierce before her capture. As for the first rumour, Briette has second sight and received limited training as a druid before her master decided she was unsuitable. She uses the small pieces of magic she knows in secret to encourage her husband's ambitions and help him in her endeavours. She did not need any magic to make a man like Paege fall in love with her.

Briette loves Paege too in her own way. He is a good man for an Angle and capable of mercy and compassion as well as hardness. It is these qualities that would make him a fine king. Briette can tell it is going to be an Angle world but it is not all clear who would rule them and ultimately much of Britain. Thus, along with the laece Aelfstan, Briette has stoked her husband's ambition. It may mean war but it is all for the greater good.

As for Aelfstan, Briette knows that he realises she has power. Briette does not like the laece, and fears what he could do, but for the moment they are allies.

Briette

Characteristics	Attributes
STR: 8	Action Points: 3
CON: 12	Damage Modifier: -1d2
SIZ: 11	Magic Points: 15
DEX: 12	Movement: 6 metres
INT: 13	Initiative Bonus: 13
POW: 15	Armour: None
CHA: 16	

Skills: Binding 59%, Culture (Celtic) 66%, Dance 78%, Deceit 79%, First Aid 73%, Healing 78%, Influence 97%, Insight 73%, Language (Angle) 64%, Language (Brythonic) 69%, Lore (Celtic) 66%, Lore (Saxon) 61%, Lore (Pagan) 45%, Sing 91%, Sleight 78%, Trance 57%, Unarmed 25%, Willpower 60%

Passions: Loyalty to Paege 60%, Love (Power) 60%, Pagan Gods 60%

1d20	Location	AP/HP
1–3	Right Leg	0/5
4–6	Left Leg	0/5
7–9	Abdomen	2/6
10–12	Chest	2/7
13–15	Right Arm	0/4
16–18	Left Arm	0/4
19–20	Head	5/5

Combat Style: Unarmed 25%

Ealdorman Cerdic

Although not yet a king, Cerdic is the ruler of southern Britain and the power behind the throne on the island of Wiht, which his forces conquered. He is a formidable strategist and unlike many Saxon warriors is ruled by logic rather than passion. He is a big man, although not as large as his son Cynric, and unusually for a Saxon wears his greying hair short. His grey eyes are narrow and calculating.

As well as logic, Cerdic is governed by his ambition and determination to make Britain a Saxon land and to be its ruler. Not just the British but other Saxons, especially King Aelle who is past his prime, stand in the way of Cerdic's ambitions, although for now Cerdic needs Aelle. Cerdic is privately convinced – and he has told nobody of this, not even his son – that the gods themselves have chosen him for this task. He relishes in this conviction.

Cerdic

Characteristics	Attributes
STR: 16	Action Points: 3
CON: 15	Damage Modifier: +1d4
SIZ: 15	Magic Points: 15
DEX: 12	Movement: 6 metres
INT: 17	Initiative Bonus: 15/12
POW: 15	Armour: Mail Hauberk, Helm
CHA: 11	

Skills: Athletics 61%, Boating 61%, Deceit 73%, Endurance 75%, Engineering 59%, Evade 69%, Influence 67%, Insight 72%, Lore (Norse Gods) 49%, Lore (Strategy and Tactics) 109%, Navigate 62%, Perception 62%, Ride 72%, Seamanship 66%, Stealth 74%, Superstition 37%, Unarmed 73%, Willpower 65%
Passions: Hate (Dumnonia) 60%, Loyalty (Southern Britain) 55%, Norse Gods 60%

1d20	Location	AP/HP
1–3	Right Leg	0/6
4–6	Left Leg	0/6
7–9	Abdomen	5/7
10–12	Chest	5/8
13–15	Right Arm	0/5
16–18	Left Arm	0/5
19–20	Head	5/6

Combat Style: Saxon Noble (Sword, Seax and Shield, Trait: Mounted Combat) 88%

Weapon	Size/Force	Reach	Damage	AP/HP
Seax	*M*	*S*	*1d4+2+1d4*	*6/8*
Sword	*M*	*M*	*1d6+1d4+2*	*4/8*
Saxon Shield	*L*	*S*	*1d4+1d4*	*4/12*

Cerdic is a cool-headed political operator. He is for the present happy to acknowledge Aelle as Bretwalda, even as he pulls away fighting men from Ceint to be his own personal followers. He has made an informal alliance with Guercha of Anglia and is now taking an interest in Mierce, to see the lie of the land. There he inclined to support Thane Icel.

There is a passion that underlies Cerdic's ambition. His wife, Elisedd, who died in childbirth, was a British exile from Dumnonia. She had high blood, and was a victim of politics, and Cerdic once promised to conquer Dumnonia for her. Since his wife's death, Cerdic trusts nobody who is not kin – trusting only his son Cynric, and nephews Stuf and Whitgar. For that matter, Cerdic is prepared to betray others who are not kin in the interests of his greater ambitions, although only when it is really worth it. The Britons already know that they cannot trust his word.

King Cissa, Son of Aella

Cissa is King Aella's eldest remaining child and rules Ceint alongside Aelle, although he is a junior partner. He is in the shadow of his dead brother, Cymen. Cymen was bold and impetuous, proud of the family name, skilled at arms and the apple of ruthless King Aelle's eye. Cissa, on the other hand is cautious and both more intelligent and more pragmatic than Cymen was.

Unusually for a Saxon, Cissa has learned to read Latin under the instruction of educated thralls, whom he treats well. Were it not for King Aelle, many men would call Cissa weak. He is handsome in a soft-seeming way and relatively slight, which leads some people to underestimate him as a warrior.

However, King Aella trusts Cissa's skills, else he would not rule as king with him. Cissa, although slight, is quick and skilled, and does not mind people underestimating him, as long as they follow and obey him. Alhough Cissa is apparently soft and politely spoken, even with his enemies, this hides a hard core. And those who serve Cissa directly love him.

King Aelle has sent Cissa away to the north, to lead Ceintish men to conquer new territories in Mierce before Anglia lays claim to them. The rumours that Aelle has sent Cissa north to toughen him up are untrue. The mission is both vital and sensitive, and Cissa the only one Aelle could trust with it.

Cissa

Characteristics	Attributes
STR: 10	Action Points: 3
CON: 11	Damage Modifier: 0
SIZ: 12	Magic Points: 14
DEX: 17	Movement: 6 metres
INT: 18	Initiative Bonus: 18/15
POW: 14	Armour: Scale Coat, Helm
CHA: 12	

Skills: Art (Poetry) 66%, Courtesy 75%, Customs 71%, Culture (Saxon) 76%, Evade 64%, Influence 69%, Insight 62%, Literacy 66%, Language (Saxon) 70%, Language (Brythonic) 70%, Language (Latin) 75%, Lore (Strategy and Tactics) 81%, Lore (Military History) 81%, Lore (Saxon) 76%, Navigate 80%, Ride 71%, Survival 50%, Superstition 35%, Willpower 48%

Passions: Loyalty to Aelle 59%, Loyalty to Ceint 54%, Love (Learning) 58%

1d20	Location	AP/HP
1–3	Right Leg	0/5
4–6	Left Leg	0/5
7–9	Abdomen	4/6
10–12	Chest	4/7
13–15	Right Arm	0/4
16–18	Left Arm	0/4
19–20	Head	3/5

Combat Style: Saxon Noble (Sword, Seax and Shield, Trait: Mounted Combat): 87%

Weapon	Size/Force	Reach	Damage	AP/HP
Seax	*M*	*S*	*1d4+2*	*6/8*
Sword	*M*	*M*	*1d6+1*	*4/8*
Saxon Shield	*L*	*S*	*1d4*	*4/12*

Ealhwyn, Daughter of Hrof

Ealhwyn is the only child of Hrof, the most powerful of King Aelle's Ealdormen. When her father retires, Ealhwyn is determined to rule in his stead. She is strong and almost as large as her bear-like father. She knows how to fight and has led warbands in battle against both Britons and Angles. Ealhwyn also knows how to inspire men and knows her father's lands; none could rule better.

Despite her prowess, and the beginnings of glory, Ealhwyn is still obedient to both her father and to King Aelle. Thus she is reluctantly betrothed to King Aelle's youngest son, Wlencing. Ealhwyn has no desire for marriage and children until she has proven herself fully as a warrior and war leader, and even then, she has no intention of ceasing to be a warrior after marriage, which is conventional for the women who follow her path. As for the atheling Wlencing, his birth has made him both arrogant and naive, and he does not understand that her role in life is to fight.

If Wlencing saw things her way, it could all be different. But he does not understand Ealhwyn or her desire not to stand in the shadows of kings and Ealdormen, or to quietly benefit from the works of her father. Ealhwyn is her father's daughter but she will not rest until she has not just won her own glory but glory that exceeds her father's and Hrof has brought her up to want nothing less.

Ealhwyn

Characteristics	Attributes
STR: 16	Action Points: 3
CON: 15	Damage Modifier: +1d4
SIZ: 17	Magic Points: 14
DEX: 13	Movement: 6 metres
INT: 12	Initiative Bonus: 13/10
POW: 14	Armour: Leather Tunic, Helm
CHA: 11	

Skills: Athletics 69%, Brawn 77%, Culture (Saxon) 64%, Endurance 90%, Language (Saxon) 63%, Locale 79%, Lore (Saxon) 65%, Lore (Strategy and Tactics) 54%, Swim 61%, Superstition 42%,Survival 74%, Track 63%, Unarmed 59%, Willpower 43%
Passions: Love (Personal Glory) 58%, Loyalty to Hrof 59%, Fear (Being stuck at home) 58%, Norse Gods 59%

1d20	Location	AP/HP
1–3	Right Leg	0/7
4–6	Left Leg	0/7
7–9	Abdomen	2/8
10–12	Chest	2/9
13–15	Right Arm	0/6
16–18	Left Arm	0/6
19–20	Head	5/7

Combat Style: Berserker (Battleaxe, Great axe, Trait: Intimidating Scream) 89%

Weapon	Size/Force	Reach	Damage	AP/HP
Seax	*M*	*S*	*1d4+2+1d4*	*6/8*
Bow	*L*	*-*	*1d6+1d4+2*	*4/4*
Spear	*M*	*L*	*1d8+1+1d4*	*4/5*

King Guercha of Anglia

Stories gather around old King Guercha, stories he encourages. Guercha was never just an ordinary warrior, or even an ordinary king. Since he lost his eye in battle – or sacrificed it like the god Woden as the stories tell it – Guercha has been able to see into the spirit world. In his prime, he had both the strength of a warrior and the insight of a laece. Now, as an old, bald man with a scraggly grey beard, he still has the latter.

When the Angle lands flooded and the crops failed, Guercha knew they would fail again and knew the future of his people lay here, in Britain, and the east coast was ready for them. He also

Guercha

Characteristics	Attributes
STR: 9	Action Points: 3
CON: 9	Damage Modifier: 0
SIZ: 15	Magic Points: 14
DEX: 12	Movement: 6 metres
INT: 16	Initiative Bonus: 14/12
POW: 14	Armour: Furs, Helm
CHA: 15	

Skills: Binding (Saxon Tradition) 62%, Culture (Saxon) 77%, Deceit 63%, Engineering 52%, First Aid 58%, Insight 95%, Language (Angle, Jute, or Saxon) 71%, Lore (Norse Gods) 62%, Lore (Saxon) 72%, Lore (Strategy and Tactics) 82%, Oratory 89%, Perception 85%, Sleight 63%, Survival 68%, Stealth 58%, Trance 53%, Willpower 98%
Passions: Loyalty to Anglia 54%, Norse Gods 59%, Fear (Anglia's Destiny won't come) 58%, Hate (King Aelle) 58%

1d20	Location	AP/HP
1–3	Right Leg	0/5
4–6	Left Leg	0/5
7–9	Abdomen	1/6
10–12	Chest	1/7
13–15	Right Arm	0/4
16–18	Left Arm	0/4
19–20	Head	5/5

Combat Style: Saxon Noble (Sword, Seax and Shield, Trait: Mounted Combat) 68%

Weapon	Size/Force	Reach	Damage	AP/HP
Seax	*M*	*S*	*1d4+2*	*6/8*
Sword	*M*	*M*	*1d6+2*	*4/4*
Saxon Shield	*L*	*S*	*1d4*	*4/12*

knows (and the chief laece of Anglia, Aelfstan, backs him here), that the Angles are destined to dominate Britain. This serves to fuel Guercha's disdain, bordering upon hatred, for his fellow king, Aelle of Ceint, who has recently had the nerve to proclaim himself Bretwalda.

Guercha, despite his visions, has doubts for his people's great destiny. He has but one child, Uffa, unlike Aelle who has several sons. Uffa has potential for wisdom but is no war leader, and Guercha's nephew Icel is the most talented of his relatives but he cannot be trusted. The king's Ealdormen have included great war leaders but none have been wise.

The king of Anglia has no true heir and so he hopes that his conquests in Mierce are sufficient to make Anglia unassailable until a true leader comes along who is capable of asserting the kingdom's dominance. Even there, after some of Anglia's conquests were reversed, Guercha has doubts.

Guercha does not share these doubts with others. His strength is in his stories of godlike foresight and power at war, and the descendant of a god cannot show such weakness.

Thane Icel of Tomworthig

King Guercha's nephew Icel is a young, talented and idealistic man. He rules the town of Tomworthig as an independent stronghold in Mierce and has taken himself out of consideration for the throne in Anglia. He maintains Guercha as an ally but is not a subject of Anglia and hates some of those Guercha has sent to Mierce, such as the brutal Ealdorman Stangar.

Unlike many of the young ambitious Saxon warlords in Britain, Icel is a modest man and does not regard himself as a mighty warlord or leader. He is both poetic and courteous in his speech, proficient at the harp and sometimes performs the role of skald, reciting his own works to music. Uffa prides himself on is recognising talents in others, both Angle and Briton, and winning their loyalty. Even mercenaries working for Icel under long term contracts come to regard themselves as his men. Under Icel's rule, Tomworthig prospers and expands in influence.

Icel keeps another part of pride, which reaches through his modesty, private. He feels that in shunning individual glory, he is the best of the viable kings for Britain. He has no ambition to

Icel

Characteristics	Attributes
STR: 11	Action Points: 3
CON: 11	Damage Modifier: 0
SIZ: 13	Magic Points: 15
DEX: 12	Movement: 6 metres
INT: 16	Initiative Bonus: 14/9
POW: 15	Armour: Scale, Helm
CHA: 17	

Skills: Art (Poetry) 62%, Commerce 78%, Courtesy 88%, Culture (Saxon) 72%, Customs 62%, Evade 54%, Influence 84%, Insight 91%, Locale 92%, Lore (Saxons) 72%, Lore (Strategy and Tactics) 62%, Lore (Military History) 62%, Musicianship 59%, Oratory 73%, Perception 46%, Ride 52%, Superstition 34%, Willpower 60%, Unarmed 53%
Passions: Loyalty to Tomworthig 60%, Norse Gods 60%, Hate Stangar 60%

1d20	Location	AP/HP
1–3	Right Leg	0/5
4–6	Left Leg	0/5
7–9	Abdomen	4/6
10–12	Chest	4/7
13–15	Right Arm	0/4
16–18	Left Arm	0/4
19–20	Head	5/5

Combat Style: Saxon Noble (Sword, Seax and Shield, Trait: Mounted Combat) 68%

Weapon	Size/Force	Reach	Damage	AP/HP
Seax	*M*	*S*	*1d4+2*	*6/8*
Sword	*M*	*M*	*1d6+2*	*4/4*
Saxon Shield	*L*	*S*	*1d4*	*4/12*

be Bretwalda but wants one day to make all of Mierce his. He is confident this will happen, one tiny step at a time. So far the kings of Ceint and Anglia and the British kings underestimate him and he has done little to antagonise them. This is another unusual attitude for a Saxon – that peace can be more profitable than war.

King Octa of Wiht

Octa was once one of the two kings of Ceint. He is a proud and bitter old man. Never tall, Octa now seems shrunken with age, although his blue eyes burn fiercely when challenged or if his passions are engaged. Octa's pride comes from being son of Hengist, first of the Saxon kings in Britain. His hate comes from Aelle now being king of Ceint and from owing the smaller power he now wields to Cerdic, a mere Ealdorman, who installed him as King of Wiht.

His men are traitors, criminals and pirates, and his enemies and those he hates are many. He resents Cerdic and wants to see him fail so that Cerdic does not challenge his authority. He hates the Britons but is willing to work with them, especially those of Dumnonia, against his other common enemies. Above all else although, he hates King Aelle and those who support him in Ceint.

Octa presents himself as an old-fashioned sort of Saxon, being a pirate and a raider, but he cannot completely hide the hate that drives him. Although the other Saxon kings have rivalries and even wars, Octa is the knife waiting at their back. There is no telling what he will do in his hatred and desperation.

Ealdorman Stangar

Many Saxon warlords are brutal in their pursuit of glory and victory in war but Ealdorman Stangar is different. He acutely enjoys inflicting brutal and deadly punishments on those who oppose him and dreaming up new and imaginative ways to inflict torment. Stangar does not look the part of the sadist, being young, dark-haired and handsome.

Stangar's tastes were born out of frustration. Under the orders of King Guercha of Anglia, he and his men easily retook the old Roman city of Ratae for the Angle cause but the neighbouring fortress of Caer Leonis has resisted him now for months and forces sallying out of there continue to damage his cause. In frustration, and seeking to goad the Britons into making a mistake or frightening

Octa

Characteristics	Attributes
STR: 10	Action Points: 3
CON: 10	Damage Modifier: 0
SIZ: 12	Magic Points: 13
DEX: 13	Movement: 6 metres
INT: 14	Initiative Bonus: 14/11
POW: 13	Armour: Leather Tunic, Helm
CHA: 13	

Skills: Athletics 53%, Art (Poetry) 41%, Boating 75%, Culture (Jutes) 68%, Deceit 97%, Evade 56%, Influence 81%, Language (Jute) 67%, Language (Brythonic) 42%, Lore (Saxon) 68%, Lore (Strategy and Tactics) 63%, Navigate 92%, Oratory 71%, Seamanship 94%, Superstition 39%, Swim 50%, Willpower 41%
Passions: Hate (Aelle) 68%, Hate (Britons) 43%, Fear (Cerdic) 43%, Norse Gods 58%

1d20	Location	AP/HP
1–3	Right Leg	0/5
4–6	Left Leg	0/5
7–9	Abdomen	2/6
10–12	Chest	2/7
13–15	Right Arm	0/4
16–18	Left Arm	0/4
19–20	Head	5/5

Combat Style: Saxon Noble (Sword, Seax and Shield, Trait: Mounted Combat) 68%

Weapon	Size/Force	Reach	Damage	AP/HP
Seax	*M*	*S*	*1d4+2*	*6/8*
Sword	*M*	*M*	*1d6+2*	*4/4*
Saxon Shield	*L*	*S*	*1d4*	*4/12*

them into surrender, he slaughtered scores of British prisoners, including children, in bloody and imaginative ways in sight of the hillfort. Even now he continues, when it is clear the plan is not working, and simply stirs up further determined resistance, not just from Caer Leonis but from Britons further afield.

Stangar

Characteristics	Attributes
STR: 15	Action Points: 3
CON: 12	Damage Modifier: +1d2
SIZ: 15	Magic Points: 14
DEX: 13	Movement: 6 metres
INT: 12	Initiative Bonus: 13/10
POW: 14	Armour: Scale, Helm
CHA: 10	

Skills: Athletics 63%, Brawn 65%, Craft (Torture) 55%,Culture (Saxon) 64%, Endurance 67%, Evade 49%, Influence 65%, Insight 56%, Language (Angle) 63%, Language (Brythonic) 43%, Lore (Saxon) 64%, Lore (Strategy and Tactics) 49%, Perception 73%, Ride 77%, Stealth 55%, Superstition 52%, Survival 66%, Unarmed 63%, Willpower 43%
Passions: Hate (Britons) 54%, Loyalty to Anglia 59%, Love (Inflicting Torment) 54%

1d20	Location	AP/HP
1–3	Right Leg	0/6
4–6	Left Leg	0/6
7–9	Abdomen	4/7
10–12	Chest	4/8
13–15	Right Arm	0/5
16–18	Left Arm	0/5
19–20	Head	5/6

Combat Style: Saxon Noble (Sword, Seax and Shield, Trait: Mounted Combat) 88%

Weapon	Size/Force	Reach	Damage	AP/HP
Seax	*M*	*S*	*1d4+2+1d2*	*6/8*
Sword	*M*	*M*	*1d6+2+1d2*	*4/4*
Saxon Shield	*L*	*S*	*1d4+1d2*	*4/12*

Still, the Ealdorman has gained fame if not glory; he is the most hated of the Angles Saxons in Mierce. Some of his own countrymen hate him as much as the Britons do, although they have yet to fall victim to him, while others are attracted to his determination. Stangar figures he may as well enjoy that reputation and strives to live up to it.

Stuf of Portus Caester

Stuf is Cerdic's nephew and is trusted by him. He shares his uncle's pragmatic view in matters of war, although Stuf's focus is personal combat and tactics with small groups of warriors rather than grand strategies. Stuf is a monster on the battlefield and rates victory far higher than honour, although when he actually closes with an enemy his style is that of a terrifying berserker rather than a cool calculating opponent.

Cerdic's nephew looks the part of a champion, with flowing light brown hair, blue eyes, polished mail armour and helm, and a wicked smile. Stuf chases glory, always taking the forefront in battles, and seeking out enemy champions and commanders. Recently his romantic streak has been tempered and he has been given more responsibility by his uncle, taking command of the fortress of Portus Caester.

Stuf knows that he needs the local Britons on his side to keep command of the fortress. He consciously apes King Aelle's attempts to turn the British who do not oppose him into allies and has promoted those who seem loyal into senior roles. Only time will tell if this policy is wise.

The new ruler of Portus Caester also knows the power of fear and public displays of brutality and does not hesitate to act against those who oppose him, or punish those who betray him. Stuf is just as cold as Cerdic and as ruthless in rule as he is in war. Stuf wants to be a good ruler but despite his best efforts he is more feared than loved. While he is content with this for now, Stuf is on the cusp; he could prove a wise and effective ruler in the future or a bloody handed tyrant.

Stuf

Characteristics	Attributes
STR: 17	Action Points: 3
CON: 16	Damage Modifier: +1d4
SIZ: 16	Magic Points: 11
DEX: 14	Movement: 6 metres
INT: 12	Initiative Bonus: 13/8
POW: 11	Armour: Mail, Helm
CHA: 13	

Skills: Athletics 91%, Boating 51%, Brawn 93%, Culture (Saxon) 66%, Deceit 56%, Endurance 92%, Evade 73%, Influence 56%, Insight 54%, Language (Saxon) 66%, Language (Brythonic) 41%, Locale 56%, Lore (Saxon) 66%, Lore (Strategy and Tactics) 69%, Navigate 54%, Oratory 59%, Perception 69%, Ride 65%, Sing 54%, Seamanship 54%, Stealth 52%, Superstition 39%, Swim 63%, Unarmed 61%, Willpower 52%

Passions: Loyalty (Aelle) 66%, Love (Fighting) 62%, Loyalty (Southern Britain) 56%, Hate (Dumnonia) 52%

1d20	Location	AP/HP
1–3	Right Leg	0/7
4–6	Left Leg	0/7
7–9	Abdomen	5/8
10–12	Chest	5/9
13–15	Right Arm	0/6
16–18	Left Arm	0/6
19–20	Head	5/7

Combat Style: Berserker (Battleaxe, Greataxe, Trait: Intimidating Scream) 106%

Weapon	Size/Force	Reach	Damage	AP/HP
Battleaxe	*M*	*M*	*1d6+1+1d4*	*4/8*
Greataxe	*H*	*L*	*1d6+2+1d4*	*4/10*

Typical Carl

Characteristics	Attributes
STR: 13	Action Points: 2
CON: 11	Damage Modifier: +1d2
SIZ: 13	Magic Points: 9
DEX: 12	Movement: 6 metres
INT: 12	Initiative Bonus: 12/11
POW: 9	Armour: Leather Tunic
CHA: 10	

Skills: Athletics 55%, Brawn 56%, Craft (Repair Weapons and Armour) 39%, Culture (Saxon) 64%, Endurance 47%, Evade 39%, Language (Angle, Jute, or Saxon) 62%, Lore (Saxon) 64%, Perception 51%, Superstition 38%, Unarmed 50%, Willpower 28%
Passions: Loyalty to Lord 55%, Love (Fighting) 50%

1d20	Location	AP/HP
1–3	Right Leg	0/5
4–6	Left Leg	0/5
7–9	Abdomen	2/6
10–12	Chest	2/7
13–15	Right Arm	0/4
16–18	Left Arm	0/4
19–20	Head	0/5

Combat Style: Fyrdman (Battleaxe, Seax, Shield, Trait: Formation Fighting) 55%

Weapon	Size/Force	Reach	Damage	AP/HP
Seax	*M*	*S*	*1d4+2+1d2*	*6/8*
Battelaxe	*M*	*M*	*1d6+1+1d2*	*4/4*
Saxon Shield	*L*	*S*	*1d4+1d2*	*4/12*

Typical Thane

Characteristics	Attributes
STR: 13	Action Points: 3
CON: 11	Damage Modifier: +1d2
SIZ: 13	Magic Points: 11
DEX: 12	Movement: 6 metres
INT: 13	Initiative Bonus: 13/11
POW: 11	Armour: Leather Tunic, Helm
CHA: 12	

Skills: Athletics 52%, Brawn 49%, Craft (Carpentry or other) 55%, Culture (Saxon) 66%, Language (Angle, Jute, or Saxon) 65%, Lore (Agriculture) 46%, Lore (Animal Husbandry) 46%, Lore (Saxon) 66%, Endurance 47%, Influence 52%, Locale 56%, Perception 62%, Survival 65%, Superstition 36%, Unarmed 40%, Willpower 42%
Passions: Loyalty to Community 55%, Loyalty to Lord 50%, Love (Fighting) 50%

1d20	Location	AP/HP
1–3	Right Leg	0/5
4–6	Left Leg	0/5
7–9	Abdomen	2/6
10–12	Chest	2/7
13–15	Right Arm	0/4
16–18	Left Arm	0/4
19–20	Head	3/5

Combat Style: Fyrdman (Battleaxe, Seax, Shield, Trait: Formation Fighting) 70%

Weapon	Size/Force	Reach	Damage	AP/HP
Seax	*M*	*S*	*1d4+2+1d2*	*6/8*
Battelaxe	*M*	*M*	*1d6+1+1d2*	*4/4*
Saxon Shield	*L*	*S*	*1d4+1d2*	*4/12*

Typical Ealdorman

Characteristics	Attributes
STR: 15	Action Points: 3
CON: 12	Damage Modifier: +1d2
SIZ: 13	Magic Points: 10
DEX: 12	Movement: 6 metres
INT: 13	Initiative Bonus: 13/11
POW: 10	Armour: Leather Tunic, Helm
CHA: 14	

Skills: Athletics 42%, Brawn 43%, Culture (Saxon) 66%, Endurance 47%, Evade 49%, Influence 85%, Insight 38%, Language (Angle, Saxon, or Jute) 66%, Lore (Saxon) 66%, Lore (Strategy and Tactics) 41%, Oratory 69%, Perception 73%, Ride 72%, Superstition 36%, Unarmed 42%, Willpower 50%

Passions: Hate (Britons or Rival) 50%, Loyalty to King 55%, or Love (Power) 50%

1d20	Location	AP/HP
1–3	Right Leg	0/5
4–6	Left Leg	0/5
7–9	Abdomen	2/6
10–12	Chest	2/7
13–15	Right Arm	0/4
16–18	Left Arm	0/4
19–20	Head	5/5

Combat Style: Saxon Noble (Sword, Seax and Shield, Trait: Mounted Combat) 87%

Weapon	Size/Force	Reach	Damage	AP/HP
Seax	*M*	*S*	*1d4+2+1d2*	*6/8*
Sword	*M*	*M*	*1d6+2+1d2*	*4/4*
Saxon Shield	*L*	*S*	*1d4+1d2*	*4/12*

Typical Skald

Characteristics	Attributes
STR: 9	Action Points: 3
CON: 9	Damage Modifier: 0
SIZ: 12	Magic Points: 14
DEX: 12	Movement: 6 metres
INT: 15	Initiative Bonus: 14/13
POW: 14	Armour: Furs
CHA: 12	

Skills: Art (Poetry) 53%, Culture (Saxon) 68%, Customs 48%, Influence 56%, Insight 49%, Language (Angle, Saxon, or Jute) 67%, Lore (Norse Gods) 43%, Lore (Saxon) 68%, Musicianship (Harp) 53%, Perception 39%, Ride 35%, Sing 53%, Willpower 48%

Passions:: Loyalty to King 55%, Love (Poetry) 50%, Norse Gods 55%

1d20	Location	AP/HP
1–3	Right Leg	0/5
4–6	Left Leg	0/5
7–9	Abdomen	1/6
10–12	Chest	1/7
13–15	Right Arm	0/4
16–18	Left Arm	0/4
19–20	Head	0/5

Combat Style: Fyrdman (Battleaxe, Seax, Shield, Trait: Formation Fighting) 65%

Weapon	Size/Force	Reach	Damage	AP/HP
Seax	*M*	*S*	*1d4+2*	*6/8*
Battelaxe	*M*	*M*	*1d6+1*	*4/4*
Saxon Shield	*L*	*S*	*1d4*	*4/12*

Typical Laece

Characteristics	Attributes
STR: 9	Action Points: 3
CON: 9	Damage Modifier: 0
SIZ: 12	Magic Points: 14
DEX: 12	Movement: 6 metres
INT: 15	Initiative Bonus: 14/13
POW: 14	Armour: Furs
CHA: 12	

Skills: Binding (Saxon Tradition) 56%, Culture (Saxon) 70%, Deceit 57%, First Aid 54%, Healing 54%, Insight 44%, Language (Angle, Jute, or Saxon) 67%, Lore (Norse Gods) 60%, Lore (Saxon) 70%, Perception 44%, Sleight 51%, Survival 48%, Stealth 57%, Trance 53%, Willpower 58%

Passions: : Loyalty to Community 55%, Norse Gods 69%

1d20	Location	AP/HP
1–3	Right Leg	0/5
4–6	Left Leg	0/5
7–9	Abdomen	1/6
10–12	Chest	1/7
13–15	Right Arm	0/4
16–18	Left Arm	0/4
19–20	Head	0/5

Combat Style: Hunter (Seax, Spear, Bow, Trait: Skirmishing) 48%

Weapon	**Size/Force**	**Reach**	**Damage**	**AP/HP**
Seax	*M*	*S*	*1d4+2*	*6/8*
Bow	*L*	*-*	*1d6*	*4/4*
Spear	*M*	*L*	*1d8+1*	*4/5*

The Saxon Campaign

Britons view Saxons as the enemy; they came to Britain as raiders and looters, murderers and pirates, and untrustworthy mercenaries. Then some of them stayed and more came as invaders, taking land, more loot and seeking to rule over or enslave the Celts. They have different ways, different codes of honour and different gods.

In this book, you play the Saxons, viewing the Celts who oppose them — and it must be remembered that many Celts already answer to Saxon lords — as an obstacle, and a source of loot, as much as an enemy. It must be noted that Saxons do not treat their enemies and captives any worse than other peoples of the age.

The Saxons have a rich culture, and codes of law, honour and freedom. The first lands in Britain went to them as payment, which the Celts tried to cheat them out of and thus they feel entitled to be here. Worse, they have to be here — in their old homes, the fields are ruined, through no fault of their own and there is fertile land here. It is surely the will of the gods that they came to settle in Britain.

They are carving out a new land for the sake of their people and winning glory on the battlefield. To them the most important things are their kin, freedom and glory. Injuries and insults must be avenged with blood feud, which is legally sanctioned, or compensated with wergeld. Every free Saxon has a say in the decisions their lord makes and need not follow a lord they do not wish to.

This concept is not so different to the Celts, really, although there are many unique cultural details. The Saxons are not monsters, and include good and bad people the same as any other folk. In a standard *Mythic Britain* campaign, it is possible to portray the Saxons as somewhat alien, as brutal savage conquerors. When playing the Saxons although, and especially in a Saxon-centred campaign, remember they are people and remember what is important to them.

When setting up a Saxon-centred game or campaign, you and the players need to give the player characters a reason to adventure together. The easiest set-up is if everyone is a highly placed servant of some minor lord, such as a king's Thane, an Ealdorman or an Atheling on the make.

It is quite possible that in character generation, one of the player characters occupies such a high rank. In this case there are several choices. The most straightforward is for everyone to serve a prince or king who is more highly placed than any of the player characters. This allows for the same sort of scenario as the above, "standard" set-up.

Alternatively, the player characters can be loose allies against a shared enemy or for some shared cause. Perhaps they have the same foe in a blood feud. Remember that kin is very important to the Saxons, so related player characters are going to be allies. The details here are up to the players and GM to work out.

Finally, if everyone is willing, the other player characters can serve the highest-ranked player character. This set-up may not be to everyone's taste, as it puts one player character in charge of everyone else, and may be better in a shorter game than a long campaign, but it in many ways, it is the most logical way to arrange things.

Designing Saxon Scenarios

Mythic Britain is a land of conflict and therefore ripe for scenario design. This is just as true for campaigns centred on Saxon characters as it is for campaigns centred on Celt characters. There are many situations that can be used to build adventures and here we single out just four types of situations. The campaign in chapters 8 to 11 gives further examples, which draw on all of these ideas, as well as others.

Blood Feud

A blood feud is a vendetta sanctioned by a lord in assembly. When a man or woman has been wronged, they and their kin may hunt down the wrongdoer, although wergild rather than death is an acceptable form of restitution. It is justice in Saxon society and must be ratified in assembly.

A character might seek to pursue a blood feud against an enemy, beginning with events seeking to get permission in a lord's assembly. Or a character or their kin might have a blood feud declared against them by an enemy, an idea leading to interesting questions: Is the cause just? Will the character stand by their kin, no matter what?

A blood feud can also take place between Thanes, with permission given by an Ealdorman, or at the most extreme between Ealdormen, with permission given by a king, although the last is extremely rare, with the king usually ordering a settlement with enough wergild to pay up. Such blood feuds will also drag in those who serve a lord — or perhaps the characters will choose to leave their lord, finding new service, which itself is a good adventure hook.

Conquest

The Saxons and Britons are at war. While the Saxons are here to take land and treasure, as this book makes clear, there is far more to the Saxons than them being the "baddies" of Arthurian legend. However, the fact remains that they are invaders and conquerors, although to their eyes they have good reasons for what they do.

A conquest scenario could involve raids or piracy, as well as large scale battles. For a more nuanced approach, ultimately, if the Saxons hold the land they take, they and the Celts will have to live in peace. How is this possible and what tensions arise in parts of the land where both peoples live?

Politics

There are several Saxon kingdoms and regions: Anglia, Ceint, Wiht, Cerdic's territories on the south coast and the patchwork that is Mierce. The people of these areas are mostly allies but there are great underlying tensions, and war between them could break out at any time.

King Guecha of Anglia resents King Aelle of Ceint. They are competing for territory in Mierce but many places stay neutral or are opposed to both — not only the Celts living there but even Guercha's nephew, Thane Icel of Tomworthig.

Then there is the fact that King Aelle fears Cerdic's growing influence; rightly so, as Cerdic believes he is ultimately to become Bretwalda of Britain and he gains territory each year. In addition, King Octa of Wiht hates Aelle as a usurper in Ceint and fears Cerdic even although he relied on him to obtain his position.

Finally, in each of these kingdoms there are rivalries between Ealdormen, either on personal grounds, or competing for influence. As you can see, war and politics is far more than a simple Saxon against Briton equation.

The Supernatural

Britain is a land where the spirits are real and druids and laeces can talk to them and sometimes have them do their bidding. The supernatural is both all-pervasive and a subtle rather than an overt force, with rare exceptions. Naturally the player characters are just the sorts of people who might experience these rare exceptions.

Supernatural forces driving scenarios include manipulative and unscrupulous laeces and druids, areas blighted or subjected to fearful superstition because of hostile *landvaettir* or other spirits, hidden things in isolated places and spirits sent to plague the player characters by enemy laeces or druids. The supernatural can also form a part of another scenario rather than being the driving force; indeed, any scenario featuring a druid or laece will involve supernatural forces to some extent.

Campaign: Blood Feuds and Dark Power

In this campaign, the characters begin in a village, Caedering, at the edge of Ceint, where the local Thane, Osbehrt, has recently transferred his allegiance to the new conquerer, Cerdic, who arrived a few years ago, in 495 AD.

Cerdic's initial foray into Britain was indecisive, although he managed to comfortably seize control of the island of Wiht and pass it on to Octa, the exiled former king of Ceint. Despite that, Cerdic is officially an ally of King Aelle of Ceint, the most powerful of the Saxon kings of Britain, and Cerdic recognises Aelle as Bretwalda.

Nevertheless, Cerdic schemes for greater conquests and for a power base of his own. His Saxons have settled on the south coast, an area that is something of a no-man's land between areas fully controlled by Ceint and the still mighty kingdom of Dumnonia, home of Arthur. Rather than face Dumnonia in open battle yet again, Cerdic's forces are pushing north.

Player characters are either locals, or else are newly arrived in Caedering with Cerdic's carls, under the command of Taethle (see below). They now serve Cerdic, directly or indirectly, and are a part of his expansion. They have local allies, rivals and enemies. The campaign comes with a number of NPCs who are suitable for player characters who have such personal connections, either by design or as a background event.

Osbehrt

Osbehrt is a King's Thane and ruler of Caedering. He is the player characters' lord at the beginning of these scenarios.

Taethle

Taethle is a commander in Ealdorman Cerdic's forces, newly arrived in Britain like many of Cerdic's followers. She and the carls she commands are newly arrived in Caedering in the first scenario.

Ceolfrith

Ceolfrith is a local Ealdorman and Osbehrt's old lord before he changed allegiance to serve Cerdic. Osbehrt has lost face and territory and has privately vowed to punish Osbehrt for his disloyalty.

Wulfric

A treacherous Thane serving Ceolfrith, hungry for more power and territory. It is rumoured he murdered his own brother to get his lands.

Dunric

A powerful laece who serves the Ealdorman Ceolfrith, although those close to them debate who is really in charge. He deals with more unsavoury spirits and magic.

The campaign consists of four scenarios, which should each occupy one or two sessions of play.

Conquest

Ealdorman Cerdic's forces arrive in Caedering to subdue the surrounding area. The player characters are assigned to scout things out, gathering information ready for the conquest. But they also face treachery from within.

Assembly

The player characters deal with a blood feud declared by a neighbouring Thane, along with possible escalation, meetings in an Ealdorman's and perhaps a king's assembly, attacks and attempts at murder.

The Cursed Hill

When the player characters return to Caedering, they find things in chaos, with tensions between Cerdic's forces and the residents of Caedering such that things are about to break. One of Cerdic's men has been mysteriously murdered and the people are blamed. As people who were out of town, the player characters are exonerated; it is up to them to solve the mystery and stop the murders. Dark magic and monsters are involved.

Uprising

In this scenario, both Cerdic and King Aelle seek to recruit the player characters to travel to a Saxon village, Taddenlaege, in the middle of Celt territory. Cerdic sends them there, looking for allies in the war with Dumnonia. The player characters find the local Celts in unrest, gathering forces to destroy Taddenlaege completely. Can the heroes prevent this and discover what is at the root of the trouble? Can they still manage to send forces to Cerdic or Aelle?

Sample Characters

The following group of characters have appropriate ties for the Blood Feuds and Dark Power campaign, and a good range of abilities. You can use them as is, as inspiration for player characters, or as non-player characters. They are created using the standard rules for starting characters.

The characters are all quite poor at the start of the campaign; this could be a factor in getting them involved in initial adventures.

Hafgan

Hafgan is a Celt who grew up in Ceint under Saxon rule. He is a free warrior, Saxon by alliance if not by blood, and a journeyman blacksmith. He acknowledges the Saxon rulers and has sworn service to Osbehrt, King's Thane of Caedering. Still, his ways, and even more so, the ways of his family, are more Celt than Saxon. Hafgan views the Saxons and Celts as people who now have to live together and hostile kingdoms — both Celt and Saxon — as enemies rather than whole peoples.

Not everyone shares these attitudes. Many Saxons view Hafgan as an inferior and many Celts view him as a traitor. Hafgan is keen to correct both attitudes, either by reasoned argument (Hafgan is an intelligent man) or by fists or weapons - (he has a vicious temper and fights like a Saxon berserker).

Hafgan	Attributes
STR: 13	Action Points: 3
CON: 11	Damage Modifier: +1d2
SIZ: 15	Magic Points: 8
DEX: 11	Movement: 6 metres
INT: 15	Initiative Bonus: 13
POW: 8	Armour: None
CHA: 11	

Skills: Art (Poetry) 19%, Athletics 49%, Boating 24%, Brawn 53%, Conceal 19%, Craft (Blacksmith) 56%. Commerce 41%, Culture (Saxon) 45%, Culture (Celt) 70%, Customs 30%, Dance 19%, Deceit 26%, Drive 19%, Endurance 52%, Engineering 55%, Evade 22%, First Aid 41%, Gambling 38%, Influence 22%, Insight 38%, Language (Brythonic) 66%, Language (Saxon) 51%, Locale 60%, Lore (Celt) 70%, Lore (Pagan) 30%, Perception 48%, Ride 19%, Sing 19%, Stealth 26%, Swim 24%, Unarmed 54%, Willpower 36%
Passions: Loyalty to Community 55%, Loyalty to Lord 50%, Love (Fighting) 50%

1d20	Location	AP/HP
1–3	Right Leg	0/6
4–6	Left Leg	0/6
7–9	Abdomen	0/7
10–12	Chest	0/8
13–15	Right Arm	0/5
16–18	Left Arm	0/5
19–20	Head	0/6

Combat Style: Berserker (Battleaxe, Great axe, Trait: Intimidating Scream) 69%

Weapon	Size/Force	Reach	Damage	AP/HP
Battelaxe	*M*	*M*	*1d6+1+1d2*	*4/4*
Greataxe	*M*	*L*	*2d6+2+1d2*	*4/10*

Although Hafgan has no intention of changing his approach, it has got him into trouble before. Hafgan once killed a Saxon Carl who insulted him in a brawl and he chose to pay wergild to the man's kin rather than face a blood feud. Hafgan will admit he was in the wrong there, after all, and he does still stand out in Saxon society. Still, he is now short of funds and keen to look for opportunities to go on to bigger and better things, at least proving himself further to Thane Osbehrt, even if such opportunities are risky ones.

Mildburg

Mildburg has held the title of Thane since her brother, Beorwald, fled into exile, although she has since lost her brother's lands. Beorwald was accused of murdering the brother of a rival Thane, Wulfric. Mildburg suspects that Wulfric killed his own brother to claim his holdings and then got greedy for Beorwald's lands. The local Ealdorman, Ceolfrith, allowed this to happen and in assembly allowed Wulfric to prosecute a blood feud against Beorwald and any kin who sided with him.

Mildburg is unsure whether to take a stand now that her brother has fled and so far has been able to delay either taking up arms against Wulfric or denouncing Beorwald. Although she will have to decide soon, Mildburg is certain she will not pay any wergild to Wulfric.

As a young woman, Mildburg was always more adept at arms rather than crafts typical for a girl but was prepared to put these aside when her brother was talking about a marriage to the unmarried King's Thane, Osbehrt, ruler of Caedering. Now that Osbehrt has left Ceolfrith's service, Mildburg has put thoughts of marriage aside and swore to follow Cerdic along with Osbehrt, who she accepts now as her lord. She is ready to win renown and perhaps gain a measure of revenge.

Aesc

Aesc is a small dark-haired man, with Celtic and Saxon blood. He is most at home in the wilderness, although he is happy enough in rough 'frontier' villages. His intelligence and stealth has also gained him a reputation for being devious; Aesc does not mind this; he knows his strengths.

Some of Aesc's cunning can be put down to an odd foresight – visions which sometimes come to him when he drinks. These began after a past event Aesc does not speak about: when he wandered into a forest grove near Old Wincen-Caestre hill, beckoned by a beautiful woman. There, he "lost" a year; when he left the grove, he had no memory of what happened in between entering

Mildburg	Attributes
STR: 12	Action Points: 3
CON: 13	Damage Modifier: +1d2
SIZ: 14	Magic Points: 11
DEX: 14	Movement: 6 metres
INT: 12	Initiative Bonus: 13
POW: 11	Armour: None
CHA: 12	

Skills: Art (Poetry) 38%, Athletics 56%, Boating 25%, Brawn 26%, Conceal 25%, Culture (Saxon) 64%, Craft (Embroidery) 26%, Customs 24%, Dance 41%, Deceit 25%, Drive 25%, Endurance 41%, Evade 43%, First Aid 41%, Healing 23$, Influence 69%, Insight 68%, Language (Saxon) 64%, Locale 34%, Lore (Military History) 24%, Lore (Saxon) 64%, Lore (Battle) 49%, Oratory 68%, Perception 23%, Ride 50%, Sing 23%, Stealth 26%, Swim 25%, Unarmed 26%, Willpower 32%
Passions: Loyalty to Cerdic 56%, Loyalty to Caedering 51%, Love Osbehrt 52%, Hate Wulfric 52%, Norse Gods 56%

1d20	Location	AP/HP
1–3	Right Leg	0/6
4–6	Left Leg	0/6
7–9	Abdomen	0/7
10–12	Chest	0/8
13–15	Right Arm	0/5
16–18	Left Arm	0/5
19–20	Head	0/6

Combat Style: Saxon Noble (Spear, Sword, Seax and Shield, Trait: Mounted Combat): 71%

Weapon	Size/Force	Reach	Damage	AP/HP
Seax	*M*	*S*	*1d4+2+1d2*	*6/8*
Sword	*M*	*M*	*1d6+2+1d2*	*4/4*
Saxon Shield	*L*	*S*	*1d4+1d2*	*4/12*

and leaving. Despite trying, he has been unable to find the grove again.

A persistent vision Aesc receives concerns Dunric, a laece who serves the Ealdorman Ceolfrith; he sees him dealing with dark forces and inflicting major acts of cruelty and torture.

Aesc's Visions

At the GM's discretion, when Aesc drinks heavily, the GM can give him a cryptic vision, which may or may not be helpful.

Eoforwine

To others, Eoforwine seems otherworldly, with a loose grasp of the physical world. He is extremely clumsy — too clumsy to make a decent warrior. Yet despite appearances, Eoforwine has a keen appreciation of his surroundings, both in the physical and the spirit world. He is a laece, and closer than most to the world of gods and spirits, especially the boar-riding fertility god Yngvi.

Despite his frequent vagueness, Eoforwine is high in the counsels of his lord, Osbehrt. He earned Osbehrt's gratitude when he saved his life after a recent illness, when his Ealdorman's laece, Dunric, had failed. This pleased Eoforwine; after all, he has a fierce rivalry with Dunric, who uses his spiritual insights for ill. Eoforwine is certain Dunric was in fact behind Thane Osbehrt's illness, though he cannot yet prove it — the malady was more spiritual than physical.

Eoforwine's wyrd is to help those communities he makes his home, however temporarily. For now, this home is Caedering, but he knows his wyrd is to have many such homes in his lifetime.

Aesc	Attributes
STR: 11	Action Points: 3
CON: 9	Damage Modifier: 0
SIZ: 10	Magic Points: 9
DEX: 12	Movement: 6 metres
INT: 16	Initiative Bonus: 13
POW: 9	Armour: Furs
CHA: 11	

Skills: Athletics 48%, Boating 35%, Brawn 21%, Culture (Saxon) 72%, Craft (Fletcher) 28%, Conceal 21%, Customs 32%, Dance 23%, Deceit 27%, Drive 21%, Endurance 43%, Evade 24%, First Aid 28%, Gambling 40%, Influence 22%, Insight 25%, Language (Brythonic) 42%, Language (Saxon) 67%, Locale 32%, Lore (Battle) 32%, Lore (Saxon) 72%, Navigate 55%, Perception 40%, Seamanship 40%, Ride 21%, Sing 20%, Stealth 58%, Survival 64%, Swim 20%, Track 70%, Unarmed 33%, Willpower 18%

Passions: Loyalty to Osbehrt 54%, Loyalty to Caedering 48%, Love the Wilderness 46%, Hate Dunric 46%, Norse Gods 54%

1d20	Location	AP/HP
1–3	Right Leg	0/4
4–6	Left Leg	0/4
7–9	Abdomen	1/5
10–12	Chest	1/6
13–15	Right Arm	0/3
16–18	Left Arm	0/3
19–20	Head	0/4

Combat Style: Hunter (Seax, Spear, Bow, Trait: Skirmishing) 83%

Weapon	Size/Force	Reach	Damage	AP/HP
Seax	*M*	*S*	*1d4+2*	*6/8*
Bow	*L*	-	*1d6*	*4/4*
Spear	*M*	*L*	*1d8+1*	*4/5*

Eolorwine	Attributes
STR: 11	Action Points: 2
CON: 11	Damage Modifier: 0
SIZ: 10	Magic Points: 16
DEX: 7	Movement: 6 metres
INT: 14	Initiative Bonus: 11
POW: 16	Armour: None
CHA: 10	

Skills: Athletics 18%, Binding 56%, Boating 22%, Brawn 21%, Craft (Fletcher) 21%, Conceal 23%, Culture (Saxon) 68%, Customs 43%, Dance 27%, Deceit 39%, Drive 21%, Endurance 22%, Evade 14%, First Aid 51%, Healing 75%, Influence 35%, Insight 60%, Locale 58%, Lore (Britain) 45%, Lore (Norse Gods) 55%, Lore (Saxon) 68%, Perception 45%, Ride 23%, Sing 26%, Stealth 21%, Survival 42%, Swim 22%, Trance 57%, Unarmed 18%, Willpower 47%

Passions: Loyalty to Osbehrt 61%, Loyalty to Caedering 56%, Love Yngvi 62%, Hate corrupt laeces 62%, Norse Gods 61%

1d20	Location	AP/HP
1–3	Right Leg	0/5
4–6	Left Leg	0/5
7–9	Abdomen	0/6
10–12	Chest	0/7
13–15	Right Arm	0/4
16–18	Left Arm	0/4
19–20	Head	0/5

Combat Style: Hunter (Seax, Spear, Bow, Trait: Skirmishing) 33%

Weapon	Size/Force	Reach	Damage	AP/HP
Seax	*M*	*S*	*1d4+2*	*6/8*
Bow	*L*	-	*1d6*	*4/4*
Spear	*M*	*L*	*1d8+1*	*4/5*

Caledonii
Votadini
Key
Terrain above 660'
Terrain above 2000'
Forest
Bogs, Swamps & Coastal Marsh
0 50 100 miles
0 50 100 km
Raida
Gododdin
Votadini
Caledonii
Middle Britain
2
Carvetii
Brigantes
Parisii
Elmet
8
Gwynedd
Cornovii
Western Britain
Ordovices
Powys
Mierce
Anglia
Gwent
Logres (Saxons)
Silures
Siluria
Ceint
Dumnonii
Dumnonia
Wiht

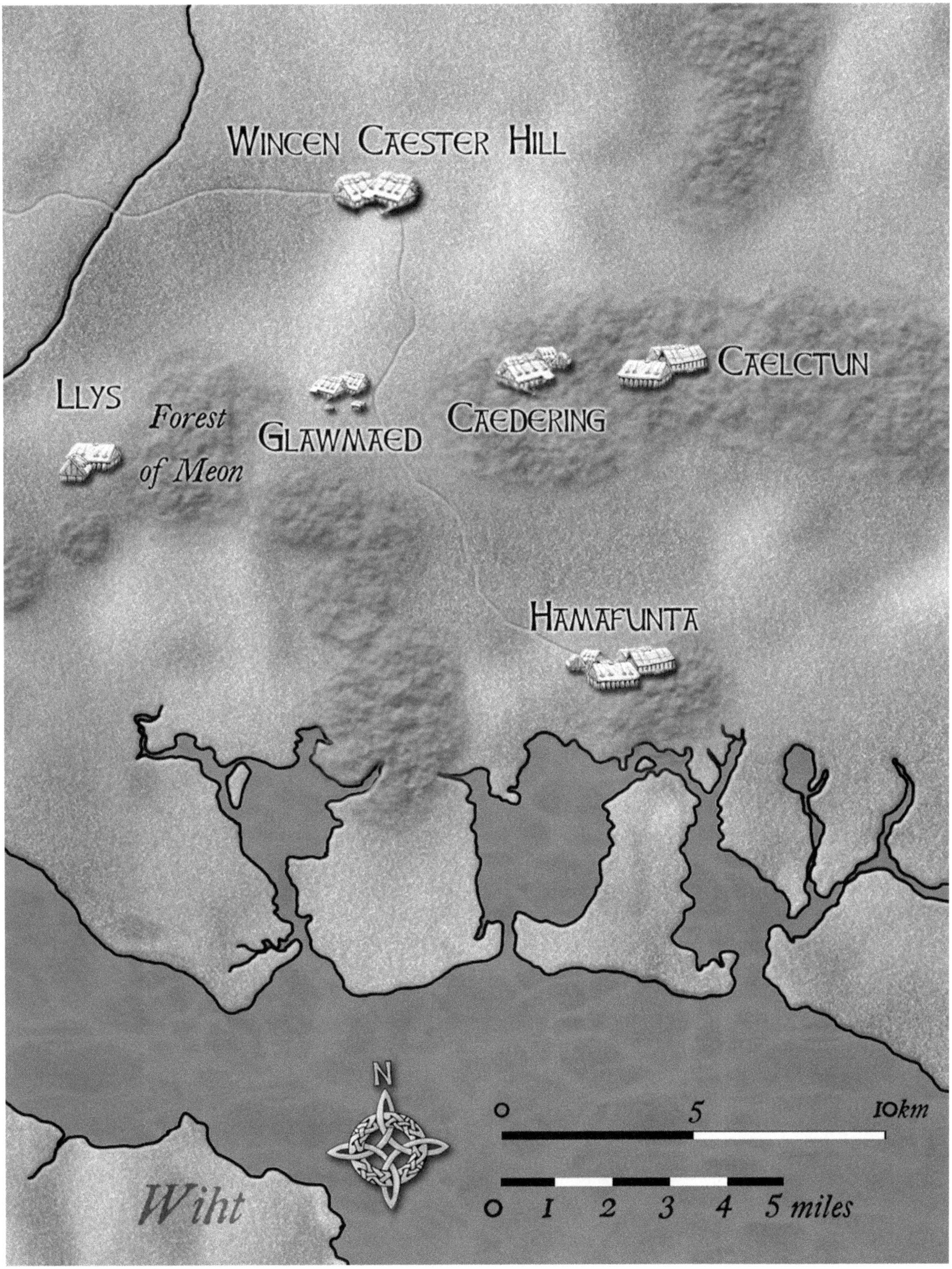
WINCEN CAESTER HILL
CAELCTUN
LLYS
Forest
of Meon
GLAWMAED
CAEDERING
HAMAFUNTA
N
0
5
10km
0 1 2 3 4 5 miles
Wiht

Conquest

Caedering, the characters' home, is a village on the western borders of Ceint, in a secure, high position on a ridge. It is surrounded by a ditch and a wooden fence made of sharpened stakes bound tightly together. Caedering is often subject to strong winds and drizzling rain, even when the weather is calmer in the farms lower down the hills, although at least the Thane's hall and houses are cosy. Unlike most Saxon villages, the houses here have wooden rather than thatched rooves.

Caedering's exposed position is a needful thing for defence; since Cerdic's landing on the south coast, the Celts to the west have been particularly aggressive and Caedering has been the target of frequent raids and attacks. The leader of the village, Osbehrt, is a King's Thane. Osbehrt's hall, where he dwells with his housecarls, is part of the walls and so the defences of the village.

In this campaign, the characters all serve Thane Osbehrt. Until recently, Osbehrt in turn served the local Ealdorman, Ceolfrith. But Ceolfrith rejected Osbehrt's request for aid against the Celt attackers; the Ealdorman sees more profit in his own raids against the Celts than in defending a village. Unfortunately, his raids also contribute to Caedering's trouble; being at the edge of Ceint's territories, it is the target of any retaliation the Celts make against the Saxons.

After the death of his wife at the hands of the Celts, which he blames on Ceolfrith's selfishness, Osbehrt changed loyalties. He travelled to Portus Caester and swore allegiance to the new power in the area, Cerdic. Cerdic immediately sent men to Caedering – men prepared to subdue the nearby Celt villages once and for all, bringing in loot and slaves, and ending the attacks.

Now that he has help, Thane Osbehrt wants to impress Cerdic and the heroes are part of this effort. They are to scout the land ahead of the invading force, getting an idea not just of the Celt forces but of the personalities involved and any allegiance(s). It is a mission of both stealth and deceptive diplomacy and is quite possible that Celts who side with the Saxons can maintain their

How Many Warriors?

Caedering holds between 30 and 40 warriors, as well as the player characters. Ealdorman Cerdic has sent another 36 warriors, under the leadership of Taethle.

independence in a new greater kingdom; such things have happened before in both Cerdic's and King Aelle's lands.

However, Ceolfrith is quietly furious at Osbehrt's change of alliance. Changing lord is normal for Saxons, when the lord does not provide but Ceolfrith has lost both face and lands. He will seek revenge and has encouraged the ambitious Thane in the neighbouring village, Thane Wulfric, to stir up trouble, hinting that Wulfric will be able to add Caedering to his own territory when matters are done. Wulfric and some of his men are present in Caedering to stir up trouble and attempt to show Cerdic's men that his new allies are nothing but liabilities.

The Feast

The scenario begins when Thane Osbehrt holds a feast to celebrate the arrival of Cerdic's men and drink to victory over the Celts. The guests (several of whom are important people of note) manage to drink Osbehrt's supplies almost dry.

Osbehrt

Osbehrt is of course Thane of Caedering. He is still a young man and has no children, although with his sad blue eyes, one gets the impression of greater age and grief. He recently lost his wife to a Celtic attack; she was outside the walls, tending the farm, when they struck by surprise. Losing his wife was the deciding factor for him turning his back on Ealdorman Ceolfrith to join Cerdic's cause.

The Thane does not so much blame the Celts for his wife's death as Ceolfrith, who should have supported him. Osbehrt does not hate the Celts but rather sees them as something like an elemental force which has to be controlled.

Osbehrt is still a fine warrior but the death of his wife has changed him. He used to be careful and take his time making decisions; he still considers strategies to his best advantage but once he commits to something he stays with it, regardless of changes or risks. He is also more prone to lose his temper. Some of Osbehrt's Carls now see him as a stronger leader but he is both more headstrong and more rash.

Others think he should remarry and are considering him and the leader of Cerdic's Carls, Taethle, thoughtfully.

Other People

The GM may wish to introduce some other people who live in Caedering or amongst Taethle's men, to add further interactions and colour. They will become more prominent in the chapter 11 scenario, The Cursed Hill.

Eadstan

A merchant based in Caedering, known for his ambition, pomposity and self-importance. Some suspect his loyalty to Thane Osbehrt.

Sunngyth

A Shieldmaiden of Caedering, well-regarded as a warrior, who sees omens everywhere. She is superstitious even for a pagan Saxon.

Bredoc

Bredoc, Taethle's second in command, is a model of Saxon piety. He is brave, dutiful and unusually sober. His major flaw is pointing out the shortcomings of others, which makes him quite unpopular.

Sigebeohrt

Sigebeohrt is a bold rash warrior, a big drinker and berserk warrior. He can be unreliable when it comes to day to day activities but is deadly in battle.

Taethle

Taethle is calm, professional and cold. Her face is young but her hair is prematurely grey. She leads the group of Cerdic's warriors who have come to Caedering, every inch the warrior; battling for victory, not lust for combat or such petty emotions as hatred. When she fights, she fights to win.

The young warrior does not seek glory but she does seek recognition for her talents. A significant victory over the Celts here, with a mere score of extra men as well as such help as Osbehrt can provide, will secure her name, both in Ceint and in Cerdic's eyes.

Taethle can come across as standoffish, although the men who follow her know her skills and trust her to help them both win and stay alive. Taethle will drink sparingly at feasts and not get involved in drunken boasting contests, games or brawls. She will not fight for fun; she fights only when she has to and then she fights to kill.

Wulfric

Wulfric, a Thane serving Ceolfrith, is not a particularly welcome guest at the feast but he is there to present his Ealdorman's interests. He is accompanied by four of his Carls. Although Osbehrt has left Ceolfrith's service, he does not want his former Ealdorman as an enemy, meaning he has to host Wulfric.

Wulfric is a handsome man, who wears his long blonde hair braided to one side in the style of the Angles. He can be pleasant company when he chooses to be but more often he comes across as cocky and deliberately annoying. He loves to taunt his enemies into making mistakes or saying things they should not. He is an able enough warrior, although he has no great love for fighting when the odds are not firmly on his side. Wulfric prefers the sudden ambush and tormenting his enemy from a position where he cannot be touched, or a position of obvious superiority.

The Thane is also a ruthless man. He murdered his brother to take his lands and title, and managed to frame another for the

Wulfric and Mildburg

If Mildburg, one of the sample player characters, is in play, Wulfric successfully blamed her brother for the murder of his own sibling. Mildburg will have to decide if she is standing by her brother or not, who has fled as a result of the blood feud.Wulfric is sure to mention Mildburg's brother to her at the feast..

horrible deed. Not only that but he successfully declared a blood feud against another Thane for the murder, managing to take his lands in the process. He is a dangerous and cunning man, who has no qualms with what he does to those who stand in his way.

At the feast, there are two main events, as well as anything that goes on directly between Wulfric and a player character enemy, or that the player characters initiate.

A Call to Arms

Thane Osbehrt calls the characters forward as the bravest and cleverest of his Carls, presenting them to the company in the hall. He is flattering and sincere, and will refer to any known exploits in the player characters' backgrounds. This is a good opportunity for the players to introduce their characters. They receive immediate acclaim from everyone present, as well as being presented with drinks and small gifts, as well as friendly questions from most of the audience and more challenging questions from Wulfric.

Taethle has something in common with Wulfric. She is less carried away with the occasion than most of the people in the halland her questions, although not unfriendly, are clearly aimed at getting some idea of the characters' capabilities.

Osbehrt asks them to act as scouts, finding the disposition of the Celts, their forces and the lay of the landscape at the present time. They are not in a position to refuse without looking disgraceful. Indeed, they should be delighted at the opportunity that Osbehrt, their lord, has presented them. Osbehrt offers a gift to each character – coins and other small valuables worth 100SP, with the promise of much more after the conquest of the nearby Celts.

There is some urgency to the mission. Taethle wants to move against the Celts as soon as possible, although she recognises the need to gather intelligence. More crucially, in the last two weeks or so, the Celts have gone very quiet, with a definite lack of raids. Thane Osbehrt suspects they are planning something.

A Riddling Contest

After much ale has been drunk, Wulfric challenges one of the player characters to a riddling contest. He suggests a "small wager" on the outcome, namely 100SP (for a starting character, this could be almost all the money he has!). Use the rules for riddles on page 30. A player character who makes an Insight test will realise Wulfric's riddles subtly insult Thane Osbehrt, then the character and finally Osbehrt's deceased wife (a nasty low blow). Of course, if confronted, Wulfric will be able to deny everything

The Riddles

I heard that something was growing in the corner,
swelling and sticking up, raising its roof.
A proud bride grasped that boneless thing,
with her hands. A lord's daughter
covered with a garment that bulging thing.
Answer: Dough

(The first riddle is one of the standard ribald sort; Wulfric's tone and gestures make it subtly insulting to Wulfric.)

Covered in a mattress of straw am I
On top does no man lie
but instead sows his seed, for he has a need
that no mere Carl can deny.
Answer: A Field

(The second is another ribald riddle delivered right in the character's face, with suggestions of sexual frustration and unmanliness.)

I have a new house in a new land
A foreigner, he lent a hand
and entered when my husband was not man
So I brought no husband, but brought my things
He dares not join me, but feasts and sings
and pecks at the ground, a raven without wings.
Where do I live?
Answer: A Grave

(The reference to Osbehrt's deceased wife is deniable but clear.)

The contest takes place near Osbehrt's chair, where he can hear. When Osbehrt's wife is mentioned, he grows visibly angry, rising from his chair and beginning to draw his sword. A character can attempt to calm Osbehrt down with a quick Influence or other relevant social skill or Passion test.

If the player characters fail to calm Osbehrt, either by choice or a failed roll, the Thane attacks, drawing his sword and making for Wulfric. A player character can try to stop Osbehrt physically; this requires an Athletics or Unarmed roll, although anyone with a Passion involving hatred for Wulfric must fail a passion roll before they can act.

If the player characters fail to stop Osbehrt, Wulfric beats a hasty retreat but one of Wulfric's men draws an axe. A heroic character might choose to do battle with the threat to his Thane. Otherwise, Osbehrt himself faces the axeman and rapidly cuts him down. There is stunned silence in the hall, as Wulfric retreats, vowing to tell the world how Osbehrt treats his guests.

If the player characters now decide to stop Wulfric from leaving, let them; otherwise he gets away. A player character who has aided Osbehrt, either in stopping him from doing something foolish, or taking up arms against the one who moved to attack him, receives his Thane's gratitude and the gift of a silver Celtic armband, worth 150sp.

This event, although dramatic, affects matters less than they might outwardly appear. Wulfric and Ceolfrith are now able to be openly hostile towards Osbehrt and Caedering, where they were secretly hostile before. Taethle certainly thinks less of Osbehrt if he attacked, or tried to, and will not trust him to take the lead when it comes to the attack against the Celts. This will increase tensions in the next adventure.

Gathering Information

Although the player characters have "volunteered" for the dangerous mission of scouting ahead of a possible invasion force, they might want some knowledge of the surrounding area before they leave. All of the player characters know that the nearest Celt settlement is Glawmaed, described below.

Each player character is allowed a standard Locale test to know more, or to find someone in Caedering to talk to who knows more. There are merchants and other people in Caedering who have travelled, although more travel east than west. Each success reveals one of the following pieces of information; a critical success reveals two things.

- Beyond Glawmaed is a larger settlement. The Celt warriors raiding Caedering probably come from there.
- Ealdorman Ceolfrith's warriors avoided that larger settlement, looking for easier pickings.
- This larger settlement is hidden within the forest of Meon.
- The forest of Meon is haunted; people have gone missing there.

Glawmaed

As a whole, the people of Glawmaed have no interest in fighting the good fight against the Saxon invader but will defend themselves if necessary. They grow an excess of food and in happier times traded with the Saxons but now the majority of it goes to the town of Llys, described below. Some of the rasher young men of Glawmaed have joined the crusade against the Saxons there but they do not mount raids of their own against Saxons unless they come rampaging on their lands.

The village is small; there are fewer than 100 people who live here and most are farmers. Glawmead can field 20 able-bodied spearmen if needs be but they are more farmers than warriors. The dwellings are typical Celt round houses, although the chief has a larger hall. The world has left Glawmaed mostly alone, as the people are not aggressive and there is little of value here for raiders to take.

Saxons who approach the village in a friendly way will be received cautiously, and watched by men armed with spears, but there will be no immediate hostility unless the player characters initiate insults or violence. It should be clear to the characters that Glawmaed will not provide any notable opposition to a Saxon conquest of the neighbourhood. Getting more out of a visit to the village requires talking to people, especially the chieftain, described below.

Observing First

Cautious (which probably means sensible) characters might try to observe Glawmaed first before going in. Should they do this, each player character who succeeds at an easy Perception roll learns one of the following pieces of information. A critical success reveals two things.

- The village is smaller than Caedering.
- The guards by the gate are armed with spears and bows. The Celt raiders who have struck Caedering were more heavily armed.
- There is a larger round house in the centre of the village and is probably a communal centre or belongs to the chief.
- The fields here appear to be very fertile.

People of Glawmaed

Gwern

Gwern is a small dark-haired man, with suspicious narrow eyes. Chieftain of Glawmaed, he is defined by his caution and aversity to risks; he ultimately desires to do what is best for the safety of himself and his village. Although an apparently uninspiring leader, he is solid and the people of Glawmaed trust his judgement thoroughly. With the exception of a few young men who want more excitement, they will go where he leads.

He has a wife and many children, some now young adults themselves. The eldest daughter, Bronwyn, definitely wants more out of life than the village and will be openly curious about visitors, even Saxons, although she does not speak their language. For his part, Gwern does speak some Saxon and is prepared to cautiously trade information.

Anyon

Anyon is a tall auburn-haired warrior, of the royal line of what was once the Kingdom of the Regnenses. He is haughty and proud of his prowess in battle. In Glawmaed, he strikes quite a glamourous figure and people watch him with respect and a little awe. Some of the young men in the village want to emulate him.

Anyon is here to boast of his success in raiding the Saxons and to persuade Glawmaed to take more of a direct role in the fight. If the chieftain, Gwern, will not hear him, he will make a direct appeal to the people. Naturally, he is far from pleased to see the player characters and will not even acknowledge them unless forced to. He pretends not to understand Saxon at all but in reality does speak a little of it.

Getting anything of value out of Gwern requires a Standard Influence, Insight or similar skill test. If Anyon is present, this will be an opposed test with his Influence skill. More than one character can try to get information, with a critical success yielding two pieces of information. Gwern is very good at prevaricating but can be pinned down with politeness and hard work.

- The Forest of Meon is haunted by spirits, who require offerings. A generous offering sometimes leads to a blessing from the spirits.
- A nearby small town, Llys, is hidden at the far edge of the Forest of Meon.
- The people of Llys are exiles from an old Celt kingdom absorbed by Ceint. They hate "your kind" (meaning the Saxons).
- The people of Glawmaed just want to be left alone to get on with their lives and not dragged into wars.
- Gwern is sure the Saxons will eventually rule the area.

If Anyon is not present, the heroes can try to get even more out of Gwern. He is half convinced that the Saxons will soon rule the area and so could be persuaded to accept a Saxon lord, such as Osbehrt, then and there. This requires at the very least a Hard skill test and Gwern will not raise the issue, although seeking information could suss it out of him.

If the player characters offer suitable incentives, such as a big gift or a marriage for Gwern's daughter Bronwyn that leads to a rise in status for her, the task of persuading Gwern to take a Saxon lord is of Standard difficulty.

The Forest of Meon

The Forest of Meon is an area of dense oak woodland crossed by ponds and streams. It is difficult to navigate; to successfully cross the forest, or even leave its heart requires, a Standard Navigation skill test or a Hard Survival test.

All paths seem to lead to a pool in its centre, a beautiful but eerie place and the home of a powerful woodland spirit. Here wild flowers grow out of season, even in the winter. A group who fails a Navigation test will find themselves here.

Within the clear pool are many ancient offerings – old Roman coins and small pieces of jewellery. The net worth of the treasure is 1,000 SP but it would take a truly courageous or foolish man to seek to claim them from the local god. The correct protocol (as a successful Lore (Pagan) or similar skill will reveal) is to make an offering and go on one's way.

One who makes an offering to the local nameless goddess will find navigation in the forest easier; reduce all difficulties of such tasks by one step. Someone who gives a particularly valuable gift will be possessed by one of the forest spirits; if the possession happens, they gain an extra two Hit Points to each location for the duration of the scenario.

On the other hand, if the player characters leave without even a small offering (a single coin suffices), or worse, try to take the treasure (which requires a Hard Athletics test), they come under attack by forest spirits. Anyone possessed by a spirit loses two Hit Points from each location for the duration of this scenario but eventually the spirit leaves.

Llys

The Kingdom of the Regnenses was a Celtic kingdom in the western parts of what is now Aelle's Kingdom of Ceint. They have been thoroughly conquered but a few who still hold out against Saxon rule retreated here, to town of Llys.

Llys was once the location of a Roman villa, which became a palace estate for the king of the Regnenses after Roman rule ended. Now it is a temple to the goddess Andraste and the centre of a small town that is home to 500 people. Of these500, there are 100 or so warriors. If the player characters stay and observe, they will not a small trickle of new warriors coming to Llys, in groups of three to five arriving every few days. Llys is recruiting.

The outside of the villa is still recognisable as a Roman mansion, although much of the stonework has been replaced. Within, the furnishings and decorations are Celtic rather than Roman and mats hide those mosaics that do not suit the building's new purpose – although a striking mythological scene portraying the goddess Minerva dropping a huge rock on the head of the god Mars is now seen as a myth of Andraste defeating the Romans and the mosaic has been altered to support this.

Andraste is the Celtic goddess of victory, ravens, and battle, and the warriors here dedicate the deaths of any Saxons they kill to the bloody goddess. They are fierce and know they will lose to the Saxons in the long run but are determined to send as many

Saxons as possible to the afterlife first. However, this fatalism does not mean they do not fight cleverly; Llys is cloaked by thick woodland, meaning its location is not obvious and the warriors from Llys sally forth in raids, using ambush tactics.

Apart from the central villa, partially converted to a temple, the older stone buildings of Llys have been demolished to make walls and the town has solid stone walls about two metres high. There is a single wooden gate in the wall. Within, and including the old villa, there are numerous round houses, in typical Celt style.

Approaching Llys

Llys is hidden near the edge of the Forest of Meon; finding it for one unfamiliar with its location requires navigating the forest, as described previously. It is easy to lose track and end up at the pool with the forest spirits, alhough those who dwell in Llys know the ways well enough for the forest not to be a distraction. Of course, this location is part of Llys's defence; few know exactly where the raiders on Saxon territory come from. And the forest spirits will surely not be pleased with a large force trooping through their domain, disturbing the trees.

The player characters need to have a closer look at the town as part of their mission. If the player characters met Anyon in Glawmaed, and did not stop him, he has raised a party of warriors within Llys. He and they are present to stop them from spying on Llys, sending word of its location and defences – or if they do, to stop them from returning. Anyon has twice as many warriors in total as there are player characters.

The player characters probably want to avoid a direct confrontation with Anyon's band, at least on even terms. Fortunately, such a large group will find it hard to stay completely hidden; they will not be able to sneak up on the characters. Passing by them without being noticed requires a group Stealth roll, opposed by Anyon's Perception skill. If the player characters are spotted, getting away requires an Athletics test, made at the level of the player character with the lowest score.

Otherwise, the player characters will find themselves in combat, outnumbered and perhaps doomed. Clever tricks to get away should be viewed generously by the Games Master.

Capture and Escape

Anyon and the Celts will accept surrender — they want to know what the player characters know — but will strike to kill rather than demanding a surrender. If captured, the player characters are taken into Llys, their gear confiscated, and they are secured in a room in the temple with a barred door. The druid Madbh will interrogate them.

She wants to know where the player characters come from, whether they plan to attack and what their numbers are. If a hero tries to lie, make a Deceit test, opposed by Madbh's Insight skill. Madbh will not torture the player characters but she will threaten them. She promises a clean death for anyone who talks but one who refuses to talk will be burned alive as a sacrifice to Andraste. Madbh is quite sincere in these threats.

Fortunately, the player characters have the chance to escape. Between interrogation sessions, they are left in the room. A standard Brawn test will break through the door or a hard Athletics test can climb out of a high up window. Someone up there could perhaps sneak around and let the others out.

Sneaking around requires a Stealth roll. On a failure, the group runs into two warriors, who now strike to kill, which could be interesting, as the player characters will be unarmed. Getting out requires climbing the wall or getting past four warriors at the gate. Stealth or trickery in the last case is possible; the warriors, after all, are looking out rather than in.

Madbh

Madbh is tall, dark-haired and imperious in manner. Every movement presents extreme confidence. Most people around her cannot refuse her commands. She knows she is doing the right thing – leading the remainder of the Regnenses to extract vengeance upon the Saxons in the name of the goddess Andraste. She is a druid and beloved by dark spirits associated to fire and the raven goddess of victory. The spirits of Meon are also friendly towards her.

Although Madbh does not have any bound spirits, her chambers have numerous torches – enough for a fire elemental to come to her aid should she need it. She cannot command the fire

elemental, but the elemental will nonetheless attack her enemies, and those who would harm Madbh.

Madbh is a fanatic, who will not be swerved a tiny bit in her views or goals, and will absolutely never give up. The slaughter of her enemies, quickly or slowly in the name of the goddess, are her meat and drink. She speaks slowly, definitely, and with deliberate relish when it comes to acts of war and bloody sacrifice.

The Ambush

The characters' problems are not yet over as they approach the ridge where Caedering is situated. On the lower slopes of the ridge, partially behind a jutting piece of cliff face, wait Wulfric's four Carls (or three, if one was cut down in Thane Osbehrt's hall).

Wulfric is not there; he has set the ambush and gone to warn the Ealdorman Ceolfrith of events in Caedering. Unfortunately for him, there are two flaws in Wulfric's plan. One is that his men are not quite as well hidden as they were; they have been waiting for some time and a Hard Perception test, made for the group of player characters, reveals their hiding place.

The other issue is that Wulfric's men are unhappy at having been left there without their Thane and are convinced that he regards them as disposable. They will readily surrender if injured or outmatched. If they surrender, they will mention they serve Wulfric, what he has ordered them to do and where he has gone. It is up to the player characters what they do with any Carls who surrender. Thralldom might be an appropriate punishment.

Conclusions and Aftermath

When the player characters return, whether in triumph or defeat, there will be consequences for what happens when the Saxons decide to subdue the nearby Celt raiders. Good intilligence leading to a precise strike on the actual target, Llys, is vital. If the player characters fail to return with this much, along with a good route through the Forest of Meon, any attempt at invasion is doomed and most of the warriors involved will be lost.

The player characters will be blamed for this, and future scenarios, rather than being a reward for good service and leading to bigger and better things, will be a chance to make amends. Meanwhile, Caedering is more exposed than ever to raids from the Britons, as well as dangers from Wulfric and Ealdorman Ceolfrith. Things are not looking good in the village.

Even with good intelligence, Thane Osbehrt feels there are good reasons to put off attacking the Celts. For one thing, with

100 warriors in Llys, the Caedering forces only number 60, even with the addition of Taethle's warriors. Attacking a walled town while outnumbered needs a plan and preferably more men.

Further, there is Thane Wulfric to worry about. His treachery will now be clear to the player characters and perhaps others. Wulfric is likely to do something against Caelctun if it is emptied of warriors. Wulfric is acting both out of personal interest and in the interests of his Ealdorman, and Thane Osbehrt's former Ealdorman, Ceolfrith. At Ceolfrith's next assembly, Wulfric asks for a blood feud against both Thane Osbehrt and the player characters, as someone wronged by them.

The next scenario involves these events.

Non-Player Characters

Thane Osbehrt

Osbehrt	Attributes
STR: 12	Action Points: 3
CON: 10	Damage Modifier: +1d2
SIZ: 14	Magic Points: 12
DEX: 12	Movement: 6 metres
INT: 14	Initiative Bonus: 11
POW: 12	Armour: Leather Tunic and Helm
CHA: 14	

Skills: Athletics 54%, Courtesy 58%, Culture (Saxon) 68%, Evade 44%, Language (Saxon) 68%, Lore (Agriculture) 48%, Lore (Tactics) 48%, Lore (Saxon) 68%, Endurance 45%, Influence 58%, Insight 56%. Locale 58%, Oratory 56%, Perception 61%, Superstition 38%, Unarmed 44%, Willpower 42%

Passions: Loyalty to Caedering 58%, Loyalty to Cerdic 38%, Love (Deceased Wife) 68%

1d20	Location	AP/HP
1–3	Right Leg	0/5
4–6	Left Leg	0/5
7–9	Abdomen	2/6
10–12	Chest	2/7
13–15	Right Arm	0/4
16–18	Left Arm	0/4
19–20	Head	3/5

Combat Style: Fyrdman (Battleaxe, Seax and Shield, Trait: Formation Fighting) 72%

Weapon	Size/Force	Reach	Damage	AP/HP
Seax	*M*	*S*	*1d4+2+1d2*	*6/8*
Battelaxe	*M*	*M*	*1d6+1+1d2*	*4/4*
Saxon Shield	*L*	*S*	*1d4+1d2*	*4/12*

Taethle

Taethle	Attributes
STR: 15	Action Points: 3
CON: 12	Damage Modifier: +1d2
SIZ: 14	Magic Points: 12
DEX: 12	Movement: 6 metres
INT: 15	Initiative Bonus: 14
POW: 12	Armour: Leather Tunic, Helm
CHA: 10	

Skills: Athletics 42%, Boating 47%, Brawn 59%, Culture (Saxon) 70%, Endurance 47%, Evade 49%, Influence 60%, Insight 42%, Language (Saxon) 65%, Lore (Saxon) 70%, Lore (Strategy and Tactics) 75%, Oratory 57%, Perception 67%, Ride 62%, Seamanship 42%, Superstition 37%, Swimming 52%, Unarmed 62%, Willpower 54%

Passions: Loyalty to Cerdic 64%, Loyalty to Men 44%, Love Battle 54%

1d20	Location	AP/HP
1–3	Right Leg	0/6
4–6	Left Leg	0/6
7–9	Abdomen	2/7
10–12	Chest	2/8
13–15	Right Arm	0/5
16–18	Left Arm	0/5
19–20	Head	5/6

Combat Style: Saxon Noble (Sword, Seax and Shield, Trait: Mounted Combat) 87%

Weapon	Size/Force	Reach	Damage	AP/HP
Seax	*M*	*S*	*1d4+2+1d2*	*6/8*
Sword	*M*	*M*	*1d6+2+1d2*	*4/8*
Saxon Shield	*L*	*S*	*1d4+1d2*	*4/12*

Taethle's Warband

Use the statistics for Typical Carl on page 74, but substitute Passions with: *Loyalty to Taethle 55%, Loyalty to Cerdic 50%, Hate (Celts) 30%*

Thane Wulfric

Wulfric	Attributes
STR: 12	Action Points: 3
CON: 12	Damage Modifier: +1d2
SIZ: 14	Magic Points: 13
DEX: 12	Movement: 6 metres
INT: 16	Initiative Bonus: 13
POW: 13	Armour: Furs
CHA: 13	

Skills: Athletics 52%, Art (Poetry) 53%, Culture (Saxon) 68%, Customs 48%, Evade 69%, Influence 76%, Insight 69%, Language (Saxon) 67%, Language (Brythonic) 37%, Lore (Norse Gods) 43%, Lore (Saxon) 68%, Lore (Strategy and Tactics) 48%, Oratory 63%, Perception 59%, Ride 57%, Sing 53%, Stealth 66%, Superstition 46%, Willpower 55%

Passions: Loyalty to Ceolfrith 45%, Love Poetry 50%, Love Tormenting Others 60%, Norse Gods 45%

1d20	Location	AP/HP
1–3	Right Leg	0/5
4–6	Left Leg	0/5
7–9	Abdomen	1/6
10–12	Chest	1/7
13–15	Right Arm	0/4
16–18	Left Arm	0/4
19–20	Head	0/5

Combat Style: Saxon Noble (Sword, Seax and Shield, Trait: Mounted Combat) 82%

Weapon	Size/Force	Reach	Damage	AP/HP
Seax	*M*	*S*	*1d4+2*	*6/8*
Sword	*M*	*M*	*1d6+2*	*4/8*
Saxon Shield	*L*	*S*	*1d4*	*4/12*

Wulfric's Carls

Use the statistics for Typical Carl on page 74, but substitute Passions with: *Fear Wulfric 55%, Hate (Celts) 50%*

Anyon

Anyon	Attributes
STR: 11	Action Points: 3
CON: 10	Damage Modifier: 0
SIZ: 12	Magic Points: 12
DEX: 15	Movement: 6 metres
INT: 13	Initiative Bonus: 12
POW: 12	Armour: Leather Tunic, Helm
CHA: 13	

Skills: Athletics 56%, Brawn 42%, Culture (Celt) 66%, Endurance 45%, Evade 45%, Influence 66%, Language (Brythonic) 66%, Lore (Celt) 66%, Lore (Pagan) 46%, Lore (Tactics) 56%, Perception 55%, Survival 65%, Stealth 58%, Superstition 56%, Sing 65%, Swim 41%, Willpower 54%
Passions: Hate (Saxons) 70%, Pagan Gods 65%, Love Madbh 50%

1d20	Location	AP/HP
1–3	Right Leg	0/5
4–6	Left Leg	0/5
7–9	Abdomen	2/6
10–12	Chest	2/7
13–15	Right Arm	0/4
16–18	Left Arm	0/4
19–20	Head	5/5

Combat Style: Warrior (Spear, Sword, and Shield, Trait: Formation Fighting) 75%

Weapon	Size/Force	Reach	Damage	AP/HP
Spear	*M*	*L*	*1d8+1*	*4/5*
Sword	*M*	*M*	*1d6+2*	*4/8*
Celtic Shield	*L*	*S*	*1d3+1*	*4/15*

Swern

Swern	Attributes
STR: 11	Action Points: 3
CON: 11	Damage Modifier: 0
SIZ: 13	Magic Points: 14
DEX: 12	Movement: 6 metres
INT: 14	Initiative Bonus: 12
POW: 14	Armour: Leather Tunic
CHA: 14	

Skills: Athletics 36%, Brawn 44%, Culture (Celt) 64%, Commerce 48%, Endurance 33%, Evade 39%, Language (Brythonic) 68%, Influence 48%, Insight 48%, Lore (Celt) 68%, Lore (Pagan) 48%, Perception 53%, Superstition 50%, Survival 68%, Willpower 58%
Passions: Loyalty (Glawmaed) 64%, Pagan Gods 44%, Love (Family) 64%

1d20	Location	AP/HP
1–3	Right Leg	0/5
4–6	Left Leg	0/5
7–9	Abdomen	2/6
10–12	Chest	2/7
13–15	Right Arm	0/4
16–18	Left Arm	0/4
19–20	Head	5/5

Combat Style: Spearman (Spear and Sling, Trait: Skirmishing) 58%

Weapon	Size/Force	Reach	Damage	AP/HP
Spear	*M*	*L*	*1d8+1*	*4/5*
Sling	*L*	-	*1d8*	*1/2*

Glawmaed Spearmen

Use the statistics for Typical Warrior on page 213 of *Mythic Britain* but Passions are: Loyalty (Glawmaed) 52%, Pagan Gods 45%

Madbh

Madbh	Attributes
STR: 9	Action Points: 3
CON: 10	Damage Modifier: 0
SIZ: 16	Magic Points: 14
DEX: 12	Movement: 6 metres
INT: 15	Initiative Bonus: 14
POW: 14	Armour: Furs
CHA: 16	

Skills: Athletics 31%, Brawn 20%, Binding (Druidic Tradition) 80%, Culture (Celt) 70%, Dance 68%, Endurance 40%, First Aid 54%, Healing 54%, Influence 87%, Insight 64%, Language (Brythonic) 71%, Language (Saxon) 51%, Lore (Pagan) 60%, Lore (Celt) 70%, Lore (Tactics) 60%, Oratory 70%, Perception 44%, Trance 73%, Willpower 78%

Passions: Loyalty to Llys 54%, Love Slaughter and Torment 59%, Worship Andraste 59%

1d20	Location	AP/HP
1–3	Right Leg	0/5
4–6	Left Leg	0/5
7–9	Abdomen	2/6
10–12	Chest	2/7
13–15	Right Arm	0/4
16–18	Left Arm	0/4
19–20	Head	5/5

Combat Style: Spearman (Spear and Sling, Trait: Skirmishing) 58%

Weapon	Size/Force	Reach	Damage	AP/HP
Spear	*M*	*L*	*1d8+1*	*4/5*
Sling	*L*	-	*1d8*	*1/2*

Llys Warriors

Use the statistics for Typical Warrior on page 213 of *Mythic Britain* but Passions are: Loyalty (Llys) 52%, Hate (Saxons) 50%, Pagan Gods 45%

The Forest Spirits of Meon

INS 5

POW 15

CHA 5

Magic Points 15

Spectral Combat 70%

Willpower 80%

Special: One touched by a forest spirit gains or loses 2 Hit Points in each hit location, depending on whether the one possessed has the spirit's favour or wrath. This blessing or curse lasts as long as the spirit stays near. It does not require full possession by the spirit but the spirit needs to succeed in a Spectral Combat roll, opposed by the recipient's Willpower, if the recipient resists.

Assembly

This scenario is an immediate sequel to the previous adventure, *Conquest*. It involves intrigue and Saxon politics and in the Saxon world, such affairs can rapidly turn bloody. The events revolve around a blood feud Thane Wulfric has declared against the characters' own lord, Osbehrt.

Thane Wulfric's home of Caelctun is only about two miles away from Caedering. Until the arrival of Cerdic's warriors in Caedering, Caelctun was used as a base for Ceolfrith to mount his own raids against the Celts. He did this while leaving Caedering to see to its own defence; in Ceolfrith's eyes, Caedering, being so close to Caelctun, was disposable.

Now Wulfric's and Ceolfrith's positions are both threatened. If Caedering can be daunted and brought into line, the crisis is averted and could even be turned to Wulfric's advantage. The death of Caedering's Thane should certainly accomplish this.

The attack on the player characters at the end of the previous scenario was intended to delay any invasion. Now Wulfric, knowing he will attain Ceolfrith's permission, has wasted no time in declaring a blood feud against Thane Osbehrt of Caedering.

Like most other decisions Thane Wulfric has made, the blood feud comes out of a sense of selfish ambition.

Caedering

After the first scenario, Thane Osbehrt trusts the heroes and desires to talk to them privately about current events. He wishes to do so outside the hearing of Cerdic's men in the village. It is not that he does not trust them, he is quick to explain, but rather because some of this is none of their business. If the player characters press him, he admits that he does not wish to show he cannot control such matters himself and fears appearing weak before Taethle, who Cerdic has just made a Thane.

The main matter that the Thane wants to talk about, and seek advice upon, is what to do about Thane Wulfric. Osbehrt does not yet know about Wulfric's declared blood feud but of course his Carls attacked the heroes. What should Osbehrt seek as recompense against this hostility? Will Ealdorman Ceolfrith defend his Thane? And should the forces from Caedering attack the Celts from the forest now or delay until matters are settled with other Saxons?

Wulfric must be planning something. It is clear that he will not let matters rest after sending his men to kill the player characters, and causing such a ruckus in Osbehrt's hall. But Osbehrt wants to find out more before he decides how to act. Perhaps a visit to his home of Caelctun could be in order.

The Attack

The first that the player characters and Thane Osbehrt hear of Wulfric's blood feud is when some of Wulfric's Carls attack. Their leader, Eorlstan, is overeager to claim the glory of dispatching their lord's enemy but he was sensible enough to bring two other Carls with him to make sure the job is done. However, Eorlstan is not so sensible that he is willing to wait until Osbehrt is alone. He does not wish to miss out on the glory and have others beat him to killing Osbehrt.

The attack happens when Osbehrt is outside of the fortified part of Caedering, surveying the farms outside of the village walls. Only the player characters accompany him when three Jute Carls come into sight from around a building where they were hiding and immediately leap to attack! They will all target Thane Osbehrt unless the player characters get in the way

As they attack, one of them boasts, "My lord Wulfric has declared a blood feud. He claims vengeance for the wrongs you have inflicted!"

The enemy will attack until one of them falls in combat and then they then seek to flee. If they cannot flee, they surrender. They will also flee if they fell Thane Osbehrt rather than staying to face the player characters.

Prisoners?

If any of the Carls who attacked are taken prisoner, it is up to Osbehrt and the player characters what to do with them. The usual punishments would be death or turning them into thralls. Thane Osbehrt favours the first course of action.

Eorlstan, if he lives, is surprised that his attack failed. He will proclaim Osbehrt and the player characters to be mighty warriors to have defeated him and his plan. This is not a clumsy attempt to get on the good side of his captors; Eorlstan is sincere in his praise. The heroes may gain the correct impression that Eorlstan, although in some ways quite charming, is not the brightest of Wulfric's Carls.

However, Eorlstan does not really want to die through hanging, as is customary for criminals. As he will tell the player characters, he always saw himself dying a warrior's death. The Carl's comrades also do not deserve execution. If the player characters offer to spare the prisoners, Osbehrt is willing to go along with this plan, although he will forbid simply releasing them or anything too merciful. Offering mercy, even if the mercy is thralldom rather than death, could persuade the prisoners to talk – this requires a relevant social skill test. A Hard social skill test can persuade Eorlstan to offer up information if offered death by the axe rather than hanging.

Eorlstan or another captured Carl can tell Thane Osbehrt and the player characters that Thane Wulfric held a feast the previous night and announced the blood feud and a reward for the killer of Osbehrt. A player character who succeeds at a Culture (Saxon) skill test will realise that a blood feud needs to be requested in assembly before one's lord. Ceolfrith's lord is Ealdorman Ceolfrith and as far as the heroes and Osbehrt are aware, he has not held an assembly recently, although he will hold one next week.

Possibly the blood feud that Wulfric has declared is not legal...

Asking the Farmers

Possibly the player characters will be interested in asking the local farmers what happened. One man, Talad, a Celt gebur, took note of the Saxons loitering near the storage building from which they attacked the Thane but did not think to report Saxon (as opposed to Celt) warriors. Since Cerdic's men arrived, there have been many strangers.

The heroes can learn nothing more of use in this way.

A New Thane?

The player characters ought to be able to defeat the attackers in the previous scene but there is a chance they fail and Thane Osbehrt is killed. If Thane Osbehrt survives, skip this subsection.

If Thane Osbehrt dies, there is the problem that he has no heir. Technically, only an Ealdorman can appoint a new heir. This means the decision belongs to Cerdic. However, someone needs to be in charge in Caedering, at least in the short term. It is likely that Cerdic will ratify whoever is currently in charge as the new Thane.

Unless the player characters choose to interfere, Taethle, the leader of Cerdic's Carls, takes charge of Caedering and sends the player characters, as the former Thane's chosen men, off to see Cerdic, as described below, to inform him and see to his wishes. Osbehrt merits a grand funeral and that can wait until his return.

Then it will be time for vengeance on Wulfric and a blood feud in return, Taethle promises them that.

On the other hand, the player characters may dislike Taethle's assumption of the role of village leader. She is a worthy leader but she does not have any ties to Caedering. A player character who puts themselves forward, and has appropriate rank, can claim the honours for themself!

To decide who can claim rule, a player character and Taethle should make competing Influence tests. The winner here has the most support in Caedering. Taethle will bow down, apparently happily, if someone has greater support than her to lead. There is no formal election but rather a feast to commemorate Thane Osbehrt and an acclamation of who is to take charge next by the assembled Carls. There is tension between the Caedering Carls and Taethle's followers but no severe insults or violence.

Hamafunta

Ealdorman Ceolfrith has an Assembly next week for those Thanes and Carls he commands. Thane Osbehrt of course no longer attends these as he is loyal to Cerdic rather than Wulfric, but in view of the attack, the next one is important. He asks the player characters to attend, to learn whether Wulfric's blood feud is legally sanctioned and whether anything can be done about it.

Thane Osbehrt will not attend himself, even if he is uninjured. He is no coward but knows that both he and Caedering itself are in danger, so it would be a poor time for the Thane to leave and besides, Ceolfrith may well consider him a personal enemy. By now, the player characters are in a position of great trust, so if they advise, they can persuade him to accompany them with a Hard social skill test. There are, as it turns out, some advantages if the player characters do persuade their lord to come along but overall it is not a good idea. Of course, if Thane Osbehrt was badly hurt in the attack, there is little question of him travelling.

Ealdorman Ceolfrith's hall is in the large coastal village of Hamafunta, named for Ceolfrith's father Hama, and the journey there is straightforward. The location of Hamafunta was important in Roman times as a junction between major roads and the site of a spring. This spring is said to be enchanted; it has never run dry, even in the driest summer, or frozen, even in the coldest

What if Osbehrt is Dead?

If Osbehrt is dead through the attack, there is still good reason for the player characters to attend Ceolfrith's assembly in Hamafunta, namely to claim vengeance for Osbehrt's death. If Wulfric's blood feud is recognised as legal, a revenge attack upon the Thane will be forbidden. An attack upon Wulfric will label the heroes as criminals rather than heroic avengers.

Whether or not the blood feud is recognised as legal, the player characters are likely to be labelled as cowards if they do not take action to avenge their lord. A Culture (Saxon) test will allow a player character to work out these nuances.

winter. Of course, the spring is still used by the Jutes who live in Hamafunta now.

A decaying Roman villa lies outside the village walls, thoroughly looted of building materials, and Ceolfrith's Hall is unusual in incorporating Roman stonework along with wood into its construction. The site itself is still of strategic importance; before Cerdic landed, it was the western edge of King Aelle's Kingdom. Now it is the westernmost of the territories King Aelle, rather than Cerdic, controls – and this is an issue, even although Ealdorman Cerdic theoretically answers to King Aelle.

The situation of Ceolfrith's hall means King Aelle needs the Ealdorman's loyalty more than most. He has awarded Ceolfrith with newly conquered lands in the area, men to command and local authority and autonomy. Without pressing reasons not to, Aelle will support Ealdorman Ceolfrith when it comes to local affairs, should this ever become an issue.

A player character who succeeds at a Lore (Saxon) or Locale test will know how Aelle depends on Ceolfrith, a dependence which grants the Ealdorman considerable freedom.

People

The player characters will be treated well at Caedering, although as visitors rather than honoured followers of Ealdorman Ceolfrith. They may get the impression they are unimportant, as Ceolfrith treats them coolly and fairly neutrally. Wulfric will already be present in Caedering when the heroes arrive. The Thane is highly honoured and sits by the Ealdorman's left hand, at the head of the table.

Before the assembly, the player characters potentially have a few days to prepare and Ceolfrith holds a feast the evening before the assembly, as well as afterwards. The main people present are:

Wulfric

Wulfric is just as unpleasant as he was in the previous scenario but mercifully, as far as possible, he blatantly ignores the characters here. He fears an attempt to goad them in front of witnesses he would like to impress could affect his reputation.

The Thane will also try to ignore any accusations or threats they make. An attempt to provoke or otherwise make him react requires a contested roll against his Willpower. If there is an attempt at open violence, Ceolfrith's housecarls will step in to break the fight up. Here is not the place.

Swithgar

Wulfric is accompanied in Hamafunta by six of his Carls. One of these men, Swithgar, leads the warriors. Swithgar is a skald but is anything but charming; he puts his talents to use in sarcasm and taunts. He is also out to goad the player characters, worsening any cause they have with evident relish. He speaks of the cowards of Caedering who need Cerdic to deal with a small number of Celts and how the traitor Osbehrt, and any who follow him, will soon die gruesome deaths when Wulfric has his way with them.

If Osbehrt is already dead, this will give Swithgar even more material to work with and he will gleefully make comments indicating the heroes' lord died disgracefully and how they are too cowardly to avenge him – not that he merits it.

Ceolfirth

Ealdorman Ceolfrith presents a cold exterior, never raising a smile even for those he favours. His wife is dead and his two sons serve in an honoured position as housecarls of King Aelle. There is nobody around him he loves and few he even likes. Ceolfrith's feasts are funished with copious food and drink, and everyone present is offered mead, for Ceolfrith likes to appear generous. Despite the excess, the Ealdorman's manner means his feasts are un-jolly events.

Behind the cold exterior, Ceolfrith never forgives or forgets a slight. He led Wulfric to believe that he would benefit from

Osbehrt's demise; Thane Osbehrt betrayed Ceolfrith, as far as he is concerned, by leaving his service. At present he honours Wulfric to encourage him; the Thane is a useful tool. He will preserve Wulfric if he can but discard him should his preservation become too much effort. It is not apparent but Ceolfrith is the true enemy here. The player characters may gain a hint of this with an Insight test.

If the heroes attempt to tell Ceolfrith anything about Wulfric, he suggests they bring it up in public at the assembly. He will outright refuse any request for a private audience.

Dunric

Dunric is Ealdorman Ceolfrith's laece and leads any religious ceremonies, such as those due to take place before the feast after the ceremony. Dunric is not a talkative man and will spend a lot of time silently watching others. In response to threats or taunts, he simply sneers – he views most people, including the player characters, as fools who are ignorant of the will and ways of the gods, and does not like to waste time on them. He may make an exception for a laece amongst the player characters though he is most likely to view them too as dangerously misguided, and so another fool.

For the moment, he is background detail unless the player characters seek to engage him.

The Assembly

At the assembly itself, there are two main items of business of interest to the player characters. The first is Ceolfrith sending more men to Caelctun, to reinforce it against possible hostile forces to the west. The player characters may read this as Caedering but Ceolfrith means Cerdic's forces here.

The second item of business, if the player characters do not get there first, is Wulfric's declaration of a blood feud against Thane Osbehrt. If the player characters speak up for Osbehrt, Wulfric adds them to the list of those he wishes a feud against; after all, they are accomplices. Wulfric names Osbehrt as conspiring to take his lands, and being responsible for the deaths of several of his Carls – any who died in the previous scenario or the attack at the start of this one. In the first scenario, if Osbehrt tried to attack him, Wulfric mentions that as a key piece of evidence. He attempts to paint Osbehrt as a dangerous deranged criminal.

Much as he would like to, Ceolfrith cannot simply agree with Wulfric's wishes; such a legal decision must be acclaimed by Ceolfrith's Carls present banging their weapons against their shields. Normally, this is an automatic thing but Ceolfrith is good enough at reading the room to not give a verdict here unless he is sure it will be supported.

Thus, although really addressing Ceolfrith or Wulfric, the player characters are in reality trying to impress the gathered Carls. Things resolve using a contested Oratory test between a player character and Wulfric. Wulfric is supported in his roll by the skald Swithgar, who adds poetic flourishes to his lord's account.

Ceolfrith does not look kindly on the player characters, however, so the player character roll is at a Formidable level of difficulty (halving the Oratory skill). For each piece of evidence a

Events at Assemblies

There are several assemblies in this chapter. As noted in chapter 3, an assembly is rounded off by a feast and such feasts can be lively affairs, especially if there are tensions from the earlier assembly.

Some ideas for events at an assembly or the feast afterwards are.

1. Contests, perhaps for a small amount of money (the equivalent of d10 SP is fairly typical, although the player characters could suggest more). Examples include riddling, wrestling (which could be decided as a contest of Brawn) and drinking contests (a contest of Physique).
2. An angry drunk questions a player character's loyalty, or right to be at the assembly. The wrong answer (or perhaps a failed Influence test) will lead to a fight.
3. A visiting skald tells a distorted tale of recent events the player characters were involved in. The skald's story either flatters the player characters excessively, or makes them look like cowards or idiots.
4. A berserk warrior takes a player character aside. The berseker critically wounded a comrade in a fight and is likely to have to pay wergild for the injury. He seeks a player character to speak out for him at the assembly for a light punishment. He has a record of such behaviour and his comrades will not speak out for him but he will owe the player character a favour, and is honourable enough to repay it.
5. A woman stands before her lord accused of treachery, dealing with the lord's enemies. Is she innocent or guilty? How the lord deals with her is an insight into his character. Clever player characters might also be able to use the incident to gain information.
6. A dull dispute over farming rights turns violent as both of those involved draw weapons and fight, not waiting the lord's judgement. The fight could be broken up, or allowed to play out as a form of settlement.

player character presents (such as the fact the feud was illegally declared, that they can testify that Wulfric goaded Osbehrt, or that they were attacked by Wulfric's men), reduce the difficulty of the roll by one level, although no further than Easy.

If the player characters lose their roll, Ceolfrith agrees to Wulfric's blood feud, both against Osbehrt and the player characters. If Wulfric's level of success is greater than that of the player characters, Ceolfrith orders their immediate imprisonment, before thralldom or execution await. The adventure could be over; otherwise, they get the chance to flee in the confusion.

If the player characters beat Wulfric in the roll, the Ealdorman dismisses the blood feud against the player characters but allows the one against Osbehrt to remain. If they achieve a higher level of success, Wulfric's blood feud is declared illegitimate, although no further action is taken. If the player characters defeat Wulfric by two or more levels of success, they have Ceolfrith's permission to pursue a blood feud against Wulfric.

If he does not get his way, which includes the death of Osbehrt, Ceolfrith plans revenge. The form of this revenge takes shape in the next scenario.

Further Events

Another Attack

Perhaps the player characters have "won" against Osbehrt in Ceolfrith's assembly, although at worst they are now also subject to Wulfric's blood feud. Regardless of what happens, a few hours after they leave, even if it is night, Wulfric and his men follow them. A Perception test, opposed by Swithgar's Stealth, reveals the pursuit. Another opposed skill test will get them to a place of comparative safety, such as Caedering, before the enemy strikes.

Otherwise combat follows. Swithgar will lead the other five of Wulfric's favoured Carls in an attack. Wulfric himself will stay back, just outside of arrow range. A player character who breaks away from the main fight can pursue the Thane and Wulfric will not flee in front of his men. Nevertheless, he has behaved in a disgraceful and cowardly way. Wulfric's men will give up the fight and flee as soon as two of them are out of action. If their Thane will not fight, why should they?

The enemy are also easy to intimidate; reduce the difficulty of any such tests by one level. The battle could be less overwhelming and final for the heroes than it first appears.

Seeing Cerdic

The player characters at this stage may well be unsure what to do next, especially if Wulfric still lives; if so, he has retreated to Caelctun. If the player characters have a plan, allow them to pursue it without interference.

But if not, Thane Osbehrt, or Taethle if she has replaced him, will ask the player characters to travel to Portus Caester, where Ealdorman Cerdic is currently in residence, to ensure that Caedering has his support against Wulfric and perhaps Ceolfrith.

If the previous attack on the player characters ended inconclusively, with them not being caught, another attack here on the way to Portus Caester is a possibility. The heroes may elect to bring a small force of Carls from Caedering. Their Thane will allow this with a suitable social skill test and having extra men is a sufficient deterrent to ensure safe passage.

Portus Caester is a Roman fortress repurposed by the Romans, now surrounded by a town of both Britons and Saxons. Many of the Britons are thralls but most are free Geburs and happy enough with their new Saxon lords. One of the larger rooms in the fortress, once a Roman barracks, now serves as Cerdic's audience chamber when he is present there. For more details of Portus Caester, see page 52.

When the heroes are admitted to see Cerdic, the Ealdorman is cool and intense in manner, and carefully considers their words. As long as the heroes are respectful, Cerdic declares that Caedering is part of his responsibility and he will stand by it in this feud. If Osbehrt was killed, he confirms Taethle as Thane; if the new Thane is one of the heroes rather than Taethle, Cerdic will confirm them if they succeed in an Easy social skill test.

A successful skill test means Cerdic also offers them the benefit of his advice. He mentions that both he and Ceolfrith are in the service of King Aelle and declares "I know Aelle. With him, forgiveness is easier to ask for than permission."

Cerdic is not directly telling the heroes to take the fight to Wulfric but that is clearly the meaning of his words. If the player characters tell Cerdic how Wulfric conducted an attack against them and escaped, he adds, "His men will not like that. That's something you can use."

He will not, however, agree to lend any forces for an attack. This is something the heroes need to manage for themselves, although they can muster a dozen Carls from Caedering to come along on the journey with a successful Influence or Oratory test.

Caelctun

Thane Wulfric's home, Caelctun, is similar in outlook to Caedering. Like Caedering, it is a ridge village, built in a secure location overlooking its surroundings. One problem Caelctun has is that both food and water need to be brought up to the village buildings from the lower lying lands and farmed fields.

Until recently, Caelctun was used as a base for Ceolfrith to mount his own raids against the Celts. He did this while leaving Caedering to see to its own defence. In Ceolfrith's eyes, Caedering, being only two miles from Caelctun, was disposable. Normally, two villages so close would share resources but the hostility between them means that things are doubled up and there is a gap between farmed land belonging to Caedering and that of Caelctun.

The player characters will be watched if they make their way into Caelctun to see to Wulfric and there are dozens of Carls present. Getting in requires either a group Stealth test to get past the watchers or a group Athletics test to climb the cliffs. If either test fails, they are spotted by a group of six ordinary Carls ready to fight, with many more ready to be present within five or ten minutes.

If they succeed, they are inside Caelctun's wooden walls, which only partially surround the village; Caelctun partially relies on the ridge for defence. Wulfric is within his hall and defended by any of the remaining elite Carls and another four ordinary Carls. The player characters can force all but the elite Carls to step back and see what happens should one of them call out Wulfric's poor behaviour in battle and succeed in an Oratory or Influence test.

Once the heroes have made it this far, they must face Wulfric and any of his warriors in mortal combat. If they succeed in slaying or crippling Wulfric, his men will not pursue vengeance or take up a blood feud on their former ruler's behalf, at least not immediately, and the heroes are free to leave. Wulfric was not well-respected...

All that remains is what King Aelle thinks of events. This last part is not necessary if Ceolfrith has given the player characters permission to conduct their own blood feud, although the player characters may with to visit Anderida after they have gone to war against the Celts, to confirm any conquests and possible new appointments as Thanes. The details of the invastion are in the next chapter.

Anderida

King Aelle's Assembly, in Anderida, takes place a month after the assemblies of Aelle's Ealdormen, so that they and others with important business arising as a result can raise them. Unless they are far distant or have other pressing business, the Ealdormen attend and those who do not attend send representatives. Not to do so is either a deliberate snub, or asking to be (perhaps literally) stabbed in the back in the dog-eat-dog world of Saxon politics.

The journey to Anderida will be routine. Anderida, like Portus Caester, is a former Roman coastal fortress on the southern shores of Britain. It is built from Roman stone extensively repaired and shored up with timber and earth works. It has been more heavily converted to Saxon use and habits than Portus Caester. In particular, King Aelle holds feasts and his audiences in a long hall that resembles a Saxon hall more than an old Roman building, albeit built of wood rather than stone. Aelle is the richest Saxon king in Britain and it shows in both the hearty and frequent feasts, and the gold ornamentation in his hall.

For more details of Anderida, see page 44.

When it comes to the player characters' business, key players present at the assembly and subsequent feast are below. The GM can easily mention other people and business here, including visitors from Anglia or Mierce, as seeds for future scenarios. After all, Aelle has claimed the title as Bretwalda, lord of the other Saxon kings.

King Aelle

King Aelle is described more fully in *Mythic Britain*, page 211. He is known as a ruthless and ferocious warlord, who offers reasonable terms to those who agree to his rule but is merciless in the face of defiance. He is a generous host and king, capable of great jollity in the feast hall, and prides himself on being able to hold his drink. Although still hale and a dangerous personal combatant, he is just beginning to turn slightly fat. His closest friends can get away with pointing this out; others are too scared.

When it comes to important business of the kingdom, either he or his coregent, his son Cissa, deals with it. With Cissa away in Mierce, Aelle has taken direct control himself. He has starting to find himself prone to hasty decisions as the strain of too much administration is getting to him. Aelle is tempted to recall his son, but by and large Aelle's ambitions as Bretwalda are undimmed and he remains a just and respected king.

Ealdorman Cerdic

Cerdic will remain mostly quiet at the assembly, as he knows that King Aelle does not trust him. Cerdic has ambitions to be a king in his own right and he hopes that King Aelle will accept that; Cerdic, for the present, is still prepared to answer Aelle as Bretwalda. But for now, it is best to avoid drawing too much attention to himself and keep an eye on fellow Ealdormen who may be plotting against them.

The player characters' interests are insufficient for Cerdic to show his hand and openly support them in the assembly. The calculating Ealdorman fears this will do more harm than good. But nonetheless, he will support them behind the scenes in what is coming. And Cerdic will make no promises to the heroes that he cannot keep.

Ealdorman Ceolfrith

If the heroes have killed Wulfric without permission, whether as part of an attack in Caelctun, or as a result of an attack Wulfric and his chosen men made against them, Ceolfrith speaks with surprising passion to condemn their actions as dishonourable and criminal. He seeks support in King Aelle's hall to gather his forces and wipe the heroes, their Thane and Caedering from the face of the Earth.

King Aelle's Assembly

Aelle's assembly is similar to Ceolfrith's, although on a larger scale. One key difference is that rather than an Ealdorman pronouncing his decision after the Carls have reacted by banging their shields, King Aelle first speaks his decision and the Carls then bang their weapons against shields in agreement. King Aelle rules with the assent of his people but he clearly does rule those in the hall, from the lowest thrall to the most powerful Ealdorman. Not even Cerdic will defy him. Aelle is a powerful and charismatic force, dominating the room even when others speak,al though he does not interrupt.

When it comes to the matter of Caedering and Wulfric, both a player character representative, perhaps with support, and Ealdorman Ceolfrith make tests involving Influence or Oratory. Ceolfrith has been working on gathering support for his proposal, which amounts to invasion of Caedering as punishment, including the deaths of the heroes and their Thane.

The player characters presumably argue against this. Maybe they go further and seek something more. The fact is that (following Cerdic's advice), they have already taken action, a fact that does not please King Aelle and he hopes to hear their reasons. If they mention Cerdic's name, Cerdic denies direct involvement while taking due responsibility as their Ealdorman.

Even if Ceolfrith defeats the player characters, he does not get his own way. King Aelle forbids him to start a war on others who are also under his rule. He will punish the heroes himself (and demands they remain for a later private audience) but forbids Ceolfrith to act against them or Caedering.

If the heroes beat Ceolfrith, King Aelle will say that their actions are legal and understandable in the light of what Wulfric has done. The matter is closed.

If the heroes not only beat Ceolfrith but gain a higher degree of success than the Ealdorman, King Aelle formerly condemns the Ealdorman and demands he pays wergild for any he or Wulfric have killed. Wulfric's blood feud was illegal and Ceolfrith was wrong to support it. With a degree of success two or more higher, Ceolfrith is willing to award Caelctun and its lands to the Thane of Caedering and promote that Thane to a King's Thane.

Conclusion

If the heroes beat Ceolfrith in the debate, Cerdic congratulates them on a job well done. He says he may well have special work for them in the future and this work will lead to firm rewards if they are willing to support him.

If the heroes lost, there is the matter of Aelle's punishment. Aelle tells them that their decisions have shown boldness and boldness has merit as long as it goes hand in hand with loyalty; the king has intervened on their behalf. As far as Aelle is concerned, they are now his men and he can call upon them for future special work. Work similar to that which the heroes performed against Wulfric.

The rivalry between Aelle and Cerdic will have consequences in the final scenario and the player characters' decisions will greatly affect how the grand affairs of state develop.

Ceolfrith has been humiliated by the characters and he vows revenge. After events at his assembly and perhaps that of King Aelle, he decides upon a subtle way to get revenge. He cannot do so by force of arms but has a powerful laece in his service. One who enjoys exercising his power and more than dabbles in the darker side of the spirit world. He rushes back to his home to instruct Dunric appropriately. The effects of this revenge are dealt with in chapter 11.

Non-Player Characters

Eorlstan

Eorlstan	Attributes
STR: 13	Action Points: 3
CON: 11	Damage Modifier: +1d2
SIZ: 13	Magic Points: 11
DEX: 15	Movement: 6 metres
INT: 10	Initiative Bonus: 11
POW: 11	Armour: Leather Tunic and Helm
CHA: 14	

Skills: Athletics 60%, Brawn 56%, Culture (Jute) 60%, Endurance 47%, Evade 44%, Influence 58%, Language (Jute) 60%, Lore (Jute) 60%, Perception 53%, Stealth 60%, Superstition 41%, Track 51%, Willpower 42%
Passions: Fear Wulfric 56%, Hate Osbehrt 51%

1d20	Location	AP/HP
1–3	Right Leg	0/5
4–6	Left Leg	0/5
7–9	Abdomen	2/6
10–12	Chest	2/7
13–15	Right Arm	0/4
16–18	Left Arm	0/4
19–20	Head	3/5

Combat Style: Saxon Hunter (Spear, Seax and Bow, Trait: Skirmishing) 64%

Weapon	Size/Force	Reach	Damage	AP/HP
Seax	*M*	*S*	*1d4+2+1d2*	*6/8*
Spear	*M*	*L*	*1d8+1+1d2*	*4/5*
Bow	*L*	*-*	*1d6+1d2*	*4/4*

Swithgar

Swithgar	Attributes
STR: 10	Action Points: 2
CON: 10	Damage Modifier: 0
SIZ: 13	Magic Points: 10
DEX: 10	Movement: 6 metres
INT: 14	Initiative Bonus: 11
POW: 10	Armour: Leather Tunic
CHA: 13	

Skills: Art (Poetry) 58%, Athletics 50%, Culture (Saxon) 73%, Customs 48%, Endurance 38%, Influence 61%, Insight 59%, Language (Angle, Saxon, or Jute) 67%, Lore (Norse Gods) 43%, Lore (Saxon) 68%, Musicianship (Harp) 53%, Perception 69%, Ride 35%, Sing 53%, Willpower 50%

Passions: Loyalty to King 55%, Love (Poetry) 50%, Norse Gods 55%

1d20	Location	AP/HP
1–3	Right Leg	0/5
4–6	Left Leg	0/5
7–9	Abdomen	1/6
10–12	Chest	1/7
13–15	Right Arm	0/4
16–18	Left Arm	0/4
19–20	Head	0/5

Combat Style: Fyrdman (Battleaxe, Seax and Shield, Trait: Formation Fighting) 65%

Weapon	Size/Force	Reach	Damage	AP/HP
Seax	*M*	*S*	*1d4+2*	*6/8*
Battelaxe	*M*	*M*	*1d6+1*	*4/4*
Saxon Shield	*L*	*S*	*1d4*	*4/12*

Ealdorman Ceolfrith

Ceolfrith	Attributes
STR: 12	Action Points: 3
CON: 12	Damage Modifier: 0
SIZ: 13	Magic Points: 13
DEX: 12	Movement: 6 metres
INT: 16	Initiative Bonus: 12
POW: 13	Armour: Leather Tunic
CHA: 14	

Skills: Athletics 40%, Brawn 48%, Culture (Saxon) 72%, Commerce 60%, Endurance 59%, Evade 59%, Influence 85%, Insight 76%, Language (Jute) 66%, Lore (Saxon) 72%, Lore (Tactics) 47%, Oratory 72%, Perception 76%, Ride 75%, Superstition 38%, Willpower 58%

Passions: Loyalty to King 55%, Love (Poetry) 50%, Norse Gods 55%

1d20	Location	AP/HP
1–3	Right Leg	0/5
4–6	Left Leg	0/5
7–9	Abdomen	2/6
10–12	Chest	2/7
13–15	Right Arm	0/4
16–18	Left Arm	0/4
19–20	Head	5/5

Combat Style: Saxon Noble (Sword, Seax and Shield, Trait: Mounted Combat) 64%

Weapon	Size/Force	Reach	Damage	AP/HP
Seax	*M*	*S*	*1d4+2*	*6/8*
Sword	*M*	*M*	*1d6+2*	*4/4*
Saxon Shield	*L*	*S*	*1d4*	*4/12*

Dunric

Dunric	Attributes
STR: 9	Action Points: 3
CON: 9	Damage Modifier: 0
SIZ: 12	Magic Points: 16
DEX: 12	Movement: 6 metres
INT: 15	Initiative Bonus: 13
POW: 16	Armour: Furs
CHA: 8	

Skills: Athletics 36%, Brawn 30%, Binding (Saxon Tradition) 74%, Culture (Saxon) 70%, Deceit 73%, First Aid 54%, Healing 54%, Language (Angle, Jute, or Saxon) 63%, Lore (Norse Gods) 60%, Lore (Saxon) 70%, Perception 46%, Sleight 51%, Stealth 57%, Trance 75%, Willpower 72%
Passions: Loyalty to Community 54%, Norse Gods 59%

1D20	Location	AP/HP
1–3	Right Leg	0/5
4–6	Left Leg	0/5
7–9	Abdomen	1/6
10–12	Chest	1/7
13–15	Right Arm	0/4
16–18	Left Arm	0/4
19–20	Head	5/5

Combat Style: Hunter (Seax, Spear, Bow, Trait: Skirmishing) 48%

Weapon	Size/Force	Reach	Damage	AP/HP
Seax	*M*	*S*	*1d4+2*	*6/8*
Spear	*M*	*L*	*1d8+1*	*4/5*
Bow	*L*	*-*	*1d6+1*	*4/4*

Dunric has a bound Aelf:

Characteristics

INT 8

POW 21

CHA 7

Skills: Discorporate 79%, Spectral Combat 78%, Stealth 65%, Willpower 92%

Special: The Aelf can drag a victim into the spirit plane with Discorporate to fight them in spirit combat. If the Aelf wins, it possesses them, causing the ailment of Paralysis (onset time 4 minutes)

The Battle of Llys

In the first scenario, the player characters, if successful ,tracked the source of the Celtic raids on Caedering to Llys. Conquering Llys would not only stop the raids but open up new territory to Saxon rule. Probably the heroes and those in charge of Caedering delayed attacking Llys until they have more warriors and have dealt with their rival Wulfric.

Although the events here follow directly from the first scenario, the events could take place at any time. But the people of Cadering cannot delay forever. If they wait for too long, Llys will have sufficient forces to go on the attack themselves.

The Saxon Forces

There are four likely sources of Saxon forces.

Caedering Fyrdmen

The village of Caedering has 30 warriors, as well as the player characters (who may fight in this formation or another)

Unit Type:	Seasoned Fyrdmen
Unit Traits:	Formation Fighting
Commander: Osbehrt	Command Skill 55%
Strength: 36	Current Damage: 1d4
Competency: 55%	Morale: 55%
Initial Formation: Line	Frontage: 18 x 2 ranks

Cerdic's Warriors

Taethle leads another force of 30 warriors in Ealdorman Cerdic's service, which together with the Caedering Fyrdmen form the core, and perhaps the entirety, of the Saxon army.

Unit Type:	Seasoned Fyrdmen
Unit Traits:	Formation Fighting
Commander: Taethle	Command Skill 60%
Strength: 36	Current Damage: 1d4
Competency: 60%	Morale: 60%
Initial Formation: Line	Frontage: 18 x 2 ranks

Caelctun Fyrdmen

If the player characters ousted Thane Wulfric in the previous scenario, they may be able to draw forces in from Caelctun. This will, at the very least, require an Influence test on the part of the leader of these forces. The leader here will be a player character.

Unit Type:	Seasoned Fyrdmen
Unit Traits:	Formation Fighting
Commander: Character	Command Skill: Lore (Tactics)
Strength: 32	Current Damage: 1d4
Competency: 55%	Morale: 40%
Initial Formation:	Frontage: 16 x 2 ranks

Ceolfrith's Reinforcements

Ceolfrith's reinforcements, sent to Caelctun in the last scenario,potentially provide another 20 warriors if the player characters can convince them to join in the fun. Osbehrt's strategy will be to distribute them between the Caedering Fyrdmen and Cerdic's warriors, increasing the frontage of each of these two units to 31 x 2 ranks.

Llys' Forces

Llys Warbands

The Llys warriors will split their forces into two equal forces of 50 each, one force commanded by Anyon (see page 89), the other by Madbh (see page 91).

Unit Type:	Seasoned Spearmen
Unit Traits:	Shield Wall
Commander: Anyon or Madbh	Command Skill: 55%
Strength: 50	Current Damage: 1d8
Competency: 55%	Morale: 60%
Initial Formation: Line	Frontage: 50 x 1 ranks

Celtic Skirmishers

The number of Celtic Skirmishers depends when the Saxons attack. If they attack immediately, there are none of these extras. If they attack within a month, there are 40 of them. If they wait longer than a month, there are 80 such skirmishers and they launch an attack against Caedering (see below). The Skirmishers are led by a man called Hywel from a village to the north-west. Hywel's abilities are the same as those of an Elite Llys Warrior, along with a Lore (Tactics) skill of 53%.

Unit Type:	Seasoned Skirmishers
Unit Traits:	Skirmishing
Commander: Hywel	Command Skill: 53%
Strength: 40 or 80	Current Damage: 1d4 or 1d6
Competency: 53%	Morale: 35%
Initial Formation: Skirmish	Frontage: 20 x 2 ranks, or 40 x 2 ranks

Elite Llys Warriors

Llys Warrior	Attributes
STR: 13	Action Points: 3
CON: 13	Damage Modifier: +1d2
SIZ: 13	Magic Points: 12
DEX: 13	Movement: 6 metres
INT: 13	Initiative Bonus: 13
POW: 12	Armour: Leather and Helm
CHA: 10	

Skills: Athletics 65%, Brawn 56%, Culture (Celt) 64%, Endurance 47%, Evade 39%, Language (Brythonic) 63%, Lore (Celt) 66%, Lore (Pagan) 46%, Perception 41%, Survival 63%, Stealth 58%, Superstition 39% Willpower 44%
Passions: Loyalty to Llys 80%, Hate (Saxons) 50%, Pagan Gods 45%

1d20	Location	AP/HP
1–3	Right Leg	3/6
4–6	Left Leg	3/6
7–9	Abdomen	3/7
10–12	Chest	3/8
13–15	Right Arm	3/5
16–18	Left Arm	3/5
19–20	Head	5/6

Combat Style: Warrior (Spear, Sword, and Shield, Trait: Formation Fighting) 65%

Weapon	**Size/Force**	**Reach**	**Damage**	**AP/HP**
Sword	*M*	*M*	*1d6+1+1d2*	*6/8*
Spear	*M*	*L*	*1d8+1+1d2*	*4/5*
Celtic Shield	*L*	*S*	*1d3+1+1d2*	*4/15*

Fire Elemental

Fire Elemental	Attributes
STR: 36	Action Points: 3
DEX: 15	Damage Modifier: +1d6
INT: 13	Magic Points: 21
POW: 21	Movement: 6 metres
	Initiative Bonus: 14
	Armour & Hit Points: 2/39

Suffers double damage from water

Skills: Brawn 92%, Evade 66%, Perception 56%, Willpower 92%
Combat Style: Elemental Combat 78% (Damage: 2d6)

Preparing for Attack

To attack Llys, the player characters need to make their way across the Forest of Meon. This will be straightforward if they already made peace with the spirits of the forest in the first scenario. Otherwise, the journey through the forest will be surprisingly tough.

There is little the forest can do to prevent such a large force making its way through but a player character guide who has been there before must make a Hard Survival roll, or else the forest has both hindered the player characters and warned those of Llys. The Saxons come across the walls of Llys ill-prepared for battle and face an immediate ambush.

If there is no ambush, before the battle, the Saxons are challenged by two Celt champions at the front of their forces. Player characters might choose to fight these champions to gain glory and demoralise the enemy, although of course the effect is the opposite if a player character loses. If Madbh has time to prepare, she calls forth a fire elemental spirit. Losing or not facing the fire elemental has the same effect on morale as losing in the initital battle of champions.

Neither Taethle or Osbehrt will face a champion; they are needed to lead their own forces. An NPC Saxon who faces a Celt champion will lose.

In the actual battle, the people of Llys naturally make use of their walls. Initial attacks will be at formidable difficulty until the Celts are pushed back from the walls or some ruse opens the gates.

Attack on Caedering

If the Celts attack Caedering, probably only the Caedering forces will be present, as well perhaps as those men led by Taethle. The Celts vastly outnumber the Saxons with 180 warriors, although the Celts' initital attacks will be at a hard difficulty until the Saxons are pushed back from Caedering's defences.

As above, the Celts will begin the challenge with their champions. Madbh will also have had time to call forth a fire elemental to attack; not dealing with the fire elemental will be the same blow to morale as suffering a loss to the Celtic champions.

To the Victor, the Spoils

If the Saxons successfully invade Llys, there is much available to all who take part, in terms of in loot or slaves; the equivalent of 200SP each. A player character who leads part of the force gains an extra 50 points as a Reward and one who defeats an enemy champion gains 13 points.

After the conquest of Llys and Wulfric's defeat, both Caelctun and Llys have need for new Thanes. A character who gains a Reward will be offered the position. Taethle will be promoted to a Thane at the end of the battle unless both positions are taken by player characters.

The rewards for successfully defending Caedering will be simple recognition as heroes and commendations to Cerdic and King Aelle. Perhaps there will be something in mind.

If Llys is conquered, Caedering assumes a position of new importance, being a centre of trade and a hub of Saxon expansion. Ealdorman Ceolfrith is sidelined, no longer controlling vital territories on the borders of Saxon territory.

The Cursed Hill

Dunric is a laece, a Saxon healer and binder of spirits. He has long had a fascination with darker power and is stronger when it comes to cursing than healing. He is in the service of Ealdorman Ceolfrith, who largely keeps him under control. Ceolfrith knows some of what Dunric has done and is capable of, and knows he can blackmail him if necessary.

After the last scenario, the Ealdorman seeks revenge on the village of Caedering and its people. Ceolfrith cannot act openly but Dunric can act covertly and the laece relishes the chance to use his power.

Dunric sets out for old Wincen-Caester hill, with a few hardened men ordered to obey him, where he knows a dark spirit — a Scaedugengan — lurks that is suitable for his needs. The spirit is too powerful for him to bind but not so powerful the laece cannot make contact and bribe the monster with human sacrifice and misery.

Elsewhere

If the player characters are now Thanes of nearby settlements, perhaps events take place when they come to Caedering to discuss policy with Taethle and Osbehrt who are by now their peers. Alternatively, the scenario could shift to the village where a player character is now in charge. There are tensions in Llys between the conquered Celts and Saxons, and in Caelctun between the villagers and new rulers.

The monster attacks the people of Caedering that very night and will continue its predations every night hence, until Caedering is empty or it is dealt with. Fortunately, where the monster came from also lies the means for its defeat but the way is not easy.

Tensions in the Thane's Hall

This tale begins when the heroes return to Caedering from a journey, perhaps after their trip to Anderida in the previous scenario. Taethle and her men have left the village to set up camp outside. They sullenly ignore the player characters but if they seek to speak to someone, Taethle will briskly say that one of her men was murdered last night. Someone in the Thane's Hall was responsibleand nobody can say who.

Taethle demands justice, her right of blood feud against the murderer, and her men support her. The murdered man was Bredoc, a Carl with Celt blood – perhaps the reason he was killed?

In Caedering, Thane Osbehrt is desperate; Taethle blames him for not being able to find the murderer. But he is sure that all of his men who were with or near Bredoc were innocent. He suspects that one of Taethle's men must have killed Bredoc. He asks the players to investigate, as they are becoming respected heroes. Being away from Caedering when the murders took place, they are not under suspicion and all parties trust them.

What if Osbehrt Died?

If Osbehrt was killed in the previous scenario, with Taethle outside of Caedering, Eadstan (see below) is acting as spokesmen for the Carls. He perhaps would like to be Thane — he feels he has earned it but is out of his depth and needs the player characters to help.

Investigations

The murder victim, Bredoc, was killed with his own axe. The murder happened while he was on watch with Sigebeorht, another of Taethle's men, who claims he saw nothing. Indeed, all of the Caedering Carls can say as much. Those in Caedering who may know something are:

Eadstan

Eadstan, a merchant, is in the process of becoming comfortably rich now that Caedering is a centre of trade. He seeks to become richer still and is hatching political ambitions. Eadstan is pompous and self-important but nonetheless loyal to Caedering, even although he may well have greater mercantile opportunities elsewhere. If he is to be an important man (as he is certain he is), he will do so in the place he has made his home, which seems at present to be the centre of major events.

He is chief in raising the idea that Bredoc must have been killed by one of Taethle's own men. An Insight roll reveals that he has no basis on which to make this suggestion. It is just his assumption that nobody in Caedering would have done the deed and the fact that he can raise his own importance by leading the Caedering voices here.

If the player characters come to Eadstan with supernatural suspicions, or later on when such goings on are confirmed, he passes on an interesting snippet of information. The laece Dunric, and a group of Carls, visited Seaxnatune, a tiny village on the slopes of Old Wincen-Caester hill, with whom he sometimes trades. He will not think to mention this as relevant unless enquiries go in this direction.

Sunngyth

Sunngyth is a warrior woman. She stands out from the other Carls, not because of her gender but because of her extreme superstition. She sees omens everywhere but nobody listens to her when she says that she does not believe that Bredoc was murdered by anyone in Caedering, or among Taethle's men. Rather she believes that a dark spirit "from the cursed hill" came and killed him while he was on watch. She has no evidence for this – just a feeling and a belief in what she saw in omens by watching the birds.

When Sunngyth learns the player characters are investigating, she seeks them out to point this out. Although Sunngyth is disbelieved by most of her fellows, and they laugh at her behind her back, in this case she is correct.

What is the Cursed Hill?

The Cursed Hill which Sunngyth refers to is the hill of Wincen-Caester, site of a barrow and ruined hill fort which pre-dates the Celts, as well as a Saxon village on its lower slopes. A relevant Lore or Locale roll reveals that spirits of darkness are reputed to guard the barrow, which belongs to an ancient warrior king who bore a magical sword. For more details, see page 117.

Winfrith

Amongst the Caedering men, Winfrith, a Carl and Caedering's armourer, was Bredoc's closest friend. Winfrith is honest to the point of bluntness and devoted to smithcraft far more than he is to fighting, of which he has a mild distaste. Despite these traits, he is respected in Caedering and seen as trustworthy.

He can provide a good insight into Bredoc's character, both the dead man's strengths and flaws. Bredoc was an upright warrior and nobody doubted his bravery, loyalty and above all his honour. If anything, he was a bit too flawless. Worse still, Bredoc was prone to pointing out the faults of others; he expected his comrades to share his virtues and was not afraid to say where they could do better. Naturally, this could be irritating and Winfrith shares freely that he and Bredoc had several friendly arguments.

Winfrith is not a man to make accusations he cannot back but he knows that Bredoc's fellow watchman, Sigebeorht, one of Taethle's men, was someone with whom he had quarrelled several times. For a Saxon Carl, excessive drinking is no sin but it is when one cannot perform his duty, or falls asleep when he is meant to be on watch. If he could, Winfrith would talk to Sigebeorht.

Taethle

Of course, speaking to any of Taethle's men means first speaking with their leader. Taethle is not willing to believe that any of her men have anything to do with Bredoc's death and it will take a Hard social skill test for the player characters to let them speak to anyone if they approach her with the suggestion that one of her men could be guilty. An easy Insight test reveals that making accusations will just make Taethle angry.

On the other hand, the war leader wants to get to the bottom of things. If the player characters take the attitude that one of her men could know something helpful, and do not suggest that one of them could have committed the murder, getting to see them only requires an Easy skill test.

Other approaches the heroes might take vary in difficulty; use the above as guidelines.

Sigebeorht

Sigebeorht, one of Taethle's men, regularly kept watch with Bredoc. He had also fallen out with his comrade, who had told him off for falling asleep while on watch several times, mainly due to the effects of drink. Last night, when Bredoc was killed, Sigebeorht was with him. Sigebeorht had also had a drink and cannot believe what he saw. When talking to others, he claims he fell asleep and others are all too willing to believe it of him, so his story has gone unquestioned.

An Easy Insight roll reveals that the Sigebeorht is lying about falling asleep. If confronted with this, he reveals what he really saw, with apologies for it being so unbelievable and begging the player characters to understand why he did not immediately reveal the truth of the matter.

Sigebeorht saw a monstrous shadow, roughly human in shape but far larger, seek to enter the hall, Bredoc challenged the creature but it was unaffected by the axe blows of both Bredoc and Sigebeorht. Sigebeorht could not stop the creature, even as Bredoc froze in place under the onslaught of its claws and the monster snatched up Bredoc's axe to slaughter its owner.

The heroes will unfortunately be unable to convince neither the people of Caedering nor Taethle and her men that "a monster did it" without further evidence.

What is the Shadow?

A Lore skill test related to magic, the supernatural or the Norse gods, reveals that the creature is most likely a Scaedugengan, a monster of forest shadows. These beings are part spirit, part material and are not affected by mundane weapons.

A Scaedugengan preys upon mortals but will confine its predations to one place unless sent elsewhere by a laece. For a laece to call one or to attempt to persuade it to plague a particular place requires human sacrifice. There are stories of this being done on a large scale.

A laece among the player characters may well seek out the Scaedugengan in the spirit world. Finding it requires a successful Trance roll; once found, the creature will seek to engage the laece in spirit combat.

Murders in the Night

That night the monster, the Scaedugengan, strikes again. It once more targets Taethle's camp, which is easier now as it is outside of the walls. Unless the player characters interfere, Sigebeorht is on watch once again and is the target. The monster is humanoid, with vast claws and a gaping maw. It engages Sigebeorht (or whoever is with him or leaps in), in combat. It is unaffected by attacks from everyone's weapons but unfortunately its attacks can affect physical creatures, although they leave no marks.

When Sigebeorht is dying, the monster finishes the Carl off with his own axe, just as it did for Bredoc, before leaving.

This is of course what happens if they player characters do not interfere. Although the monster is immune to weapons, it can be grappled and so prevented from attacks. A laece who attempts to bind or engage the being in spirit combat will also cause it to flee, although if the laece pursues in the spirit world they will have to face it alone. This is not to be advised.

All being said, if the player characters planned things even reasonably well, there will be more witnesses to the attack, even if there is nothing they can really do. If the player characters do not find a way to oppose the monster, there will be more attacks – it will strike again each night, taking one victim each time, even from within Caedering's walls.

What do the Characters Know?

Seeing the monster face-to-face any player character with magical or pagan Lore skills will realise that the creature is a Scaedugengan, as described on page 37. No roll is needed.

If Taethle and her Carls return, not everyone is happy to see them back. Eadstan, self-appointed spokesmen of the Carls of Caedering, publically demands an apology from Taethle for accusing the Carls of Caedering of murder. Taethle is angered by this and points out through clenched teeth that two of her men were killed by the creature. However, Eadstan will not back down.

The player characters can make a social skill check using Influence or Oratory, depending on how the roleplaying goes, to attempt to calm things down. On an ordinary success, matters are publicly civil, even if tempers are still sore. On a critical success, the characters sooth both sides. If the player characters do not succeed, Taethle and her men again leave Caedering; on a critical failure, they have worsened the situation and things come to blows between Taethle and Eadstan; the latter is likely to lose the fight.

What about Osbehrt?

If Osbehrt is still Thane, he can silence Eadstan, albeit too late to stop all damage. He cannot, however, hush Taethle. If the player characters fail and Taethle leaves, Osbehrt goes after her. Taethle and her men will return the next night at Thane Osbehrt's insistence, still fuming but at least practical.

The Sword and the Hill

The next stage of the scenario, assuming the heroes cannot defeat the Scaedugengan on their own merits, potentially involves a trip to Old Wincen-Caester hill. This need not be the only solution to the problem. Of course, the longer the player characters delay, or spend away from Caedering, the more people die.

Relevant clues leading to Old Wincen-Caester Hill include:

- Sunngyth's omens pointing to Old Wincen-Caester hill as the origin of the evil.
- The knowledge that a magical sword may lie beneath Old Wincen-Caester hill (one character may make a Locale skill test).
- A player character prone to visions having one of the hill — both the barrow and of the laece Dunric (see page 101) calling up something, surrounded by hanged men in a village.
- Eadstan has heard that the laece Dunric has been seen in the village of Seaxnatune on the lower slopes of the hill, accompanied by a small group of Carls.

The Thane may also order the heroes to go to the hill to investigate, being unable to think of other options. The hill is just over seven miles from Caedering — half a day of travel on foot without the heroes pushing themselves.

The Ruined Village

On the west slopes of the hill is a tiny Saxon village — little more than an independent farmstead — called Seaxnatune. This farmstead, although ruled by a King's Thane loyal to Aelle, had little to do with the Saxon lands to the south. Although in many ways on the frontier, it was always closer to nearby Celt settlements and never a staging post for war and conquest. The old Thane, Aescfrith, wanted to stay out of the way of politics and such matters.

Seaxnatune is no more and when approaching it the stink of death and smoke hangs in the air. The 30 or so people who lived there are all dead, slaughtered, with many now hanging from the few nearby trees. They are dead almost down to the last man, woman and child. Even for a hardened Saxon warrior, the scene is a gruesome sight. The remains of the wooden houses still smoulder from the fires that burned them down.

A search of Seaxnatune finds the only survivor – a young girl, Idris, hiding under the body of her father. Idris is incoherent with fear and grief, and likely to do nothing but scream when the player characters find her. An Influence test may calm Idris enough to persuade her to talk. On a failed test, Idris will calm down eventually with kind treatment but not until the next day.

Idris can tell the heroes of the "bad men" killing everyone, under the directions of "the sneering man with the teeth necklace" who chanted prayers to Skadi as people were killed. He then spoke to a "shadow monster with big claws from the barrow". The heroes will recognise Idris' description of the laece Dunric — and some magical ritual calling down the Scaedugengan.

The girl can also direct the heroes to the barrow near the top of the hill. Without finding and talking to her, this requires a half day of searching and a player character to succeed in a Perception or Locale test.

The Hill and the Barrow

The hill is a chunk of chalk downland and is surprisingly beautiful, being full of wild flowers and blue butterflies. It is an easy climb. The barrow on the east side is always in shadow. Nearby the

air feels stuffy and there is a faint musty smell. It is strangely silent; observers will note that the local wildlife avoids the area.

The barrow has not been exposed to the world. Getting in requires digging, which will be a lengthy process without tools. Inside, the barrow lies shrouded in darkness, which no light, not even magical, can penetrate. If a player character attempts to take a torch inside, it rapidly dims and then goes out. Within, partially in the spirit world, lurks a Niflung, a dragon-shaped spirit of darkness, watching over the treasure 1,000 years or more after it was first placed there, with the dead king.

The treasure consists of numerous silver coins, a gold torque and a bronze sword. One who tries to find the sword by touch can do so, although a Perception check is needed for a character in a hurry. The Niflung will physically manifest should anyone try to take any of the treasure from the barrow, appearing as a shadowy and vague dragon shape of pure darkness. It voicelessly demands the return of what was taken. Anyone with a connection to the spirit world can understand the darkness spirit, although it makes no sound.

If the Niflung is defeated either in physical combat or in spirit combat by a laece, the darkness lifts and the heroes can seize the treasure without further hindrance. The value is 5,000SP.

The heroes can also negotiate with the Niflung. On a successful Influence or other relevant test, the Niflung will agree to terms – they are to replace any piece of treasure they take with two of their own (or just one of their own on a critical success) of similar value. When it comes to replacing the sword with something, a hero can donate a sword of their own. Although unenchanted, it is steel rather than bronze and the darkness spirit knows its value.

Naegling

The sword is a bronze broadsword, quite blunt with time, and it appears useless. However, the sword is enchanted with the Folk Magic spell Bladesharp. When someone picks it up, the dust and corrosion falls away, leaving a sharp blade which inflicts 1d10 damage. This process costs the sword wielder one Magic Point.

Any scene in which a character draws the sword, the spell again takes effect, giving the above damage and costing one Magic Point. The sword's wielder knows the weapon's name is Naegling, while the name of the king or chief to whom it once belonged is long forgotten.

A third option is Stealth, perhaps involving a character sneaking into the barrow while the Niflung is distracted by negotiations or combat.

Conclusion

Once they have the sword, the player characters are free to take on the Scaedugengan in Caedering. The monster will have continued its rampage, killing a victim each night. Naturally, if the player characters manage to defeat it, they are acclaimed as great heroes and with this mighty deed, their fame begins to spread. This leads directly to the offers in the next scenario.

Fighting the Scaeduengan

The Scaedugengan is a tough foe. Only a hero with the sword from the barrow can harm it physically. A laece in the party can engage the creature in spirit combat at the same time as the physical fight.

Other player characters, although they cannot harm the Scaedugengan physically, can certainly attempt to make combat manoeuvres to help.

Little trace remains of Dunric or his Carls, although Dunric again reappears in the next scenario and the player characters have the chance to end his threat. If the heroes search for clues, a Survival test at Formidable difficulty helps them find a trail near the remains of Seaxnatune. This leads to the neighbourhood of Taddenlaege, in the next scenario before petering out. This is an alternative lead in to that scenario, or perhaps an added personal motivation for the heroes to go there.

Even the Ealdorman Ceolfrith believes that Dunric has gone too far with his massacre and disowns any association with him. The heroes may choose to attempt to end Ceolfrith for condoning this, although this will be extremely difficult to prove and proof is needed if they wish to act legally.

Non-Player Characters

Eadstan

Eadstan	Attributes
STR: 11	Action Points: 3
CON: 11	Damage Modifier: 0
SIZ: 13	Magic Points: 12
DEX: 12	Movement: 6 metres
INT: 14	Initiative Bonus: 13
POW: 12	Armour:
CHA: 13	

Skills: Athletics 53%, Brawn 52%, Commerce 56%, Culture (Saxon) 68%, Endurance 50%, Evade 49%, Insight 55%, Influence 46%, Language (Jute) 68%, Lore (Saxon) 68%, Perception 54%, Riding 54%, Superstition 37%, Willpower 44%

Passions: Loyalty to Caedering 55%, Love Wealth 50%

1d20	Location	AP/HP
1–3	Right Leg	0/5
4–6	Left Leg	0/5
7–9	Abdomen	0/6
10–12	Chest	0/7
13–15	Right Arm	0/4
16–18	Left Arm	0/4
19–20	Head	0/5

Combat Style: : Fyrdman (Battleaxe, Seax and Shield, Trait: Formation Fighting) 53%

Weapon	Size/Force	Reach	Damage	AP/HP
Seax	*M*	*S*	*1d4+2*	*6/8*
Battelaxe	*M*	*M*	*1d6+1*	*4/4*
Saxon Shield	*L*	*S*	*1d4*	*4/12*

Sigebeorht

Sigebeorht	Attributes
STR: 14	Action Points: 2
CON: 11	Damage Modifier: +1d2
SIZ: 14	Magic Points: 14
DEX: 12	Movement: 6 metres
INT: 11	Initiative Bonus: 12
POW: 14	Armour: Leather Tunic
CHA: 10	

Skills: Athletics 56%, Brawn 58%, Culture (Saxon) 64%, Endurance 47%, Evade 39%, Language (Saxon) 61%, Lore (Saxon) 62%, Lore (Norse Gods) 32%, Perception 75%, Superstition 53%, Unarmed 50%, Willpower 48%

Passions: Loyalty to Taethle 55%, Love Drink 50%

1d20	Location	AP/HP
1–3	Right Leg	0/5
4–6	Left Leg	0/5
7–9	Abdomen	2/6
10–12	Chest	2/7
13–15	Right Arm	0/4
16–18	Left Arm	0/4
19–20	Head	0/5

Combat Style: : Fyrdman (Battleaxe, Seax and Shield, Trait: Formation Fighting) 53%

Weapon	Size/Force	Reach	Damage	AP/HP
Seax	*M*	*S*	*1d4+2+1d2*	*6/8*
Battelaxe	*M*	*M*	*1d6+1+1d2*	*4/4*
Saxon Shield	*L*	*S*	*1d4+1d2*	*4/12*

Sunngyth

Sunngyth	Attributes
STR: 13	Action Points: 2
CON: 11	Damage Modifier: +1d2
SIZ: 13	Magic Points: 12
DEX: 12	Movement: 6 metres
INT: 14	Initiative Bonus: 13
POW: 12	Armour: Leather Tunic
CHA: 10	

Skills: Athletics 55%, Brawn 56%, Culture (Saxon) 64%, Endurance 50%, Evade 39%, Language (Saxon) 64%, Lore (Saxon) 68%, Lore (Norse Gods) 68%, Perception 57%, Superstition 78%, Unarmed 50%, Willpower 44%

Passions: Loyalty to Taethle 55%, Love Norse Gods 70%

1d20	Location	AP/HP
1–3	Right Leg	0/5
4–6	Left Leg	0/5
7–9	Abdomen	2/6
10–12	Chest	2/7
13–15	Right Arm	0/4
16–18	Left Arm	0/4
19–20	Head	0/5

Combat Style: : Fyrdman (Battleaxe, Seax and Shield, Trait: Formation Fighting) 65%

Weapon	Size/Force	Reach	Damage	AP/HP
Seax	*M*	*S*	*1d4+2+1d2*	*6/8*
Battelaxe	*M*	*M*	*1d6+1+1d2*	*4/4*
Saxon Shield	*L*	*S*	*1d4+1d2*	*4/12*

Winfrith

Winfrith	Attributes
STR: 12	Action Points: 2
CON: 11	Damage Modifier: +1d2
SIZ: 16	Magic Points: 11
DEX: 12	Movement: 6 metres
INT: 13	Initiative Bonus: 12
POW: 11	Armour: Leather Tunic
CHA: 10	

Skills: Athletics 54%, Brawn 58%, Craft (Make and Repair Weapons and Armour) 65%, Culture (Saxon) 66%, Endurance 47%, Evade 39%, Language (Jute) 63%, Lore (Saxon) 65%, Perception 54%, Superstition 50%, Unarmed 49%, Willower 42%

Passions: Loyalty to Caedering 55%, Love Craftsmanship 50%, Norse Gods 40%

1d20	Location	AP/HP
1–3	Right Leg	0/6
4–6	Left Leg	0/6
7–9	Abdomen	2/7
10–12	Chest	2/8
13–15	Right Arm	0/5
16–18	Left Arm	0/5
19–20	Head	0/6

Combat Style:: Fyrdman (Battleaxe, Seax and Shield, Trait: Formation Fighting) 55%

Weapon	Size/Force	Reach	Damage	AP/HP
Seax	*M*	*S*	*1d4+2+1d2*	*6/8*
Battelaxe	*M*	*M*	*1d6+1+1d2*	*4/4*
Saxon Shield	*L*	*S*	*1d4+1d2*	*4/12*

Monsters

The Niflung

The Niflung is a dragon-shaped spirit of darkness. When it manifests, it flows and breathes darkness itself, which envelops a single opponent within 10 metres. This attack does 1d6 damage to every hit location and cannot be parried, only Evaded. Further, escaping the freezing darkness requires an opposed Athletics, Brawn or Evade roll.

After the initial attack of freezing darkness, the Niflung attacks normally with its Elemental Combat skill. The Niflung is physically present and vulnerable to ordinary weapons as well as spirit combat.

Niflung	Attributes
STR: 36	Action Points: 3
DEX: 15	Damage Modifier: +1d6
INT: 13	Magic Points: 21
POW: 21	Movement: 10 metres
	Initiative Bonus: 14
	Armour:/Hit Points: 2/39

Skills: Brawn 92%, Evade 66%, Perception 56%, Willpower 92%
Combat Style: Elemental Combat 78% (Damage: 2d6)

The Scaedugengan

The Scaedugengan is a monster around nine feet tall, with a great maw and vast claws, surrounded by darkness. The creature is partially manifest physically, meaning it can use its spectral combat to inflict physical wounds. These attacks leave no mark but do damage normally and cannot be parried with mundane weapons. Similarly, the creature cannot be harmed with mundane weapons.

The monster likes to cover up the magical nature of its attacks by finishing off a victim using their own weapon.

Note that the monster regenerates all Hit Point and Magic Point loss after 24 hours without incident. If hurt, the Scaedugengan goes away to hide and recover, before seeking revenge.

Nitlung	Attributes
STR: 36	Action Points: 3
DEX: 15	Damage Modifier: +1d6
INT: 13	Magic Points: 21
POW: 21	Movement: 10 metres
	Initiative Bonus: 14
	Armour:/Hit Points: 2/39

Skills: Brawn 92%, Evade 66%, Perception 56%, Willpower 92%
Combat Style: Elemental Combat 78% (Damage: 2d6)

Uprising

A dozen years ago, King Aelle of Ceint lay claim to territories outside the usual boundaries of his kingdom. These new territories are near the old ruined Roman city of Calleva Atrebatum and were intended to lay the grounds for a later expansion into the area - an expansion that never happened, as Ceint ran into other problems and conflicts.

The Celts in the area never became Saxon subjects but rather allies of Ceint against their common enemy, the Kingdom of Dumnonia. A new King's Thane, Tadda, founded the large village, Taddenlaege and came to an arrangement with the Celts. Over time, Taddenlaege and the Celts have built up fair relations and mutual trade

These relations are backed by three dozen carls at the Thane's command, able to defend Taddenlaege and Saxon interests in the area, inflicting punishments on the Celts for raids and other misdemeanours. It i a rough sort of peace.

But the peace was never going to last; Tadda, although King Aelle's man, is a second cousin of the new great Saxon power in Britain, the Ealdorman Cerdic. Cerdic wants Tadda on his side, both to gain a beach head in the region in his own name and to be able to gather warriors from the region for his ongoing war with Dumnonia. Neither Cerdic nor Aelle have quite grasped how tenuous Tadda's grip here is.

In this scenario, Cerdic and Aelle both seek to send the player characters to the area. They both want troops from Taddenlaege, with similar ends in sight. Unfortunately, matters are more complex than they first appear. Leofstan, a war leader serving King Octa of Wiht, is in the area to stir up trouble. Octa and Ealdorman Ceolfrith have a secret alliance. Octa will always do what he can to inconvenience King Aelle of Ceint and does not want Cerdic to gain more power and allies. The idea is that the trouble here will prevent both Cerdic and Aelle from making use of possible forces and allies in the area, thus slowing their expansion. Ideally for Octa, Cerdic or Aelle will have to divert forces to the area, although matters have yet to advance that far. And Ealdorman Ceolfrith, having been embarrassed by King Aelle, and considering himself a rival of Cerdic, shares the cause.

Leofstan and his men have attacked and burned several Celtic villages. They have killed many Celts and made many more homeless. Worse, Leofstan has been joined by the laece, Dunric, villain of The Cursed Hill, and the three Carls who worked with him in that scenario. In the villages, any who did not hide or flee were sacrificed to dark aspects of the Saxon gods at the insistence of Dunric. Dunric does not lead the small warband but his influence has undeniably led to the worst atrocities, including people burned alive or hung from trees to slowly strangle to death.

The Celts do not know that Leofstan's men form a separate group and are nothing to do with Taddenlaege. The atrocities have had an impact and led many Celts into violent opposition against Thane Tadda's holdings and influence. Worse, before the atrocities began, the band visited Taddenlaege, and the laece Dunric cursed Thane Tadda, leaving him 'elf-shot' and Taddenlaege without leadership.

And the player characters now walk right into this mess.

The Mission

The player characters have probably met both Cerdic and King Aelle in previous scenarios and possibly owe King Aelle their help. Now their previous exploits show both leaders the heroes' potential.

Firstly, Cerdic himself seeks out the heroes. This is already a sign of great opportunity. Cerdic will explicitly bring up any notable acts of heroism or success in the previous scenarios. It is clear he wants something; probably something dangerous.

The Games Master should use Cerdic to relay the following information:

- Taddenlaege is a large walled village ruled by Tadda, a King's Thane loyal to King Aelle of Ceint.
- The area is not fully under Saxon control, allthough apparently at peace.
- Cerdic wants the player characters to see that the area is secure and persuade Tadda, who is Cerdic's second cousin, to join his cause, sending what armed forces he can – Saxon but also Celt if possible – to Cerdic's banner to help him fight Dumnonia.
- A laece matching Dunric's description (the necklace of teeth) has been recently seen in the area.

Play Cerdic as cold and icily determined, and hint that impressing him will bring great rewards. Cerdic is polite to the player characters and makes a request rather than giving a command, even if they are his Carls. This request is, granted, hard to refuse but if they carry out the mission successfully, Cerdic will be in the player characters' debt. When the matter of payment is raised, Cerdic mentions lands and the status of a Thane for a player character leader.

Further Standard checks on relevant Lore skills or an Easy check on a Locale skill applying to the area can also reveal some of the following. Each character can attempt a check for a piece of information. A critical success will reveal two pieces of information.

- Taddenlaege is near the ruins of a Roman city, Calleva Atrebatum. The old Roman road between Calleva Atrebatum and the Celtic city of Caer Cradawc, once known by the Roman name of Venta Belgarum, at the borders of Dumnonia is still an active trade route.
- Calleva Atrebatum is haunted by Roman ghosts.
- The Celts in the area belong to the Atrabetes tribe. They are pagan rather than Christian and enemies of the Kingdom of Dumnonia. This is good news for Cerdic's cause.
- Thane Tadda certainly has too few men to assert much control over the area.

Before the heroes get a chance to set out, another man approaches – a woman, Ealhwyn, Daughter of Hrof (see page 48), who is here as an emissary of King Aelle. She gives the king's instructions, which are rather similar to those of Cerdic, although instead of sending the men to Cerdic, they are to send them to Aelle in Anderida. Something is going on – after all, Cerdic is an Ealdorman nominally in King Aelle's service – but Cerdic will not be available to ask and Ealhwyn does not know.

Aelle is willing to give "great rewards" for success, although precisely what that means is left vague.

Getting There

The region around Taddenlaege is on gentle hills with heavy forest cover, apart from large clearings around Calleva Atrebatum and Taddenlaege itself. It is good hunting ground for deer and boar.

However, on the journey here it is the heroes who are being hunted – by Celts displaced by the slaughter in their villages and out for revenge.

A group of Celt hunters will attempt to follow the player characters without being noticed, in order to strike suddenly at night when most of the travelling party are asleep. Ask the player of the character with the highest Perception skill to make a roll, opposed by the Stealth skill of Caradoc, the Celtic leader, at 45%. If the check succeeds, the player characters will know they are being followed and hunted.

A critical success even reveals the exact locations of the pursuers; failing that, the player characters can try to lure out the pursuers, or track and trick them with other skills.

If the characters do not spot the Celts, they strike suddenly by surprise at night. Mechanical details for Caradoc and his associates are at the end of this scenario. There is one fewer Celt than there are player characters, which discourages them, even in their lust for revenge, from a direct assault without the benefit of surprise.

Caradoc and the others are based in the Roman ruins of Calleva Atrebatum, which is now a base for those Celts who have been made homeless or taken up arms in the cause. Naturally, this is not something the Celts will readily reveal to the player characters, even if they are captured.

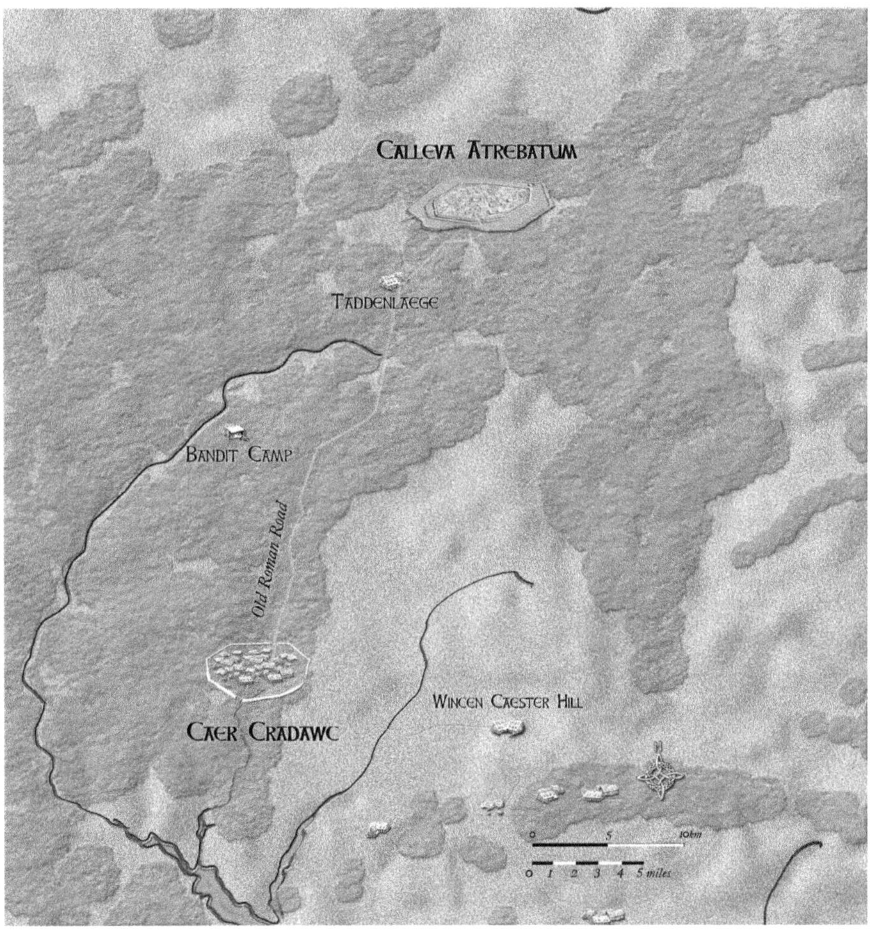

The Celts are in a cold rage. None of them speak Saxon but those who understand Brythonic will hear them express their hatred of the Saxons who have slaughtered innocent people and burned their villages to the ground, and especially of the Saxon "witch" who had people hanged and burned alive, even defenceless women and children.

The player characters may well recognise the atrocities as consistent with actions of the laece Dunric, from previous scenarios.

Caradoc and his allies will not respond to threats or violence to make them talk. The one thing that could, with a suitable skill test, persuade them to open up, is a promise to bring those who destroyed their homes and kin to justice. If the players do not figure this out for themselves, a successful Insight test suggests this is a good route to take. If the player characters make such promises, the Celts will not be shy about doubting the value of a Saxon's sworn word but a successful Influence or similar test will bring them round.

Taddenlaege

Taddenlaege is somewhere between a large village and a small town and sits in the centre of a cleared area of forest, surrounded by farmed land. The people here are farmers and woodsmen, and the axes of Carls more often hew wood than foes. Although at need, they still make worthy warriors.

A ditch and wooden stockade fence with two gates surrounds the town. Within are nearly 100 buildings, also made of wood. Most of these buildings are typical two storey Saxon houses, with thatched rooves and the lower floor below ground. These houses belong to six extended families, which include free Carls, dependents and Gebur servants, and a few thralls. Unlike most communities, the thralls here are of Saxon rather than British blood.

As well as the houses, there are a dozen burs; out-buildings near the walls. These single room buildings serve as workshops, storage and lodgings for those visitors who are not put up in the Thane's Hall.

The Thane's Hall is the largest building in the village and stands in the centre of Taddenlaege. While not as impressive as the hall of an Ealdorman or king, the building is still large enough to seat all of the village's free Carls — nearly 50 men — at feasts. It is a tall building with a yellow-painted gabled wooden roof.

As well as the Thane's Hall, there are two lesser halls belonging to the heads of the most powerful families here. Probably the player characters will stay at one of the burs rather than the Thane's Hall or one of the family halls. This could be construed as an insult but Taddenlaege is currently in a crisis. Bands of Celts — and some say Saxon bandits — are attacking people outside the walls and nobody is really dealing with the problem. Thane Tadda is ill and incoherent, and the village has no leadership.

The major NPCs in Taddenlaege are:

Thane Tadda

Thane Tadda is a decisive leader with a gift for bringing people with different needs together. He does this by imposing his own unique vision on everyone rather than seeking compromise. Tadda is skilled at making others see the benefits of his way of doing things and in finding common interests with possible followers and allies.

He has even found common ground with the local Celts, helping them see the benefits of a Saxon presence when it comes to trade with the Saxon lands to the west and for allies against a shared enemy, Dumnonia. Some Celts were even coming to acknowledge Tadda's rule, although the attacks by Leofstan's bandits have ruined this.

Unfortunately, Tadda is feverish and says little that makes sense at the moment. He is in fact possessed by an Aelf, a curse inflicted on him by the laece Dunric who works with the bandits.

Braeca, Son of Tadda

Braeca, the Thane's 20 year old son, is trying to rule in his father's stead now that Tadda is ill but he does not yet have what it takes. Braeca lacks experience as a warrior and all but the most loyal Carls are reluctant to follow a man unproven in battle. He tries to be conciliatory but this comes across as weak and indecisive.

Without aid, or his father's recovery, Braeca will not last for long.

Rowenna

Rowenna, head of one of the two powerful families in Taddenlaege, is a recent widow. Her husband, Bedic, died three weeks ago at the hands of the bandits. Bedic was a merchant and one of the first victims. Rowenna was a warrior in her youth and now that she is widowed and her children have grown up, she has taken up arms yet again, for vengeance and, it must be said, the sake of glory.

What Rowenna wants is action and revenge against both the bandits and the Celts. She has sent out her men — Carls associated to the family — and they have traced the centre of the Celtic uprising to Calleva Atrebatum. She is now gathering her forces and trying to persuade others in Taddenlaege to join her. The other power in town, Garbold, a head of a rival family, has spoken out against a "rash" attack but Rowenna will push forward even without his aid.

Garbold

Garbold, head of the richest family in Taddenlaege, is a good leader. He knows how to reward those who follow him and inspire loyalty. He is welcoming to potential allies and ruthless with enemies. He projects an air of heartiness and hospitality.

It is really unfortunate that he has these positive qualities, as Garbold is plotting with Taddenlaege's enemies, Leofstan and the bandits, to replace Tadda as Thane. In doing this, Garbold will place himself in alliance with King Octa rather than King Aelle,but Garbold does not care which distant king he answers to.

Garbold meets with the bandits regularly in a bur that lies outside of Taddenlaege's walls. Understandably, he is reluctant to take up arms to hunt them down (pointing out quite reasonably that nobody knows where they are based) but he is equally against attacking the Celts. In truth, he is both stalling for time and sowing seeds for his future rule, saying the warriors do not yet know the numbers of the enemy and it might be wise to wait for help from King Aelle — and if he will not hear, to look for another king to follow.

Events in Taddenlaege

Tadda and Braeca

Probably, when the heroes first arrive, they will seek to meet Thane Tadda. Tadda's housecarls will inform the heroes of the Thane's ailments but they will be able to see his son Braeca.

Braeca's weakness and indecision should be apparent to the player characters. They could persuade him with an Influence or other social skill test to help their cause but possibly few will go along with Braeca's decision, especially if it's radical. Even Braeca

will advise the heroes to seek out Rowenna and Garbold, the leaders of the two major families in town.

The Thane's son will inform the player characters of the existence of the Celt uprising. He also mentions that he has seen Garbold meeting with strange folk not from the village in one of his burs. He did not say anything to Garbold and as far as he is aware, Garbold did not know he was there. Braeca has not made a connection between the men Garbold has met and the bandits, although the player characters may (correctly) infer this.

Braeca is a superstitious man, and believes that his father is "elf-shot". Surprisingly, he is quite correct in this. If the player characters have a laece among them and can convince Braeca to let him see the Thane, the laece can cure Tadda by casting out the sickness spirit by defeating it in spirit combat. The sickness spirit clutching at the Thane is easy to see for a laece who enters a trance.

If the spirit is vanquished, Tadda will take time to recover but is immediately coherent.

The Aelf

Characteristics
INT 8
POW 21
CHA 7

Skills: Discorporate 79%, Spectral Combat 78%, Stealth 65%, Willpower 92%

Special: The Aelf can drag a victim into the spirit plane with Discorporate to fight them in spirit combat. If the Aelf wins, it possesses them, causing the ailments of Confusion (onset time 2 days) and Maiming (onset time 3 hours later).

Rowenna and the Celts

Rowenna will not seek out the player characters but will receive them if they go to her. She is preparing to sally forth with whoever she can gather against the Celts and asks the player characters to join her in that quest; she can leave as soon as tomorrow but is hoping to find more allies in the village. Rowenna is disappointed in Garbold not backing her up in taking action. She thinks he is a coward, although has so far stopped short of calling him that; blood feuds have started for less.

It will take a good deal to dissuade Rowenna from attacking the Celts; at the very least, it needs a Hard test in a relevant skill to the argument the player characters use. If the player characters discover the location of the bandits and tell Rowenna, they present a better target for more immediate action, although Rowenna sees that the Celts still have to be dealt with afterwards.

Garbold and the Bandits

Once he hears of the player characters, Garbold will invite them to a feast and even (if they inspire him) invite them to stay in his hall. At the feast, beer and mead flow, and the rules of hospitality mean the player characters cannot openly decline it. During the drinking, there are riddle contests, with drinking penalties for losing. It is a rowdy time for all.

The player characters each need to make an Endurance test to avoid becoming drunk. A Lore (Saxon) or similar skill to do well at riddles or a Deceit or Sleight roll to avoid drinking without being caught out will also work. A player character who has too much to drink has the difficulty of any social skills involving subtlety increased by one step.

Unfortunately for those who over-imbibe, subtlety is needed in this situation. Garbold waits until late in the evening to grill the player characters about their intentions. If the heroes reveal that they potentially suspect Garbold of wrongdoing, the family leader will try to win them over, revealing that his scouts have discovered the hiding place of the bandits. He intends to send some of his men there to remove them on the next night and the player characters are welcome to join them.

An Insight skill test reveals that Garbold is setting up a trap.

Calleva Atrebatum

A group of 60 Celt warriors, both from the villages that the bandits destroyed and others attracted to the cause, have set up camp within the crumbling ivy-covered walls of the ruined Roman city of Calleva Atrebatum. The city has a reputation for being haunted, owing to the way the wind howls through buildings and portions of the wall where bricks and stone blocks are missing.

For this reason, most people avoid the ruins. This makes it an ideal place for the Celts to gather in large numbers and prepare their attacks. In their bitterness and anger, the Celts have embraced the city's haunted reputation.

The Celts are a formidable force and the walls provide protection. They will attack Saxons who simply ride in. If Rowenna's force attacks, they will be overmatched by the Celts and forced to flee when half of their number are killed, while the damage to the Celts will be minimal.

The key here is either stealth or diplomacy. The Celt warriors will disperse if their leader, Orin, is killed or surrenders. They will also follow Orin's direction should he find a new foe to attack other than the Saxons of Taddenlaege.

Guards watch the walls but they are not fully manned. Getting in requires an Easy Athletics roll to climb the walls and an opposed Stealth roll so as not to be noticed. Only one Stealth roll is needed for the whole group of heroes; a player character with a high score can coordinate. The GM should reward clever methods to distract or bluff the Celts.

Rowenna's forces attacking certainly provide an adequate distraction. In this case, the player characters can seek out Orin and his two bodyguards, described below. Orin is easy to find, as he is the one giving all the orders.

Within the walls, the old crumbling houses are largely unoccupied and provide plenty of places to hide. There are tents and even wooden huts within the old market area, where the Celts have set up their camp. The largest of these huts is the dwelling of Orin, chief of the exiles and people seeking vengeance.

Orin has a reputation as a fierce leader but even he has trouble keeping the group together. He is guarded by two young men — twin brothers called Taran and Turi — who are the only two survivors from Orin's village and have appointed themselves to protect him.

If the player characters have persuaded the Celts to let them in, perhaps through trickery, they can negotiate with Orin, although they must leave their weapons with Taran and Turi. Otherwise, a social skill test is required to persuade Orin to talk at all and not immediately attack with his bodyguards — and more Celt warriors arrive to help in 1d4 rounds.

Assuming the player characters manage to talk to Orin, they discover that he wants public vengeance on those who destroyed the Celt villages and the Saxons either gone from this area or answering to a local Celt leader. He has no ambitions to lead here himself but is the obvious candidate.

With a successful Influence or other relevant social skill test, Orin is prepared to answer to a Saxon king in return for this. With a successful Hard test or a critical success, Orin will give another concession. He is even willing to send warriors to help Cerdic fight Dumnonia if the player characters bring it up.

The people of Taddenlaege will not be happy with these terms if the player characters go this route but Cerdic is potentially perfectly content.

The Bandits

The Saxon bandits led by Leofstan are not easy to find. Garbold knows the location of their woodland camp and as noted above will send the player characters there with three of his Carls but these men eventually will turn on the player characters and side with the bandits, once they get the chance.

If the player characters are prepared for this, both knowing about the trap and able to spring it from within, this is one way to get to the bandits. Another way, which Rowenna or Thane Tadda (if coherent), will suggest, is to set up a trap of their own.

The bandits often attack traffic taking the old Roman road to Caer Cradawc – the old Roman city of Venta Belgarum. If the player characters go disguised as a trade caravan, four bandits will indeed attack. These bandits do not care for simple robbery; they are here to spread chaos and will kill travellers before looting rather than making threats. But a captured bandit will reveal where the others are with a simple social skill test.

There are 13 bandits in total, including their leader, Leofstan, and the laece Dunric. Leofstan is eager to talk; if he is to go down for his crimes, he will take those he serves with him. Leofstan gladly reveals Garbold as an accomplice and King Octa as the man whose instructions he's following. Three of the bandits came with Dunric from Ealdorman Ceolfrith to help with the endeavour; Ceolfrith and Octa have a secret alliance. Leofstan comes across as petty and sadistic, as well as annoyingly chatty.

Of course, if the player characters seek the bandits without back-up from the Celts or people in Taddenlaege, Leofstan will be likely to have the upper hand. He will capture rather than kill the player characters; he wants to find out if they work for anyone important who might come for him.

Clever heroes can actually find out more from Leofstan while captured; a social skill test can goad Leofstan into talking. If the player characters are clever, they might be able to buy their own lives, although perhaps not their honour.

Dunric

Leofstan is accompanied by the laece Dunric. Dunric does not serve Leofstan but is an equal partner in his enterprise. He views the attacks on the villages as an opportunity to make sacrifices to the aesir, in particular Skadi, the goddess of winter destruction. After calling the powerful spirit he summoned in The Cursed Hill, Dunric felt a rush of power. He is now making further sacrifices to Skadi in the hope of being able to repeat his success. He came to serve Leofstan and lent the bandit leader those Carls with him, not out of a sense of fellow feeling or belief in the cause but rather because it was an expedient way to sacrifice lots of people.

He plans to continue these sacrifices after Skadi is repaid in an effort to gather more power again.

Dunric is just as surly, sneering and contemptuous of others as he was before. The laece certainly values his own life above that of fools such as the heroes. He will not get involved in any fighting unless the odds are clearly in his favour or he is cornered. In the case of a big attack against the bandit camp, Dunric will flee. He will seek to release his bound spirits against any player characters who break away from the main fighting to pursue him; most NPCs will be too scared to pursue a man of such fearsome magical power.

The laece is heading for a stream a few hundred metres away, where he will release his most powerful spirit, a bound Nikor, and seek to escape while the Nikor delays pursuers. If he cannot make the stream, he will still release the Nikor but have it occupy his own body.

Conclusion and Aftermath

The events of this scenario can lead in many directions. If the player characters restored Thane Tadda to health, Rowenna will fall into line with her Thane's commands. Garbold, however, is worried that the Thane knows or will find out that he has betrayed him. He will leave Taddenlaege with his most loyal Carls to join the bandits if they are still around. If not, he will have to travel further afield. He can certainly show up again to menace the player characters in future scenarios.

Another future menace is Dunric, if he manages to escape.

Cerdic will be pleased with the player characters if they dealt with the Celts and even more pleased if they recruited them to his cause. He possibly also knows that King Octa is acting in a way that undermines him and will have to be dealt with. More immediately, if Cerdic has the requested forces, he now has the resources to launch an attack on Caer Crawdawc.

If this attack succeeds, Cerdic will name himself as king in his own right, not an Ealdorman subject to King Aelle and Caer Crawdawc, which he renames as Wincen Caester becomes his new capital.

In terms of rewards, Cerdic is happy to give gifts amounting to 500SP for moderate success in the mission, which was more complex than planned. He will raise the amount to 1,000SP for going beyond the call of duty. If the heroes were successful, he will call on them again and award lands – possibly further lands than held previously – making one of them a Thane if they are not so already. Of course, these lands are on a dangerous frontier.

On the other hand, the heroes may have chosen to support King Aelle. In this case, Cerdic does not have the forces he needs to attack Caer Crawdawc by himself. If the player characters were able to send armed men to Aelle, negotiations between the King and Ealdorman lead to a joint expedition against Caer Crawdawc. If this succeeds, Cerdic still rules and renames the city but as a subject of King Aelle, at least for now.

Aelle's rewards are similar to those offered by Cerdic but any Thane named by Aelle will be a King's Thane and so higher in status. Aelle's priority is not so much Octa of Wiht but Ealdorman Ceolfrith, who now needs to be removed from his position. This act is going to be costly in manpower unless the player characters have a better idea.

Non-Player Characters

Caradoc

Caradoc	Attributes
STR: 11	Action Points: 3
CON: 13	Damage Modifier: 0
SIZ: 13	Magic Points: 14
DEX: 12	Movement: 6 metres
INT: 14	Initiative Bonus: 12
POW: 14	Armour: Leather Tunic
CHA: 12	

Skills: Athletics 53%, Brawn 54%, Culture (Celt) 64%, Endurance 51%, Evade 44%, Language (Brythonic) 64%, Language (Saxon) 34%, Lore (Celt) 66%, Perception 54%, Stealth 55%, Superstition 50%, Survival 57%, Unarmed 50%, Willpower 42%

Passions: Loyalty to Orin 54%, Hate (Saxons) 59%, Celtic Gods 44%

1d20	Location	AP/HP
1–3	Right Leg	0/6
4–6	Left Leg	0/6
7–9	Abdomen	2/7
10–12	Chest	2/8
13–15	Right Arm	0/5
16–18	Left Arm	0/5
19–20	Head	0/6

Combat Style: Hunter (Dagger, Sling, Bow, Trait: Skirmishing) 68%

Weapon	Size/Force	Reach	Damage	AP/HP
Dagger	*S*	*S*	*1d4+1*	*6/8*
Bow	*L*	-	*1d6+2*	*4/4*
Sling	*L*	-	*1d8*	*1/2*

Celt Hunters

As for Caradoc but 2 Action Points, Initiative Bonus 11 and the following Passions: Loyalty to Comrades 50%, Hate (Saxons) 50%

Orin

Orin	Attributes
STR: 13	Action Points: 3
CON: 11	Damage Modifier: +1d2
SIZ: 13	Magic Points: 12
DEX: 13	Movement: 6 metres
INT: 14	Initiative Bonus: 12
POW: 12	Armour: Leather Tunic and Helm
CHA: 14	

Skills: Athletics 66%, Culture (Celt) 68%, Endurance 57%, Evade 46%, Influence 58%, Insight 56%. Language (Brythonic) 68%, Language (Saxon) 38%, Lore (Celt) 68%, Lore (Strategy and Tactics) 58%, Oratory 68%, Perception 64%, Superstition 40%, Unarmed 51%, Willpower 34%

Passions: Loyalty to Celts at Calleva 52%, Hatred (Saxons) 72%, Pagan Gods 42%

1d20	Location	AP/HP
1–3	Right Leg	0/5
4–6	Left Leg	0/5
7–9	Abdomen	2/6
10–12	Chest	2/7
13–15	Right Arm	0/4
16–18	Left Arm	0/4
19–20	Head	0/5

Combat Style: Warrior (Spear, Sword and Shield, Trait: Formation Fighting) 81%

Weapon	Size/Force	Reach	Damage	AP/HP
Spear	*M*	*L*	*1d8+1+1d2*	*4/5*
Sword	*M*	*M*	*1d6+2+1d2*	*4/8*
Celtic Shield	*L*	*S*	*1d3+1+1d2*	*4/15*

Orin's Bodyguards & Other Celts

Use statistics for Typical Warrior on page 213 of *Mythic Britain*. Passions: Loyalty to Orin 70%, Hatred (Saxons) 50%

Thane Tadda

Tadda	Attributes
STR: 14	Action Points: 3
CON: 12	Damage Modifier: +1d2
SIZ: 14	Magic Points: 11
DEX: 12	Movement: 6 metres
INT: 14	Initiative Bonus: 11
POW: 11	Armour: Leather Tunic and Helm
CHA: 13	

Skills: Athletics 41%, Brawn 43%, Culture (Saxon) 66%, Culture (Celt) 46%, Endurance 58%, Evade 49%, Influence 70%, Insight 38%, Language (Saxon) 66%, Language (Brythonic) 46%, Lore (Saxon) 66%, Lore (Strategy and Tactics) 51%, Oratory 54%, Perception 63%, Ride 52%, Superstition 36%, Unarmed 52%, Willpower 42%

Passions: Loyalty to Taddenlaege 55%, Love (Power) 50%

1d20	Location	AP/HP
1–3	Right Leg	0/5
4–6	Left Leg	0/5
7–9	Abdomen	2/6
10–12	Chest	2/7
13–15	Right Arm	0/4
16–18	Left Arm	0/4
19–20	Head	5/5

Combat Style: Saxon Noble (Sword, Seax and Shield, Trait: Mounted Combat) 77%

Weapon	Size/Force	Reach	Damage	AP/HP
Seax	*M*	*S*	*1d4+2+1d2*	*6/8*
Sword	*M*	*M*	*1d6+2+1d2*	*4/8*
Saxon Shield	*L*	*S*	*1d4+1d2*	*4/12*

Braece

Braece	Attributes
STR: 10	Action Points: 2
CON: 10	Damage Modifier: 0
SIZ: 13	Magic Points: 7
DEX: 10	Movement: 6 metres
INT: 14	Initiative Bonus: 11
POW: 7	Armour: Furs
CHA: 11	

Skills: Athletics 40%, Brawn 30%, Culture (Saxon) 68%, Customs 48%, Endruance 44%, Influence 54%, Insight 46%, Language (Saxon) 65%, Lore (Strategy and Tactics) 43%, Lore (Saxon) 68%, Oratory 51%. Perception 36%, Ride 35%, Sing 51%, Superstition 36%, Willpower 34%

Passions: Loyalty to Taddenlaege 55%, Love (Tadda) 52%

1d20	Location	AP/HP
1–3	Right Leg	0/5
4–6	Left Leg	0/5
7–9	Abdomen	1/6
10–12	Chest	1/7
13–15	Right Arm	0/4
16–18	Left Arm	0/4
19–20	Head	0/5

Combat Style: Saxon Noble (Sword, Seax and Shield, Trait: Mounted Combat) 55%

Weapon	Size/Force	Reach	Damage	AP/HP
Seax	*M*	*S*	*1d4+2+1d2*	*6/8*
Sword	*M*	*M*	*1d6+2+1d2*	*4/8*
Saxon Shield	*L*	*S*	*1d4+1d2*	*4/12*

Rowenna

Rowenna	Attributes
STR: 11	Action Points: 2
CON: 11	Damage Modifier: 0
SIZ: 13	Magic Points: 15
DEX: 12	Movement: 6 metres
INT: 13	Initiative Bonus: 12
POW: 15	Armour: Leather Tunic
CHA: 12	

Skills: Athletics 36%, Brawn 33%, Commerce 75%, Courtesy 38%, Culture (Saxon) 66%, Customs 59%, Endurance 36%, Evade 54%, Influence 69%, Insight 56%, Locale 59%, Lore (Saxons) 66%, Lore (Strategy and Tactics) 39%, Oratory 54%, Perception 51%, Ride 52%, Superstition 42%, Unarmed 53%, Willpower 60%

Passions: Loyalty to Taddenlaege 55%, Norse Gods 50%, Hate (Garbold) 40%, Hate (Celts) 50%

1d20	Location	AP/HP
1–3	Right Leg	0/5
4–6	Left Leg	0/5
7–9	Abdomen	2/6
10–12	Chest	2/7
13–15	Right Arm	0/4
16–18	Left Arm	0/4
19–20	Head	0/5

Combat Style: Fyrdman (Seax, Battleaxe and Shield, Trait: Mounted Combat) 68%

Weapon	Size/Force	Reach	Damage	AP/HP
Seax	*M*	*S*	*1d4+2*	*6/8*
Battleaxe	*M*	*M*	*1d6*	*4/8*
Saxon Shield	*L*	*S*	*1d4*	*4/12*

Garbold

Garbold	Attributes
STR: 12	Action Points: 3
CON: 9	Damage Modifier: +1d2
SIZ: 16	Magic Points: 10
DEX: 12	Movement: 6 metres
INT: 14	Initiative Bonus: 11
POW: 10	Armour: Leather Tunic and Helm
CHA: 14	

Skills: Athletics 46%, Brawn 41%, Courtesy 49%, Commerce 58%, Culture (Saxon) 68%, Endurance 37%, Evade 54%, Influence 70%, Insight 61%, Locale 59%, Lore (Saxons) 68%, Lore (Strategy and Tactics) 50%, Oratory 40%, Perception 57%, Ride 52%, Superstition 36%, Unarmed 53%, Willpower 40%

Passions: Love (Power) 50%, Hate (Thane Tadda) 50%, Hate (Celts) 45%

1d20	Location	AP/HP
1–3	Right Leg	0/6
4–6	Left Leg	0/6
7–9	Abdomen	2/7
10–12	Chest	2/8
13–15	Right Arm	0/5
16–18	Left Arm	0/5
19–20	Head	5/6

Combat Style: Saxon Noble (Sword, Seax and Shield, Trait: Mounted Combat) 59%

Weapon	Size/Force	Reach	Damage	AP/HP
Seax	*M*	*S*	*1d4+2+1d2*	*6/8*
Sword	*M*	*M*	*1d6+2+1d2*	*4/8*
Saxon Shield	*L*	*S*	*1d4+1d2*	*4/12*

Leofstan

Leofstan	Attributes
STR: 10	Action Points: 3
CON: 9	Damage Modifier: 0
SIZ: 13	Magic Points: 13
DEX: 12	Movement: 6 metres
INT: 14	Initiative Bonus: 11
POW: 13	Armour: Leather Tunic and Helm
CHA: 13	

Skills: Athletics 46%, Brawn 41%, Culture (Saxon) 68%, Culture (Celt) 38%, Deceit 67%, Endurance 37%, Evade 56%, Influence 61%, Language (Saxon) 67%, Language (Brythonic) 44%, Lore (Saxon) 68%, Lore (Strategy and Tactics) 63%, Perception 58%, Stealth 75%, Superstition 53%, Willpower 56%

Passions: Hate (Celts) 68%, Love (Carnage) 43%, Norse Gods 58%

1d20	Location	AP/HP
1–3	Right Leg	0/5
4–6	Left Leg	0/5
7–9	Abdomen	2/6
10–12	Chest	2/7
13–15	Right Arm	0/4
16–18	Left Arm	0/4
19–20	Head	5/5

Combat Style: Saxon Noble (Sword, Seax and Shield, Trait: Mounted Combat) 67%

Weapon	Size/Force	Reach	Damage	AP/HP
Seax	*M*	*S*	*1d4+2*	*6/8*
Sword	*M*	*M*	*1d6+2*	*4/8*
Saxon Shield	*L*	*S*	*1d4*	*4/12*

Leofstan's Bandits

Bandits	Attributes
STR: 11	Action Points: 2
CON: 11	Damage Modifier: 0
SIZ: 13	Magic Points: 12
DEX: 12	Movement: 6 metres
INT: 13	Initiative Bonus: 12
POW: 12	Armour: Leather Tunic
CHA: 12	

Skills: Athletics 54%, Brawn 54%, Craft (Repair Weapons and Armour) 39%, Culture (Saxon) 64%, Endurance 47%, Evade 41%, Language (Saxon) 62%, Lore (Saxon) 64%, Perception 53%, Stealth 55%, Survival 55%, Superstition 49%, Unarmed 50%, Willower 42%

Passions: Loyalty to Leofstan 35%, Love (Carnage) 50%, Fear (Dunric) 35%, Norse Gods 30%

1d20	Location	AP/HP
1–3	Right Leg	0/5
4–6	Left Leg	0/5
7–9	Abdomen	2/6
10–12	Chest	2/7
13–15	Right Arm	0/4
16–18	Left Arm	0/4
19–20	Head	0/5

Combat Style: Saxon Hunter (Seax, Spear, Bow, Trait: Skirmishing) 55%

Weapon	Size/Force	Reach	Damage	AP/HP
Seax	*M*	*S*	*1d4+2*	*6/8*
Bow	*L*	*-*	*1d6+2*	*4/4*
Spear	*M*	*L*	*1d8+1*	*4/5*

Dunric

Dunric	Attributes
STR: 9	Action Points: 3
CON: 9	Damage Modifier: 0
SIZ: 12	Magic Points: 16
DEX: 12	Movement: 6 metres
INT: 15	Initiative Bonus: 13
POW: 16	Armour: Furs
CHA: 8	

Skills: Athletics 46%, Brawn 41%, Binding (Saxon Tradition) 84%, Culture (Saxon) 70%, Deceit 73%, Endurance 31%, Evade 36%, First Aid 54%, Healing 54%, Language (Angle, Jute, or Saxon) 63%, Lore (Norse Gods) 60%, Lore (Saxon) 70%, Perception 46%, Sleight 51%, Stealth 57%, Trance 85%, Willpower 72%

Passions: Loyalty to Community 54%, Norse Gods 59%

1d20	Location	AP/HP
1–3	Right Leg	0/5
4–6	Left Leg	0/5
7–9	Abdomen	1/6
10–12	Chest	1/7
13–15	Right Arm	0/4
16–18	Left Arm	0/4
19–20	Head	0/5

Combat Style: Saxon Hunter (Seax, Spear, Bow, Trait: Skirmishing) 48%

Weapon	Size/Force	Reach	Damage	AP/HP
Seax	*M*	*S*	*1d4+2*	*6/8*
Bow	*L*	*-*	*1d6+2*	*4/4*
Spear	*M*	*L*	*1d8+1*	*4/5*

Dunric's Spirits

Dunric has the aid of the aelf and the Nikor. The Nikor is a water spirit. It manifests physically, either with a large body of water, or by occupying Dunric's body. In the latter case, Dunric transforms into the Nikor, taking on its physical form as a watery demonic horse, with the attributes below.

Aelf	Attributes
INT: 8	Action Points: 3
POW: 21	Damage Modifier: 0
CHA: 7	Magic Points: 21

Skills: Discorporate 79%, Spectral Combat 78%, Stealth 65%, Willpower 92%

Special: The Aelf can drag a victim into the spirit plane with Discorporate to fight them in spirit combat. If the Aelf wins, it possesses them, causing the ailment of Paralysis (onset time 4 minutes)

The Nikor	Attributes
STR: 31	Action Points: 3
DEX: 15	Damage Modifier: +1d6
INT: 13	Magic Points: 20
POW: 20	Movement: 6 metres
	Initiative Bonus: 14
	Armour/Hit Points: 3/40

Skills: Brawn 82%, Evade 72%, Perception 65%, Willpower 94%
Combat Style: Elemental Combat 87% (Damage: 2d6)

bibliography

There are a number of things, above and beyond my staples of Arthurian lore and Dark Ages history that I read in the course of writing this book. This bibliography adds to that in Mythic Britain when it comes to Saxon-themed campaigns.

There are two strands here: the fictional and the historical. When it comes to fiction, my favourite of them all is actually the epic poem *Beowulf*, surely the most famous of all the Anglo-Saxon works of literature. There are many translations and retellings out there. My personal recommendation for those new to it is Seamus Heaney's translation, which is very readable, and captures the story and the poetry. There are many other excellent translations. Retellings on the other hand vary in quality, and some are not at all faithful to the original work beyond a very broad outline; the story, characters, and themes sometimes differ. In no faithful form of the tale did Beowulf kill a dragon by making use of a swarm of bees.

Finally, when it comes to Beowulf, I would be doing an injustice if I did not mention J.R.R. Tolkien, best known of course for The Hobbit and Lord of the Rings. Tolkien's work on the poem led to it becoming as well-known as it is today. The Rohirrim culture in Lord of the Rings is explicitly based on Anglo-Saxon culture, and the Rohirrim poems have the same style as Anglo-Saxon works.

Although heroic Anglo-Saxon poetry is the best known, some, such as The Wanderer and The Seafarer are more mystical "wisdom poems", and capture more aspects of the Anglo-Saxon view of life. Finally, the Exeter Book contains over 90 riddles. Tolkien's riddles in The Hobbit are also in the Anglo-Saxon style.

When it comes to the historical and historical fantasy fiction, much of it is set later in time, usually in the Viking Age. Of those listed here, Conscience of the King (A. Duggan) and Dawn Wind (R. Sutcliff) take place in an earlier time. The Way of Wyrd is a novel with the purpose of teaching the author's view of Anglo-Saxon magic and views of fate, and influenced the magic chapter presented here.

As for non-fiction, the book that kindled in me an enthusiasm to write an Anglo-Saxon RPG book was Michael Wood's In Search of the Dark Ages, based in his television series, which ran from 1979 to 1981. Other inspirational easy reads were Life in Anglo-Saxon England (R.L. Page) and Barbarians: Secrets of the Dark Ages (R. Rudgley). The last book in particular casts the early Saxons and other "barbaric" people of the general time-frame (meaning within a few centuries) in a more sympathetic than usual light.

Fiction

The Way of Wyrd (B. Bates)
The Last Kingdom and sequels (B. Cornwell)
Conscience of the King (A. Duggan)
Last Light of the Sun (G.G. Kay)
Dawn Wind (R, Sutcliff)
The Hobbit (J.R.R. Tolkien)
The Lord of the Rings (J.R.R. Tolkien)

Classics

The Anglo-Saxon Chronicles
Beowulf
The Exeter Book Riddles
The First Poems in English (M. Alexander)
The Anglo-Saxon World, An Anthology (Introduction and Translation, K. Crossley-Holland)
Finn and Hengest (J.R.R. Tolkien)

Non-Fiction

The Real Middle Earth: Magic and Mystery in the Dark Ages (B. Bates)
The Anglo-Saxons (edited by J. Campbell)
Bloodfeud: Murder and Revenge in Anglo-Saxon England (R.A. Fletcher)
Anglo-Saxon Mythology, Migration, and Magic (T. Linsell and B. Partridge)
The Anglo-Saxon World (N.J. Higham and M.J. Ryan)
Exploring the Northern Tradition: A Guide to the Gods, Lore, Rites, and Celebrations from the Norse, German, and Anglo-Saxon Traditions (G. Krasskova)
Life in Anglo-Saxon England (R.L. Page)
The Roman Shore Forts (A. Pearson)
Anglo-Saxon Art, Myth, and Material Culture 4th to 7th Century: Wayland's Work (S. Pollington)
Barbarians: Secrets of the Dark Ages (R. Rudgley)
A Feast of Creatures (C. Williamson)
In Search of the Dark Ages (M. Wood)
Kings and Kingdoms of Early Anglo-Saxon England (B. Yorke)

index

C

D

E

F

G

index

R

S

T

U

V

W